R.M.S. QUEEN ELIZABETH

THE ULTIMATE SHIP

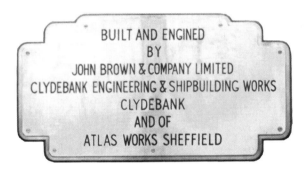

BUILT AND ENGINED
BY
JOHN BROWN & COMPANY LIMITED
CLYDEBANK ENGINEERING & SHIPBUILDING WORKS
CLYDEBANK
AND OF
ATLAS WORKS SHEFFIELD

R.M.S. QUEEN ELIZABETH

THE ULTIMATE SHIP

by
Clive Harvey

Published by

Carmania Press

PO Box 56435, London, SE3 0SZ

Artwork and production by Christopher Mason.
Printed by Tisak Zambelli, Rijeka, Croatia.

ISBN 978-0-9543666-8-1 First published 2008

CONTENTS

Front endpapers. Just launched, the hull of the *Queen Elizabeth,* the World's biggest liner, is manoeuvred into the fitting out basin at the John Brown yard at Clydebank.

Frontispiece. A Moran tug nudges the *Queen Elizabeth* in mid-Hudson at the start of another transatlantic voyage from New York. The Jersey shore can be seen in the background.

Rear endpapers. Death of a Queen. Ravaged by fire, the *Queen Elizabeth* lies in Hong Kong harbour. The plans for her to have a new career as a university cruise ship have come to nought.

ACKNOWLEDGEMENTS

As is usually the case, this book would not have come to fruition were it not for the kindness, help and generosity of several people. The use of their photographs and the sharing of their memories have been invaluable. I really wish that I could thank my dear but now late friend Christopher Hurd-Wood. I know, as with my previous books, he would have been a fund of information. As it was, his partner, Alan Thomas, very kindly gave me two scrapbooks that had been compiled by Chris during the 1940s and 1950s. At the time that he gave them to me (as we sorted through Chris's vast collection in preparation for it to be sent to auction) he had no idea how utterly invaluable these would be. So I must extend very special thanks to Alan, who unknowingly helped to get this book launched. Thanks must also go to Steven Moore for all his hard work in transposing the fantastic collection of photographs of Stephen Berry onto CD and of course thank you to Stephen Berry for allowing me to use his remarkable pictures. Arthur Crook has once again been exceptionally generous both with photographs and information, especially regarding the fire on board *Seawise University*. Gordon Ghareeb was also generous in allowing me to use his account of the time that the *Queen Elizabeth* spent in Florida and David Hutchings shared with me other information about that unfortunate period. As a result of the information Martin Grant passed to me, I hope that I have been able to correct an often-held misconception regarding the earliest days of the *Queen Elizabeth*; and John Shepherd's insight into life in the Purser's Office was both fascinating and invaluable. Thank you also to Bob Boorman, John Dockray and the late Laurence Dunn, whose collection is now owned by Peter Newall. I am hugely indebted to Charles Dragonette, Maurizio Eliseo and Ian Johnston for supplying valuable, additional material at very short notice and also to Claudio Ernè for his contribution to the careful restoration work on the illustrations.

I am thrilled at being able to use Don Stoltenberg's sensational painting as a dust jacket illustration. To me it sums up all the excitement and drama that was the *Queen Elizabeth*. I am also honoured that John Maxtone-Graham has contributed his perceptive Foreword.

Thank you to Anthony Cooke of Carmania Press for suggesting the project (despite my initial misgivings) and for editing and publishing the result. A word of thanks ought to go to my long-suffering partner, Clive J Baker, who probably got well and truly fed up with hearing about the *Queen Elizabeth*.

In these days of Internet chat I should perhaps also extend a thank you to all those people on the LinersList who contributed to the sometimes seemingly endless discussions regarding the *Queen Elizabeth* – and sometimes even the *Queen Mary*. Believe me, every posting was read avidly!

Finally, my considerable gratitude goes to Chris Mason for his computer skills and his innate understanding that has enabled him to create a layout for the book which is exactly as I had envisaged and also for rising to the occasion when last minute changes became necessary.

INTRODUCTION

I was never much of a fan of the *Queen Mary* – I was always a *Queen Elizabeth* man. There was just something about her cleaner lines and, although enormous, at 83,000 tons she had a look of elegant and yet understated power. It was a look that I felt was denied her older near-sister, with her three funnels and all those huge square ventilators. To me it seemed as though the *Queen Mary* was always crying 'look at me!' whereas the *Queen Elizabeth* just didn't have to. It was as if she really knew that she was faster, more efficient, better designed and altogether the superior ship.

Yes, there is no doubt that I preferred the *Queen Elizabeth*, yet like hundreds of thousands before me, I never saw her; and yes, my heart did skip a beat when I first saw the *Queen Mary* at Long Beach. As a child of the 1950s I was well aware of the 'Queens', even though living far from Southampton. Their magic was remarkable. How else could I, as a five-year-old in a remote Norfolk village, have painted a 'self-portrait' in my version of what I thought a naval uniform looked like, as captain of the *Queen Elizabeth*? Curiously, 53 years later I still have a very clear memory of doing this! Yet when the idea of this book was suggested I was far from inspired. Huge trans-Atlantic liners are not what you might call 'my thing'. In general, I prefer my ships to be of a more human scale. Then, due to the unfortunate passing of a very dear friend, I acquired some scrap books and there, preserved within their pages, was a veritable treasure trove of newspaper and magazine cuttings recording the early career of the *Queen Elizabeth* and thus the book was born.

Her first arrival in New York was every bit as thrilling – no, more so – as any perfectly stage-managed peacetime maiden arrival. No ship has ever had such a remarkable entry into service. (The *Queen Elizabeth* is working her magic on me again – as indeed she has throughout the time that I have spent writing this book. Occasionally, so enthused have I been with some aspect of her or her career, I have probably bored some people rigid by talking incessantly about her.)

The *Queen Elizabeth* was undoubtedly a 'drama-Queen.' True, compared to the *Queen Mary*, she quietly got on with her trans-Atlantic career but that entry into service was high drama, albeit initially cloaked in secrecy, and she ended in an equally dramatic fashion. Whilst she slipped, oh so quietly, from Southampton for the final time it was drama from then onward. Yes, it was tawdry; yes, it was messy; and yes, I am sure that the old ship was at times appalled by what was happening to her. (You see, her magic takes over and it is difficult not to imagine her with a spirit of her own.) Rusting and downgraded, she was anxious to leave the appalling mess that was her Florida management. Later, in the sunshine of Hong Kong harbour she gleamed anew.

If only ………

Hers was a story that I did not much want to write and yet it is a story of sheer excitement, glamour and drama. It is a story that would occasionally even bring tears to my eyes as I wrote it. And to think that in 1968, as she neared the end of her trans-Atlantic career, Cunard dared to promote their new liner with the slogan 'Ships have been boring long enough!' Prepare then to be bored ………

Clive Harvey,
Norwich, April 2007.

FOREWORD

Too often, the first *Queen Mary* and *Queen Elizabeth* are indiscriminately paired, both in service and aesthetic appreciation. Though they did enjoy an unique, profitable duality, they were by no means sisters, displaying as they did contrasting profiles and interiors. In this fascinating history, Clive Harvey documents the second of Cunard-White Star's immortal duo.

Queen Mary was conventionally old-fashioned, with three, guy-wired funnels, eight square top-deck ventilators of brobdingnagian proportions, a vertical cut-water, a forward well-deck and sheltered bridge ends. The hull's most distinctive feature was that half-submerged knob of a cruiser stern, implemented to lengthen her waterline.

She first sailed to New York in June 1936, delayed by a two-year lay-up on the stocks. The keel of her future consort, *Queen Elizabeth*, was laid down on John Brown's building berth #4 only days after the *Mary*'s launch. A very different vessel rose above Clydebank's chimneypots, sea miles removed from Cunard's generic *Aquitania* prototype; in fact, she seemed more closely allied to *Normandie*. What remarkable irony: though *Queen Mary* became *Normandie*'s late 30s arch-rival, *Queen Elizabeth* emerged as the perfect design contemporary of the French liner. She had the same clipper stem with central anchor, free-standing funnels rooted to the Sun Deck, a flat forepeak from bridge screen to prow, a sleek, white upper strake dashing unobstructed sternward and a profile devoid of the *Mary*'s dense clutter. And her fitting out revealed interior décor that was lighter, brighter and more provocative than Cunard-White Star's norm. Whereas *Queen Mary* seemed a fusty holdover from the 1920s, *Queen Elizabeth* sported the incontestable chic of the late 1930s.

Fitted out after hostilities began, *Queen Elizabeth* was rushed from the Clyde to New York in March 1940 without sea trials, dry docking or passengers, manned by a scratch crew from *Aquitania*. That hasty, improvised debut did not permit the scrupulous fine-tuning every liner requires; worse, she was immediately transformed into a troopship,

yet another jarring expediency never anticipated by her builders.

Queen Elizabeth was neither as happy nor easy-working a ship as the *Mary*, and one can only guess that the exigencies of her tumultuous early years contributed to the problem. The first 'Queen' to be restored to peacetime guise in October 1946, *Elizabeth* did inaugurate Cunard-White Star's legendary two-ship weekly service, conceived seventeen years earlier.

Long after that service ended, *Queen Mary* has always hogged the retrospective limelight; because she was first or because she still survives, tethered somnolently in California's Long Beach? It is hard to know. Nevertheless, Clive Harvey has splendidly redressed that imbalance. In this well-considered *Queen Elizabeth* panegyric, he has sorted out the differences between the two and ushered the customarily neglected — not only second but also second-ranked — 'Queen' into deserved prominence. I have no difficulty agreeing with Harvey for I crossed on the *Elizabeth* about a dozen times yet only once on the *Mary*. To be fair, it was not a matter of preference, merely the accidental conveniences of her sailing schedule.

Though *Queen Elizabeth* did tie up near imprisoned *Normandie* briefly in New York, the two never sailed as rivals. Her life ended just as badly. Retired unsuccessfully as a waterfront attraction in Florida's Port Everglades, she was bought by Chinese shipping magnate C.Y. Tung and renamed *Seawise University*. After limping from Florida to Hong Kong and being re-fitted, she was torched by malcontent Chinese shipwrights and capsized — final, tragic *Normandie* parallel — into the waters of Junk Bay.

Bravo, Clive Harvey! *Queen Elizabeth* sails on and we are all the richer for your dogged research, graceful prose and perceptive aperçus. Required reading for the buffs — and super buffs — no less than every interested passenger.

John Maxtone-Graham,
At sea, 2007.

R.M.S. QUEEN ELIZABETH

Chapter I

A DARING DASH

She appeared to have it all: the perfect pedigree – owned by perhaps the most illustrious of shipping lines. She was the largest ship in the world and in all probability, until the advent of the ss *United States*, the fastest. When she entered commercial service she was certainly the most luxurious and she was, without doubt, the epitome of the ideal Atlantic liner with the right level of modernity but with that certain deference to the past. Her first voyage was one of the very highest drama - and with hindsight - excitement. Yet, despite all of this, she was forever in the shadow of her older near-sister - a ship more traditional (if not just old-fashioned) in both appearance and machinery and, even by the late 1940s, a little dated in her décor.

* * * * * *

On Thursday the 7th March 1940, even *The Daily Telegraph*, normally one of the more sober of newspapers, could scarcely contain its jubilation with its headlines: 'The *Queen Elizabeth* at New York – Secret Maiden Voyage Across Atlantic – To Be Laid Up In Berth Next To *Queen Mary* – 'Planes Fly Out To Greet World's Biggest Ship'. The report 'From our own correspondent, New York, Wednesday Night' was no less enthusiastic:

"Shipping circles in New York were surprised late this afternoon to learn that Britain's new giant liner, *Queen Elizabeth*, had secretly crossed the Atlantic. The 85,000-ton ship, the largest in the world, is due to dock here at nine o'clock to-morrow morning [3 p.m. British Summer Time] and all arrangements have been made for her reception. The secret of her extraordinary maiden voyage had been well guarded. Not the slightest hint of it had been allowed to escape from official quarters in New York. Even to-night, when 'planes were preparing to set off with reporters and photographers to meet the great Cunard-White Star liner as she comes up river, British officials declined to make any comment.

"American reporters who hurried to the docks, however, were quick to note the preparations which had been made. The *Mauretania*, which with the *Queen Mary* has been laid up here since the war began, had been moved from her berth at the Cunard-White Star's huge pier on one side of which the *Queen Mary* is moored. It was immediately assumed that it had been done to make way for Britain's new liner. It is learned authoritatively that the *Queen Elizabeth* reached Halifax, Nova Scotia after a dash across the North Atlantic and left the Canadian port early today." (This was sheer speculation on the newspaper's part as there is no record of the *Queen Elizabeth* making a stop at Halifax on that first voyage. It was in fact of the utmost urgency to ensure that she was safely in New York harbour as quickly as possible.)

"Coastguard authorities admitted that they had been advised that she would make the journey down the American coast today. At a late hour tonight British officials continued to profess complete ignorance of the whereabouts of the liner, but shipping circles here in New York were convinced that she would dock here tomorrow morning.

"That the *Queen Elizabeth* should be brought to New York for the duration of the war is not in itself a matter for surprise since the two famous British vessels and the French liner *Normandie* are already here. That it should apparently have been done without the knowledge of any except those most intimately concerned has caused great astonishment.

"The monthly cost of maintaining the *Queen Mary* and the *Normandie* in their berths here is about £5,000 for each liner."

That same evening the Cunard-White Star company issued a statement in New York explaining their reasons for moving the 83,673-ton *Queen Elizabeth* from the Clyde when they did: "Only twice a year when the tides are unusually high is there ample depth of water in the river to navigate a ship of her great size safely to the open sea. Such a tide occurred in the latter part of last month and, as anticipated, the *Queen Elizabeth* was taken to sea at that time. In view of the circumstances it was decided that she should proceed to America, which she did, leaving last Saturday and arriving today after an uneventful voyage at a moderate speed. No attempt at an unusually high speed was made. The ship carried no passengers or cargo and was under the command of Captain J. C. Townley. The interior accommodation of the *Queen Elizabeth* is not wholly completed. No plans have been made for the vessel beyond tying her up at Pier 90, along with the *Queen Mary*, in line with the arrangements in effect for all other ships of the company stopping at an American port. No visitors will be allowed on the pier or the ship during her present stay in New York."

The unexpected arrival in New York of the *Queen Elizabeth* caused such a stir that the American newspapers devoted more space reporting on her safe arrival than they had given to the first visit of her companion ship, *Queen Mary*.

◁ Shepherded by tugs, the grey-painted *Queen Elizabeth* begins the tortuous journey down the Clyde for an unknown destination. With Europe at war, she faces an uncertain future.

They told in both words and pictures the story of what the *Daily Mirror* called the 'triumphant docking' of the largest liner in the world. Despite being incomplete and painted in drab grey, the *Queen Elizabeth* was still hailed as being the most beautifully designed ship afloat – this despite the fact that keen disappointment was felt regarding the 'no visitors' ruling. Most of the newspapers applauded the decision to move the liner to New York. *The New York Times*, confident that Nazi Germany would be defeated, wrote: "The British were right in not leaving such a ship to the mercy of air attack at home. Their luxury liners will have a job to do when the war is over." *The Herald Tribune* commented: "The stringency of British censorship and the staunchness of British self-control are illustrated in this practically classic example." *The Indianapolis Star* said that the liner's arrival was 'a triumph for the British Navy', while *The Kansas City Times* called it evidence of the British ability to keep a secret and another demonstration of the British mastery of the seas. "Beyond doubt," said *The San Francisco Chronicle*, "many Nazi pilots dreamed of giving the *Queen Elizabeth* a couple of bombs down the stack. That dream is over now."

Some newspapers gave prominence to a report, denied by the Cunard-White Star Line, that some of the crew had threatened to strike before sailing to the United States and had agreed to make the voyage only after receiving a bonus of £30. The line also denied that 30 seamen had left the *Queen Elizabeth* at Greenock because they feared the dangers of the Atlantic crossing, saying that when it was made known that New York was the destination, some of the crew, chiefly for domestic reasons, were unable to make the trip and asked to be allowed to return home. A bonus promised to the crew was to compensate for any inconvenience involved and had nothing to do with any question of risks. Those crew members who were taken off the ship were sworn to secrecy regarding her ultimate destination. Even so, once they had disembarked the liner they were taken aboard the tender *Romsey* (which was normally down in Southampton) and she remained in a nearby loch until after the *Queen Elizabeth* had sailed and was well out into the Atlantic.

William Simms, the foreign editor of the Scripps Howard newspapers, put a fantastic suggestion forward: "Some circles," he said, "are alleging that London and Berlin 'made a deal' over the *Queen Elizabeth* and the *Bremen*." Presumably he meant that an agreement had been made that ensured both liners safe passage across the Atlantic. (The 51,731-ton *Bremen* had been homeward bound, without passengers, when war broke out. She took refuge in Murmansk before later reaching Germany.)

The newspapers and broadcasting companies were eager to make the most of the surprise arrival of the *Queen Elizabeth*. It was the biggest 'war story' the city had yet had. They sent out 'planes carrying photographers to meet the ship as she approached from the direction of Nantucket. As early as 7.45 a.m. one broadcaster flew over her and sent listeners a description of the scene. Soon after passing the Ambrose Light, which marked the entrance to the harbour, at 9.15 a.m. the *Queen Elizabeth* reached Quarantine and a doctor went aboard - to avoid revealing her position she had refrained from obtaining a clearance by wireless. Newspaper reporters were waiting there aboard a cutter which, it had been announced, would leave early in the morning 'on the assumption that the ship might be coming in'. Even at that hour officials were still refusing to admit that the ship was the *Queen Elizabeth*. None of the reporters was allowed on board and it was indicated that the liner would remain a sealed ship for all but official visitors. Even members of the United States Naval Intelligence Service were barred from her.

Having missed the tide, she did not dock in New York until 5 p.m. In spite of very strong winds which hampered the operation, it was done without mishap while twelve 'planes circled overhead. As she passed the *Queen Mary* the two liners saluted each other by dipping their ensigns. A chorus of sirens from other ships greeted the new liner and then fell silent as she moved slowly to her mooring, her own sirens booming an acknowledgement to the greeting. Meanwhile, the occupants of nearby skyscrapers with a view of the event launched a shower of torn paper into the streets in the time-honoured manner of welcome to a new visitor.

Once she was securely alongside, Mr. Newbold Morris, president of the New York City Council, went on board to greet Captain Townley on behalf of the city. Afterwards he told the waiting pressmen that Captain Townley had said that no submarines had been seen and that the naval escort of four destroyers had been dropped after one day out. A member of the *Queen Elizabeth*'s crew was reported as having said that on the Wednesday the liner had made 748 miles and reached 31.6 knots for a time. Obviously immensely proud of her, he was quoted as saying: "I believe that the ship is capable of between 35 and 36 knots". When Captain Townley went ashore to meet representatives from the press on the pier he was rather more modest, stating that she had averaged 24½ knots on the voyage and he called her 'an ideal sister ship to the *Queen Mary*'. However, he did go on to say that his chief engineer was satisfied that she would prove to be the fastest ship in the world, adding with remarkable understatement: "It is unique to leave without trials and find yourself in New York".

Never before had an express passenger liner crossed the North Atlantic without running the usual series of acceptance trials. In the case of the *Queen Elizabeth*, whose engines were credited with 200,000 shaft-horsepower, these would normally have been of the very first importance. Thus the responsibility that sat upon the shoulders of Captain Townley as he took the untried *Queen Elizabeth* out into the Atlantic was immense in all respects. He had trained in sail and had joined the Cunard Line in 1904, as Fourth Officer of the *Saxonia*. In 1912 he became First Officer of the *Pannonia* and, in 1913, Chief Officer of the Blue Riband holder

Mauretania. His first command was the cargo steamer *Thracia*, in 1915. Subsequently he was master of the *Brescia*, *Pavia* and *Tyria*. The first passenger vessel that he commanded was the *Aurania*, in 1926. He was Staff Captain of the *Aquitania* in the following year, returning to *Aurania* for about a month before taking command of the *Lancastria* in 1928. Following that, he had commanded the *Carmania* and *Aquitania* and had relieved Captain Irving for a voyage aboard the *Queen Mary*.

American shipping men were much interested to see that the liner had been equipped with a magnetic mine protector device, a series of cables running all the way around the exterior of the hull, midway between the upper decks and the waterline. However, what really left the Americans in awe was Britain's mastery of the high seas, making such a journey possible, and the manner in which thousands of people in Scotland and England, who must have known the secret, kept it until the *Queen Elizabeth* had arrived in New York.

If British officials had hoped that the arrival of the *Queen Elizabeth* would be allowed to pass un-noticed they were disappointed. New Yorkers were thrilled by the circumstances in which she made her first visit to the port and they were determined to ensure that she had an appropriate welcome. A crowd, which was estimated to be at least 10,000 gathered at the docks in the morning as soon as they had received word of her approach. It was not known then that she had missed the tide and they would have a wait of several hours before she would be able to proceed to her pier.

Chief Inspector Costuma personally took charge of the arrangements, posting an extra 100 policemen and 100 detectives near the dock.

The New York evening papers devoted the greater part of their front pages to photographs of the *Queen Elizabeth* and description of her arrival. Typical headlines were: 'Super liner foils subs' - *Journal American* (quite ignoring the fact that Captain Townley had categorically stated that no submarines had been spotted). '*Queen Elizabeth* sails in safely' - *World Telegram*. 'She's here - and safe - the *Queen Elizabeth*' - *New York Post*. The newspapers, in describing the voyage, freely used such adjectives as 'spectacular' and 'dangerous'. *The New York Times* called it 'a new epic of sea adventure', while *The Daily News* declared that the crossing 'represented

▽ For so many months a seemingly permanent fixture on the Clyde, the *Queen Elizabeth* attracts a gradually growing crowd as she leaves the birthplace to which she will never return.

△ Full steam ahead. *Queen Elizabeth* speeds towards New York and safety during her secret dash across the North Atlantic.
▽ On arrival, she is greeted by the Statue of Liberty. Already the news is spreading in Manhattan.

△ Surrounded by rivercraft, the new *Queen* heads towards her Hudson River berth for the first time. The occasion may lack the glamour of a maiden arrival in peacetime, but the excitement is no less intense.

one of the most daring feats of the present conflict'. In London, when asked to comment on the successful voyage of the *Queen Elizabeth*, the First Lord of the Admiralty, Mr. Winston Churchill said: "Splendid; very good work indeed. I never had any doubt about her getting over".

The *Queen Elizabeth* had left her fitting-out basin at John Brown's yard on the 26th February, a fact which was not made generally known until after her arrival in America. It took about five hours for her to be towed the 15 miles down the Clyde to the Tail of the Bank. The task of manoeuvring her from the fitting-out basin had begun

nearly four hours before high water. Then the liner, which was without her lifeboats, was coaxed by three tugs from the basin shortly after noon and her length was clear by 1.10 pm. Near the Rashilee Light, practically at the same spot at which the *Queen Mary* touched the bank, the bows of the *Queen Elizabeth* were caught by the incoming tide. After 50 minutes of manoeuvring, the stern tugs got control of the ship and pulled her back for close on a thousand feet. The *Queen Elizabeth* then went on at some speed and arrived at Bowling at 3.35 pm. With extreme caution the difficult Bowling bend was negotiated. When she was safely out of the Clyde some brief engine and essential compass trials were carried out and were completed in three days. Then, with little ceremony, the largest liner in the world was handed over to her owners with the formalities taking place in the unlikely location of the space designated one day to become her Third Class dining room.

Obviously to aid her safe passage across the Atlantic, Cunard had indicated that the *Queen Elizabeth* would be drydocked in Southampton after having undergone trials. This ruse was almost uncovered when surprised dock officials in Southampton reminded Cunard that they had not received any docking plans from them. So faked documents were hastily prepared so as not to arouse further suspicion. It has generally been reported that Captain Townley and his crew had no idea of their destination until the liner was already at sea. This was obviously not the case: hence the 30 crew members who were allowed to leave the ship at Greenock and return home upon learning that she would be heading for New York. Likewise, it has been stated that Captain Townley was unaware of the *Queen Elizabeth*'s destination until the arrival of the King's messenger, who had been despatched by the First Lord of the Admiralty on the 2nd March. However, he must have been involved in some way in the discussions between the Cunard Line management and the Admiralty and thus the documents carried by the King's messenger were but confirmation of the plans he had already been involved with. Indeed, once it was reported that the ship had arrived safely in New York, Mrs. Townley was reported as saying from their home near Basingstoke: "Oh yes, I knew about the trip, and I knew the date on which my husband was due to start the voyage. It was a bit of a strain while I waited for news of the ship's safe arrival, and it is a great relief now that the suspense is over".

Of course, the announcement of the arrival of the *Queen Elizabeth* in New York raised many questions regarding why she was sent there and her potential use during the hostilities. While on the 8th March 1940 the Shipping Correspondent of *The Daily Telegraph* appeared to answer some of these, it seems very likely that they were not in fact questions put to the paper by the readers, but more likely something created between Cunard and the Admiralty to give the impression

that, along with the magnificent French liner *Normandie*, the two Cunard 'Queens' would sit out the war, quietly out of harm's way.

"Why could not the ship be put to ordinary commercial use instead of being laid up?"

"Because in wartime there is no possiblity of running her at a profit, for even if she could be filled with passengers every voyage, insurance would be prohibitive."

"Could not a fast ship be employed as an auxiliary cruiser in war time?"

"Speed alone is no qualification for such duty. Not only would the ship present a tremendous target but there are few berths which could accommodate her when not at sea. She would be neither handy nor economical in any service but that for which she was designed."

"Could she be converted into an aircraft carrier?"

"No doubt it could be done but only at very great expense in money, time and labour, and then the objections which would bar her use as an auxiliary cruiser would still apply."

"Why not lay the ship up in this country instead of in American waters?"

"There are very few berths suitable for such a huge vessel in this country which will not soon be required for the many other new merchant vessels under construction. Moreover, the owners of the ship have a suitable berth in New York for which they have to pay rent in any case."

It is generally accepted that, since it had been 'made known' that the *Queen Elizabeth* would be making her way to Southampton after the completion of her trials, Luftwaffe bombers were flying over the English Channel on the day that she was due, poised to destroy her. However, what was referred to in those early days of the conflict as 'the Phoney War' continued through until the 10th May 1940 and the Ministry of Home Security Daily Intelligence Reports, which were issued at 12-hourly intervals by the War Room at the Home Office in Whitehall, reveal that Saturday 2nd March 1940, and the several days afterwards, were extremely quiet. These reports, prepared at the time as information was received from the twelve regions into which England, Scotland and Wales had been divided for Civil Defence purposes

QUEEN ELIZABETH BERTHS AT NEW YORK

The Queen Elizabeth moves to her berth under the skyscrapers of New York. Behind the new liner, almost entirely obscured by the smoke, is her sister ship, the Queen Mary. On the right are the Normandie and the Mauretania. (Aerial view received by radio.)

in July 1939, were secret and were not for publication and are therefore fairly accurate and frank descriptions of each day's major incidents. The Daily Intelligence Report for the 2nd March, the day that the *Queen Elizabeth* left Scottish waters and headed towards New York, stated: "No enemy action has been reported. At 2315 hours last night an explosion occurred at Messrs. Whiteley's Stores, Bayswater. No personal injury was caused, but three large plate glass windows were blown out. IRA activity is suspected". On Sunday 3rd March the report was somewhat similar: "There have been no reports of enemy action over the British Isles during the period", though apparently there was a fire in a Glasgow factory that caused £3,000 of damage. Also, a mine which had been washed up at Dungeness the previous day exploded and caused damage to some nearby bungalows.

Monday 4th March: "There has been no action by the enemy today. No. 11 Region (Edinburgh) reports that the captain and 12 men of the Swedish vessel *Langahohn*" (*sic.* – actually *Langaholm*) "landed at Orkney yesterday. Five men were also rescued from a raft and landed at Kirkwall." Thus the reports continued for day after day: "No action by the enemy." It was not until the 16th March that there was an attack by the Luftwaffe on the British fleet's anchorage at Scapa Flow in the Orkney Islands. The air raid caused the death of a British civilian, the first of the war.

While building, the *Queen Elizabeth* was insured on a value of £4,500,000, of which £3,760,000 was covered in the open market, the balance being insured by the Government. When the liner was placed on risk under her full marine policies, the value was increased to over £5,000,000, of which the Government carried a proportion. When the marine risk was arranged underwriters were kept in ignorance of her destination, though doubtless they made a shrewd guess at it.

▽ With her hastily applied wartime grey paint worn away by the Atlantic waves, the *Queen Elizabeth* is manoeuvred alongside her New York berth at the end of that first dangerous crossing.

The Rt. Hon Lord Aberconway.
(Chairman, John Brown & Co., Ltd.)

Mr. S. J. Pigott,
(Resident Director, John Brown & Co., Ltd.)

Sir Percy Bates,
(Chairman, Cunard-White Star, Ltd.)

The *Aquitania* from whose design the
Queen Mary and *Queen Elizabeth* evolved.

Chapter 2

ORIGINS OF YARD NUMBER 552

By the late 1920s the North Atlantic passenger trade had undergone considerable change and Cunard Line was facing both declining passenger numbers and an increasingly elderly fleet. To replace the ships on a one-for-one basis was pointless; instead the whole operation of passenger carrying needed rethinking. In fact it was simple: larger and therefore faster but fewer ships were required. Cunard's rival, White Star Line, had gone through a similar thought process and in 1928 they placed an order with Harland & Wolff for what looked set to become their most beautiful ship, the 60,000 gross tons, 1,010 feet long *Oceanic*. Her first keel plates were laid just ten days after the order was announced but it was not too long before the work was proceeding at a rather slow pace. Then, on 23rd July 1929 it ceased altogether with White Star stating that it had been deferred temporarily pending final decisions regarding the propulsive machinery. However, it was known that White Star's parent company, the Royal Mail Steam Packet Company, was suffering from financial problems and there was no possibility of White Star being able to finance the construction of the liner on its own. Thus work on what would have been Britain's first 1,000 foot liner ceased altogether.

Cunard Line followed White Star's lead by laying the keel, at the John Brown shipyard on 1st December 1930, of Hull Number 534 - the first of two super-liners. It was planned that they would be larger than any liners previously built and together they would be able to provide a regular weekly trans-Atlantic service: a service that at the time required three ships. Each of the new pair would be expected to make the crossing in five days with a two-day turnaround. It seemed however, that barely had the plan been formulated than it began to slip from Cunard's grasp. The promise of up to five years of steady work building the two ships faded. As a direct consequence of the Depression, Cunard, along with every other passenger shipping line, watched their passenger lists dwindle and their debts rise. Work on 534 was suspended just a year after it had begun.

Meanwhile, across the English Channel, work on T6, the hull of what would become the flagship of the Compagnie Générale Transatlantique, continued. She was launched on 29th October 1932 and became *Normandie*. After several months even CGT had begun to wonder whether they would be able to continue with their glorious project and the pace of the work in the shipyard was slowed. It seemed that the world was in turmoil and that the two partially completed giant liners were particularly vulnerable. In the event, however, both become potent symbols of recovery, not only to their respective nations but to the world in general. The management of CGT were struggling to survive, attempting to rehabilitate the company, to secure its future and that of *Normandie* by persuading the French Government to settle the terms of the state's aid in legislation that would not come up for a vote until June 1935. On the other hand CGT had to defend itself against a violent campaign of denigration that had been started by various parties whose interests had been injured at the time of CGT's earlier insolvency and the government's intervention. Vigorous opposition

▽ The Cunard-White Star express liners' great rival, the French *Normandie*, which vied with the *Queen Mary* for the Blue Riband of the Atlantic throughout the late 1930s.

was voiced against the company and as a consequence the completion of the liner. Further complaints were heard from the stockholders of CGT who had lost virtually all of their investment at the time of the government's reorganisation of the company. In the end it was the call to uphold national prestige that was the greatest of arguments. The French government approved a loan and the work on *Normandie* resumed its earlier pace. She was an inspiration! France would after all become the first nation to put a liner of over 1,000 feet in length into service.

Depression creates depression and it was not just the laid-off workers at the John Brown's shipyard who were suffering as a result of the suspension of work on 534. Thousands of workers up and down the country, the suppliers of just about everything that would go into the ship, to power her, to fit her out and to decorate her, all were suffering – along with the men and women who could ultimately crew her. For two years, as it seemed that her future hung in the balance, she was the subject of much political debate, her champion being the Labour Member of Parliament for Dumbarton Burghs, David Kirkwood. He urged the resumption of work on the partially completed hull, saddened as he was by the sight of vast unemployment in his constituency. He saw that the assurance of employment for many thousands of people had enormous appeal. It would be a symbol, and a potent one, to the country at large of a beginning of the end of the Depression in the enormous number of sub-contracting industries up and down the country. Of course, national pride as well as the prestige for Cunard Line was not to be ignored. The increased pace of work on *Normandie* was just the push that was needed.

Thus Cunard's board of directors approached Neville Chamberlain, Chancellor of the Exchequer, for government help. Chamberlain was a very astute businessman and was welcoming to the idea of the government giving Cunard a helping hand but he had his eye on a slightly different scenario from that envisaged by the Cunard directors. It was Chamberlain's view that competition on the North Atlantic between the two struggling companies, Cunard and White Star, was mutually destructive. Instead, a merger between the two lines would establish a strong British presence, making the new company once and for all a force to be reckoned with. While a series of meetings between Chamberlain and the directors of both Cunard and White Star was held during December 1933 to finalise the details of the amalgamation of the two companies, the impending merger had already become common knowledge during that summer. This was undoubtedly due to White Star Line being totally against such a drastic move. Indeed, they were so violently opposed to it that they went as far as trying to get an injunction to stop the proposal, but they failed. In the end, the perilous state of their finances probably made the White Star Line management realise that they had no real option but to concede to Mr. Chamberlain's plan.

In the 26th August issue of the American magazine *Business Week*, in the column 'Ships in the News' was the headline 'Cunard-White Star merger reported imminent. May revive work on Cunard's biggest. Italian Line captures transatlantic Blue Ribbon with speedy voyage of *Rex*.' The article read as follows:

"German shipping had its fling at the headlines 3 years ago when the *Bremen* and *Europa* rushed into transatlantic fame by capturing the Blue Ribbon of the Atlantic for speed – held for more than 20 years by the *Mauretania* of the Cunard Line.

"Scarcely had these North German Lloyd liners won this victory when Lloyd, with Hamburg American, set the pace in shipping competition by pooling services and schedules. The project never developed into a genuine merger until Chancellor Hitler stepped into power in Berlin. Reorganisation now is much more complete. Rival pride is going by the board and is replaced by genuine economics.

"Italy pushed into the limelight a year ago when all Italian shipping was rationalized by Mussolini. Competing lines in the North American service were put under control and schedules of the three old lines were reorganized under a single direction of the Italian Line.

"Then came the *Rex* and the *Conte di Savoia* seeking the cream of the luxury traffic to Europe for the southern route. Only last week the *Rex* raced across the Atlantic from Gibraltar in slightly more than 4 days, captured for the Mussolini fleet the Blue Ribbon which North German Lloyd has held. In 'Steamship Row' in New York there is talk of friendly competition for the record from the *Savoia*.

"The British lines pushed into the limelight this week with the rumour that the Chancellor of the Exchequer is about to announce the merging of the two great British shipping lines in the North Atlantic trade, Cunard and White Star. Almost simultaneous with the announcement, the British government is expected to back a public bond issue of £2½ millions to finance the completion of Cunard's mystery ship - No. 534 - still standing in the building stocks along the Clyde with only the hull completed.

"The news is no surprise. Like all other shipping lines, Cunard and White Star have both felt the pinch of the Depression. Both have asked for aid in meeting the competition of government subsidized vessels in the highly competitive North Atlantic service. White Star has just gone through a purging in the general 'wash-up' of the Royal Mail Steam Packet Co. (a Lord Kylsant holding until he was found guilty of fraud) of which it is a part.

"When the two companies first asked for government aid, they were warned that it would be given only after they had worked out a merger plan which would bring about healthy cooperation in place of the keen competition which they now offer each other. Both lines operate between channel ports and New York. They have, together, some of the fastest vessels on the run. Cunard schedules the *Berengaria*, the *Aquitania* and – when not in the special cruise service – the

⚠ Power unleashed. The *Queen Mary*, the first of Cunard-White Star's two great super-liners, makes an imposing sight as she runs her trials in the Clyde.

Mauretania. White Star features the *Majestic* and the *Olympic* and fills the new cabin class motor vessels – *Britannic* and *Georgic* – on every crossing.

"Cunard's new super-liner was planned before the depression. It was to cost more than $30 millions, was to gross 73,000 tons, and probably compete with the fastest liners in the service. Every modern luxury was to be included from air-conditioned public rooms to special arrangements for carrying automobiles. Only a few weeks ago King George dedicated the new dry dock in Southampton built especially to accommodate the new giant and a sister ship which were planned to maintain a weekly service between New York and the channel ports. There is no prospect that the second ship will be built now, even under the merged management.

"France is having financial difficulties with her great contender in the North Atlantic trade – the French Line – but with government aid is continuing construction of the *Normandie*, to be the largest vessel afloat, to compete in speed and luxury 'with the best'. The *Normandie* is progressing slowly, will probably schedule its maiden voyage as soon as there are signs of a genuine pick up in transatlantic passenger travel."

The terms of the British government's offer were generous but Chamberlain was indeed adamant: neither Cunard nor White Star would be able to survive independently and there was no possibility of the government offering to support both companies. The only way in which money would be loaned to complete 534 would be for the two rivals to merge. The offer was of a total of £9,500,000, with £3,000,000 to be used for the completion of 534, £1,500,000 as working capital and £5,000,000 set aside for the construction of the companion vessel. In the end, faced with the inevitable, the directors of the White Star Line had to concede to the merger. Once all parties were in agreement it appears that the offer was accepted with what amounted to almost indecent haste, for by the end of January 1934 the loan had been approved by Parliament. However, it was not finalised for several months. It did in fact take some time to work out the definitive terms and complete the final arrangements for the merger. Then, on the 3rd April, to the sound of a pipe band, the workforce returned to the John Brown shipyard and work resumed on 534 – the liner that would in five months time, on the 26th September, become the *Queen Mary*. On the 10th May 1934 the North Atlantic services of the two companies were officially merged, becoming known from then on as Cunard-White Star Line. A radical shake-up of the former White Star fleet followed, with the withdrawal from service and sale for scrap of the liners *Calgaric*, *Albertic* and *Adriatic*. The already laid up emigrant carrier *Vedic* was also sold for scrap at this time. Two other liners, *Ceramic* and *Ionic*, which had been employed on the run to Australia, were transferred to the Shaw, Savill & Albion Line. The grand liner *Olympic* would have barely a year of service in the newly formed fleet, being withdrawn and placed in lay-up on the 12th April 1935 and sold to be broken up later that year.

Two years and one month after the pipe band had led the shipyard workers back through the gates of the John Brown yard to resume work on 534 she was ready to depart on her maiden voyage. The *Queen Mary* departed Southampton for New York on the 27th May 1936. Over the following months she proved to be extremely popular, despite a tendency to roll in almost any kind of sea at all. Then in August she grasped the legendary Blue Ribbon from her great rival, *Normandie*. In fact the two liners would spend the rest of the 1930s battling over this ephemeral but potent symbol of Atlantic supremacy, with *Normandie* winning it back again in March 1937 and retaining it until August 1938, when the *Queen Mary* managed an Atlantic crossing in just 3 days, 20 hours and 42 seconds. In 1937, her first full year of service, *Queen Mary* carried 56,895 passengers. Both CGT and Cunard had after all timed it well, for in 1935 the number of passengers carried from Europe to the United States improved as the economies of the countries on both sides of the Atlantic were beginning to recover from the worst effects of the Depression. The directors of what was now Cunard-White Star Line began to feel rather more secure, somewhat more confident. With their eyes firmly set upon ordering the running mate to the *Queen Mary*, they retired both the *Olympic* and *Mauretania* in 1935 and the *Majestic* was earmarked to go in the following year.

In a letter to Neville Chamberlain, written on the 13th May 1936, Sir Percy Bates, Chairman of Cunard-White Star Line, set out the company's case for the companion vessel to the *Queen Mary*. Both *Aquitania* and *Berengaria*, whilst still serving the company well, were over twenty years old and thus no match for their impressive new fleet mate. For Cunard-White Star to realize its aim (and that of the Chancellor) to be the pre-eminent company on the North Atlantic the time was right to bring to fruition the plan for the matched pair of express liners. Sir Percy envisaged that it would not be until 1940 that a second such liner could be put into service, by which time *Aquitania* and *Berengaria* would be seriously dated, elderly and struggling to maintain the company's schedule.

The result of the negotiations that followed was that the Treasury agreed to release the promised £5 million towards the construction of a new ship. In June 1936 the Chancellor announced in the House of Commons that he had received a letter from Cunard-White Star seeking authority to use the sum available under the North Atlantic Shipping Act for the construction of a sister ship and that he had agreed in principal. While he also stated that Cunard had received preliminary tenders from various yards, they were negotiating in the first instance with John Brown and Company who had a slip almost ready for the work (and their experience in building giant liners was second to none). While tender documents were sent out to various yards for the contract it was perhaps inevitable that it should go to John Brown's yard at Clydebank, the builders of the *Queen Mary*. Indeed, according to a letter written by Sir Percy Bates on the 11th July 1936 to John Brown's Sir Thomas Bell, as far as the Chancellor of the Exchequer was concerned '… this tender business was all a farce and that the order was in Brown's pocket from the start'. William S. Morrison, Financial Secretary to the Treasury, announced in the House of Commons on the 28th July that the Chancellor had given his final assent to the money being released – after having received ample evidence from Cunard that their choice of yard had been the correct one. The formal contract was signed on the 6th October 1936 and the first keel plates were laid two months later, on the 4th December.

Although Cunard-White Star Line were in receipt of total payments of £9,500,000 from the government to aid the construction of the *Queen Mary* and the *Queen Elizabeth*, this was really a loan. For although the two liners would certainly be 'Ships of State', Cunard-White Star – unlike the owners of the national flagships of most other countries, which had been built with state aid and were underwritten with state subsidies - would have to repay this loan and the 'Queens', along with the rest of the fleet, would have to make a profit.

It was no secret that the companion vessel to *Queen Mary*, which was built on the same slip as her, would be named *Queen Elizabeth* – although for her initial period of construction she was designated Number 552. The numbering appears to have been almost arbitrary as Sir Thomas Bell had proposed that the new liner be given the hull number 535, following on from the number given to the *Queen Mary*. However, Sir Percy Bates had asked the yard 'to think of another good one'. Why 552 should have been chosen as being any 'better' than 535 must remain a mystery.

The building of a ship comparable to the *Queen Mary* was to continue the vision of Samuel Cunard of maintaining a weekly express service to and from the United States - but this time with just two liners. The ships were designed to leave Southampton and New York each week and to pass each other in mid-Atlantic. The timetable meant that one ship departing from Southampton on a Wednesday must then leave New York on the following Wednesday for Europe. The speed required for a regular weekly service of this nature was determined by simple mathematics. The ship leaving Southampton, for example, could not proceed at full speed until she was clear of the Isle of Wight on her way to Cherbourg, and would not sail from the French port until about eight hours after her departure from Southampton.

Similarly, about five hours was the time it took between passing the lightship off New York and being secured in her berth there. At the terminal ports the process of disembarking passengers; refuelling the ship and supplying her with boiler water, stores, provisions, clean linen and the like; and cleaning the entire passenger accommodation for over two thousand people had been reduced to a fine art after years of experience of operating large and luxurious liners on the Atlantic run. This 'turn-around' could, if the need arose, be completed within just twenty-four hours. However, Cunard Line were well aware that passengers did not like leaving or embarking in the middle of the night, so a period of about fifty hours generally elapsed from the time a ship reached her berth until she had embarked her new set of passengers and was ready to sail again.

All of those delays had to be deducted from the actual time available for steaming across the Atlantic. Therefore, in order to maintain a weekly service with two ships required a speed of about 28½ knots. High speed meant expense and since express liners such as the *Queen Elizabeth* and the *Queen Mary* were not designed to carry any great quantity of cargo, it followed that they had to be sufficiently big to accommodate the large number of passengers needed to produce the necessary working revenue over and above the amounts earned by the carriage of the mails. The number of passengers, in their respective classes, was laid down in the light of experience and the speed was determined with due regard to the delays mentioned and others which might be caused by bad weather conditions.

As before the building of any liner, 'tank tests' were run using a variety of models, each of them 200 inches long. The testing tank was about 400 feet long, twenty feet wide and ten feet deep. Attached to a special carriage fitted with intricate and delicate recording instruments, the models were drawn through the water at speeds proportionate to the designed speed of the ship and the results were recorded. Some 8,000 tank experiments were carried out before the shape of the ship was finally decided upon, these models travelling over one thousand miles as a result. Seaworthiness and behaviour in bad weather were also recorded by creating artificial waves in the tank and noting the effects upon the models.

Likewise, the shape and size of the funnels was determined by placing a scale model of the ship, complete with superstructure, boats, ventilators, funnels and other deck equipment, inside a wind tunnel. Suction fans were used to draw air through the ventilators and to pump smoke up the funnels, while a head of wind of any strength could be produced by another fan. The effects were all filmed through plate-glass windows in the tunnel and the effects of using various combinations and shapes of funnels were observed. This enabled the best arrangement to be made for ridding the open deck spaces of funnel smoke and gases.

Sir Percy Bates and the management of Cunard-White Star were agreed that the new ship would not just be a sister to the *Queen Mary*, nor an evolutionary development of her. Her design had to be based upon the very latest revolutionary developments that had taken place in both naval architecture and marine engineering. There was no better ship on the North Atlantic to study than the French Line's *Normandie*. Although vastly different in appearance, the *Queen Mary* and *Normandie* were similar in many respects and both had undergone structural changes since their introduction to enhance their performance and sea-keeping qualities. There was, inevitably, intense rivalry between the two liners. It was not an unusual occurrence for an engineer, technician or designer from one shipping line to book passage on a liner belonging to a competitor company in order to observe their differences and this is what Cunard did. They sent one of their designers for a voyage aboard *Normandie*. On her entry into service in May 1935, *Normandie* had stunned the world with her clean-lined, advanced profile and unique styling. The grace of her elegantly tiered after decks had no equal on the North Atlantic and the fact was that she was fast, very fast indeed. Her turbo-electric power plant was combined with a revolutionary hull design (which was in fact somewhat less than beautiful out of the water, with bulbous lines amidships that contained her bilges). Once afloat, with these bilges hidden, *Normandie* was all grace. She had an unusually long and fine entry at the waterline, which was hollowed out under flaring upper strakes, thus reducing her bow wave to a minimum. The amount of turbulence around her hull, even at high speed, was minimal, whereas the *Queen Mary* was surrounded by a lather of churned up water. While *Queen Mary* ultimately managed to achieve a faster Atlantic crossing than *Normandie*, she needed every bit of her additional forty thousand horsepower in order to obtain that fraction of a knot of extra speed.

The *Queen Mary* was in effect an evolution of the design of *Aquitania*, with her cruiser stern being a token gesture towards modernity. When she entered service, alongside the likes of *Bremen*, *Europa* and *Conte di Savoia* as well as *Normandie*, she already looked outdated. Similarly with her interior. There is no doubt that *Normandie* leaned to excess in her interior décor with astonishingly opulent public rooms of grand and dramatic statement. The *Conte di Savoia* was every bit as stunning in her refined modernity while the German twins were perhaps less bold but nonetheless very striking. On her entry into service the publication *Architect and Building News* dismissed the interiors of the *Queen Mary* as 'mild but expensive vulgarity'. Every one of her public rooms glistened with panelling of exotic woods. The fact that it has been described as being 'modern but not too modern' says a great deal and one can understand Cunard's objective in sending an incognito observer aboard *Normandie*. Nevertheless, the *Queen Mary* enjoyed enormous popularity: there were those passengers who appreciated the homely touches that Cunard gave to her grand public rooms. Indeed, such was her success that Cunard were able to begin to pay back instalments on the government loan.

Chapter 3

CONSTRUCTION

Without fanfare or ceremony, construction of the *Queen Elizabeth* began on Friday the 4th December 1936 with the laying of her keel plates. Initially, the work was given a very high priority, with the shipyard crews working around the clock. She was known at that time as No. 552 although just about everyone had come to accept that she would be given the name *Queen Elizabeth*. However, it would not be until February 1938 that Her Majesty the Queen gave her consent for the ship to bear her name.

In the light of the experience gained in operating the *Queen Mary* and of subsequent developments in shipbuilding and design (as well as impressions gleaned from the voyage aboard *Normandie*), many refinements would be made to the new ship with the result that the two 'Queens' would in fact be far from sister vessels. At 1,031 feet in length and, it was estimated at the time of her launch, with a tonnage of 85,000, the *Queen Elizabeth* was to be the largest and longest vessel ever constructed. The most obvious change in her outward appearance was that she was to have two funnels instead of the *Queen Mary*'s three. This was associated with a reduction in the total number of boilers, from twenty-four main water-tube units to twelve of larger size and output. Further research had also enabled her designers to produce a new form of hull, one feature of which was a stem with a greater rake forward, thus giving the increase of overall length by thirteen feet. Her other principal dimensions remained unaltered from those of the *Queen Mary*. Apart from the funnels, the other very obvious external change was the deletion of the separate forecastle and the enclosing of the forward well-deck, thus giving a flush main deck from the bows to the superstructure. The upper works of the *Queen Elizabeth* were also redesigned with a more refined superstructure added. The reduced space required for funnel casings allowed for a complete rearrangement of the passenger accommodation, though the style of the cabins was largely similar on both ships. Air-conditioning was also provided in the main public rooms.

There was however, much about the basic construction of the *Queen Elizabeth* that was very similar to that of the *Queen Mary*. The hull castings were about the same size as the *Queen Mary*'s and were the largest steel castings ever made at that time. Her stern frame was made in five pieces and extended from the keel to the upper part of the hull. It contained the gudgeons to take the rudder pintles and the opening for the rudder stock and had a total weight of 190 tons. The outer propeller shaft brackets, each in two pieces, weighed 180 tons; the inner shaft brackets, 120 tons; and the stem piece, 125 feet in height and built up in five sections, 60 tons. In all, about 1,000 tons of liquid steel of special quality were required to produce the odd 600 tons finished weight of all these castings.

As with the *Queen Mary*, much of the machinery for the new liner was made either in John Brown's own works or came from the area around Glasgow. There were, however, many contractors and sub-contractors around the industrial cities elsewhere in the United Kingdom who were providing essential items which went towards her creation. As the complex maze of steel began to take on the recognisable shape of a ship, fabrics and leather as well as timber, in some cases of rare and exotic types, were acquired to become panelling and wall coverings.

Captain Taprell Dorling, D.S.O., R.N. was given the opportunity to visit the ship during the early stages of construction, in February 1938. He wrote: "On a blustering morning in February, I was first taken to see the uncompleted hull of 'Number 552', the great vessel … Plated to the height of the main deck, something over one hundred feet above ground level as she lay on the building slip, she dwarfed everything in her vicinity. Encircled by the forest of cranes, masts and gantries used in her construction, her wall side, unpainted and rusty-red, marked with the symmetrical patterning of overlapping plates and tier upon tier of rivets, dwindled foreshortened into the distance like some immense block of buildings.

"Much superstructure remained to be added. Without it, and in the absence of boats, funnels and masts, it was difficult to recognise that stupendous mass as a ship – indeed, as anything designed to float, much less to contain within herself the strength and motive power to enable her to withstand the strains and stresses of being driven at great speed through that most unstable of elements, the sea.

"The uncompleted main deck of 'Number 552,' as I saw it, bore no resemblance whatever to the deck of a ship. The midship structure, seven tiers of it a workman told us, still remained to be added. What we saw was a huge, partly-plated expanse, sloping slightly upwards towards the bows, and 118 feet wide. It was something over 300 yards long – or about the length of three rugby

◁ At this early stage in her construction, the *Queen Elizabeth*'s double bottom and the bulkheads for her bunkers are in place but the scene is dominated by the shipyard cranes.

◁ Although she is far from complete, the vast new ship's bow already dwarfs her surroundings at the John Brown yard. She is to be the biggest liner in the World.

△ The *Queen Elizabeth* begins to take recognisable shape. The curves of her superstructure suggest that her design has been influenced by that of the *Normandie*.

△ The giant hull sparkles in the sunshine on the day before the launch. In the foreground is the stand from which the Queen will perform the ceremony.

▷ This profile view of the new ship's shapely stem clearly shows the aperture for her bow anchor. Unlike the *Bremen* and *Europa* and other contemporary express liners, she does not have a bulbous forefoot.

football grounds between the goal-posts placed end for end.

"Workmen swarmed. The air was full of the deafening clangour and rattle of automatic drills and riveters. Rusty-looking steel plates were being pushed and coaxed into position preparatory to being bolted and then riveted to each other and the steel beams beneath. I remembered that every one of the frames and beams of the huge hull, indeed every component of individual shape, had long since been 'laid off' in the mould loft. In other words, after the shape of the ship had been decided upon, after exhaustive calculation and experiment, full-scale drawings of every part of her skeleton were marked off on the huge expanse of wooden flooring in the mould loft, in a bewildering maze of chalk lines and curves crossing and re-crossing in every direction and incomprehensible to the uninitiated. From these lines the curves were taken off with wooden battens for the actual framework of the ship, while wooden patterns were made of the heavier plates with every curve laid off and every rivet-hole marked.

"Standing amidships on this great expanse of deck, over one hundred feet from the ground, one felt more than

ever convinced that the structure was really part of a huge building. No water was visible, nothing but those gaunt cranes, and the roofs, steeples, towers and chimneys of a great city stretching into the dim, smoky distance. Here and there were open spaces and clumps of trees as yet barren of foliage. To the west were the flat, green meadows of Renfrew, while between them and the ship ran the River Clyde. But no river could be seen from where I stood and looked. The ship seemed so massive and immovable, as though destined to remain where she was for all time.

"We went below to explore her interior, to see cavernous spaces deep down in the hull presently to be occupied by her boilers, turbines and a mass of other machinery. No bulkheads or dividing walls had yet been erected on the passenger decks and the huge restaurant on 'R' Deck, with its rusty steel floor and ceiling, was only recognisable as such by the letters painted on the ship's side. Angle irons riveted to the deck marked the layout of certain other compartments, more painted symbols designating their eventual uses as the cold pantry, larder, glass and china storerooms, the restaurant manager's office, and the like.

R.M.S. QUEEN ELIZABETH

△ Making assurance doubly sure, a shipyard official inspects the slender cord which Her Majesty Queen Elizabeth will use when she launches the new liner.

"Moving aft we came to some tourist cabins, already compartmented and in the process of being lined with wood to try out certain fittings and furniture. Lower down was the tourist class swimming-pool, unrecognisable as such, with its dressing boxes and gymnasium nearby.

"Below, where the bulkheads were already in place, the ship was a bewildering labyrinth to one unfamiliar with her internal arrangements. It was difficult to realise that in two years' time this huge steel shell, manned by a crew of over 1,200, and provided with all the comforts of three differently-priced hotels for over 2,300 passengers, together with all the amenities of a city in the way of shops, amusement and entertainment, will be driving to and fro across the Atlantic."

In 1840 the first Cunard liner, *Britannia*, was described as being a 'mammoth' ship. She was of 1,154 gross tons. The developments during the 100 years that separated that 207 - feet long paddle steamer from the steel shell of Number 552 were almost incomprehensible. The actual launching weight of the structure that would become the *Queen Elizabeth* was estimated to be somewhere about 37,000 tons. All aspects of the launching of the ship had initially to be worked out in theory even before the contract was accepted. Many experiments were carried out in the builder's tank using a 200-inch model of the ship, built exactly to scale and fitted with propellers and all the usual launching appendages. In order that the flow of the water round the hull could be simulated with fair accuracy, the contours of the bottom of the river were reproduced in clay in the tank. A succession of miniature launches, with velocities, stresses, resistances and buoyancy carefully recorded, all provided the essential data.

For the actual launch itself, many factors needed to be taken into consideration, such as the inclination, breadth and camber of the lubricated launching ways along which the ship would move, supported by the moving ways packed tightly under her bottom, and the fore poppets - steel and timber constructions temporarily attached to the ship on either side of her bow that would transfer to the launching ways the weight of the V-shaped bow, which could not otherwise be supported. The thrust brought upon the fore-poppets at the moment the stern portion of the ship becomes water-borne and lifts, while the bow is still in effect ashore, is immense and is the most critical moment of a ship's existence. It would be all the more so with a vessel the size of the *Queen Elizabeth*. There were further calculations regarding the effect of the chain drags which, by means of a whole web of wire hawsers that were temporarily bolted to her sides, would restrain the ship as she moved into the water. The launching of the *Queen Mary*, equally complex and fraught with difficulties given her vast size, went perfectly and it was hoped and expected that the same would hold true for the *Queen Elizabeth* but nothing could be taken for granted.

The work continued at quite a rapid pace, for by the beginning of April 1938 much of the hull steelwork was complete. By the end of August 1938 the propeller bosses were bolted into position. While the workers at the John Brown yard continued their efforts on Number 552 with her launching date getting ever nearer, a shadow of worry hung over those late summer months of 1938. The situation in Czechoslovakia was deteriorating, with Hitler rejecting demands that he reduce the scale of his manoeuvres. As if to highlight the seriousness of the political situation, on the slipway next to the partially completed *Queen Elizabeth* the Royal Navy's newest battleship, HMS *Duke of York*, was under construction, having been laid down on the 5th May 1937.

It had been planned that their Majesties King George VI and Queen Elizabeth would attend the launching ceremony on Tuesday 27th September 1938. But in view of the political tension and with many fearing the possibility of another war, the Prime Minister, Mr. Chamberlain, advised the King not to attend. On the day before the launch an official statement was issued from Buckingham Palace.

"At the request of the Prime Minister the King has cancelled his journey to Clydebank tonight. The Queen, accompanied by Princess Elizabeth and Princess Margaret, will carry out the programme as arranged …"

A knot of onlookers gazes at the hull, still on the slipway. The project to build this enormous liner was hugely important to the economy of the Glasgow area.

As if to match the political situation, the day was grey, wet and miserable. The *Queen Elizabeth*, however, shone, for unlike the *Queen Mary* at her launching, she had been painted in her correct Cunard livery of black hull, red boot-topping with a white line above it and white superstructure. At this time her superstructure was devoid of any windows or openings. These would be cut at a later date but were left uncut in order to give the upper parts of ship additional strength and stiffness during the critical time of her launching. Before arriving at the shipyard, the Royal party was taken to the Empire Exhibition, which had opened in Glasgow the previous year. A highlight of the exhibition was an eighteen-foot long model of the new liner. At 3 pm, on their arrival at the shipyard, the Queen and the Princesses were met by Sir Percy Bates, Chairman of the Cunard-White Star Line, The Rt. Hon. Lord Aberconway, Chairman of John Brown & Co., Ltd., and Mr. S.J. Pigott, Resident Director of John Brown & Co., Ltd. The Queen, who was in fact still in mourning for her mother, Lady Strathmore, who had died on 23rd June, wore grey, with a smart small hat. While the Queen apparently looked fragile and thinner than she had earlier in the year, she delivered the pre-launch speech, in reply to the loyal address by Sir Percy Bates, with confidence.

"I thank you for the kind words of your address.

"The King has asked me to assure you of the deepest regret he feels at finding himself compelled at the last moment to cancel his journey to Clydebank for the launching of the new liner.

"This ceremony, to which many thousands have looked forward so eagerly, must now take place in circumstances far different from those which they had hoped.

"I have, however, a message for you from the King. He bids the people of this country to be of good cheer, in spite of the dark clouds hanging over them, and indeed, over the whole world. He knows well that, as ever before in critical times, they will keep cool heads and brave hearts; he knows, too, that they will place entire confidence in their leaders, who, under God's providence, are striving their utmost to find a just and peaceful solution to the grave problems which confront them.

"The very sight of this great ship brings home to us how essential it is for the welfare of man that the arts of peaceful industry should continue - arts in the promotion of which Scotland has long held a leading place.

"The City of Glasgow has been for Scotland the principal doorway opening upon the world. The narrow waters of the Clyde have been the cradle of a large part of Britain's mercantile marine. So it is right that from here should come our foremost achievement in that connection - the greatest

The hull of the *Queen Elizabeth* slides down the ways and enters the water, a moment of great tension and of maximum stress for her structure.

of the ships that ply to and fro across the Atlantic, like shuttles in a mighty loom, weaving a fabric of friendship and understanding between the people of Britain and the people of the United States. It is altogether fitting that the noblest vessel ever built in Britain, and built with the help of her Government and her people, should be dedicated to this service. I am happy to think that our two nations are today more closely linked than ever before by a common tradition of freedom and a common faith. While thoughts like these are passing through our minds, we do not forget the men who have brought this great ship into being. For them she must ever be a source of pride and credit - and, let me add, affection. I congratulate them warmly on the fruits of their labours.

"The launching of a ship is like the inception of all great human enterprises, an act of faith. We cannot foretell the future, but, in preparing for it, we show our trust in a Divine Providence and in ourselves. We proclaim our belief that by

the Grace of God, and by man's patience and good will, order may yet be brought out of confusion and peace out of turmoil. With that hope and prayer in our hearts we send forth upon her mission this noble ship."

It was the first time that the general public had heard the voice of the Queen, which was broadcast over the airwaves (and film of the event was shown on Pathe News in cinemas). There was a symmetry to this because when Queen Mary had performed the naming ceremony of the liner *Queen Mary*, it too was the first time that the general public had heard her voice.

After the speeches there followed a pause in the proceedings to await the moment when the tide was at its correct state. It was during this time that the Queen was presented with an album of photographs of the new liner at varying stages of the construction. However, it appeared that the *Queen Elizabeth* was unwilling to wait a moment longer and, regardless of tide or royal personage, slowly she began to move down the slipway. The Queen and the officials around her looked momentarily startled but quickly she released the bottle of wine, which fortunately managed to break against the receding hull and as it did so she said: "I name this ship *Queen Elizabeth* and wish success to her and all who sail in her." As the newly-named liner thundered down to meet the waters of the Clyde, the crowd, estimated to be at least 250,000, cheered loudly and the river craft sounded their whistles and sirens. The eighteen bundles of chains, weighing in total 2,350 tons, that were secured to the ship's sides with steel cables attached to eye bolts, roared and rattled and then the *Queen Elizabeth* was afloat. Tugs took control of her, with the *Paladin* and *Flying Eagle* at her bows: they eased her 1,031 feet length towards the fitting out berth.

After the launch ceremony the Queen and the Princesses departed but the other guests gathered in the Mould Loft, which had been transformed from its usual role of being the space where the scale drawings of sections of the ships were made up into wooden templates, into the venue for a post-launch tea. In a speech Sir Percy Bates said that the launch of the *Queen Elizabeth* was bringing closer the fulfilment of a long-held dream of many shipowners: a weekly transatlantic ferry service maintained by two ships. He continued: "The ship you have seen launched is no slavish copy of her sister.

I described the sister, the *Queen Mary*, as the smallest and slowest ship that would do the job. Naval architecture and marine engineering have not stood still since we contracted for No. 534 and we tried hard to make use of their progress to get functional requirements for the sister ship expressed in a smaller hull. We found it impossible. For our schedule we need no more speed than the *Queen Mary* has got. There is no sense in having one-half of a weekly service faster than the other. Yet technical advances made it absurd for us to repeat what we had done. There had to be changes. These changes have cost us little or no money. They can hardly be needed in speed, though I think No 552 – the *Elizabeth* – might travel a little faster than No. 534, but they can be expressed in economy in the weekly job of crossing the Atlantic."

A lavish book of hand-tinted coloured photographs, by Stewart Bale, of the construction of the liner and of scenes of the launch was produced as a very special souvenir of the event. In it was a quote from H.G. Wells' 'Outline of History':

"Before the nineteenth century there were no ships in the world much over 2,000 tons burthen, now there is nothing remarkably wonderful about a 50,000 ton liner. There are people who sneer at this kind of progress as being a progress 'in mere size', but that sort of sneering merely marks the

Flanked by the flags of John Brown and Cunard-White Star, the Royal Standard flies proudly as the Queen names the ship. The young princesses are at their mother's side.

intellectual limitations of those who indulge in it. The great ship or steel frame building is not, as they imagine, a magnified version of the ship of the past: it is a thing different in kind, more lightly and strongly built, of finer and stronger materials; instead of being a thing of precedent and rule of thumb, it is a thing of subtle and intricate calculation. In the old house or ship, matter was dominant - the material and its needs had slavishly to be obeyed; in the new, matter has been captured, coerced, changed. Think of the coal and the iron and sand, dragged out of the banks and pits, wrenched, wrought, molten and cast to be flung at last, a slender glittering pinnacle of steel and glass six hundred feet above a crowded city ..."

The souvenir book went on to say: "and to continue this striking illustration, think of it in terms of that mighty ship launched by Her Majesty the Queen at Clydebank on September 27th. Here, indeed, is a thing of 'subtle and intricate calculation'; here, indeed, is the epitome of the genius of the marine engineer and naval architect linked with the accumulated knowledge of the Cunard-White Star company, whose practical experience is the life-story of the Atlantic steam ferry; here, indeed, is a vessel which, though her vast dimensions may make her the largest ship in the world, is the very antithesis of 'progress in mere size' in that she is the smallest and slowest vessel to carry out the service between Europe and North America for which she is intended. That is the attainment which lies behind the conception and construction of the great ship honoured by Her Majesty the Queen with the name Queen Elizabeth."

While the launching of the Cunard-White Star Line's new flagship made front-page news on the 27th September, just three days later it was Neville Chamberlain – now the Prime Minister – making the headlines. He had returned to England from talks with Hitler in Munich. Emerging from the aircraft at Heston aerodrome in North London, he promised "Peace in our time!"

While there remained that possible chance that another war could be averted, work continued on Clydebank as before. Cunard's sights were still firmly on the introduction in 1940 of their two-ship express service. On the 22nd August 1939 Cunard-White Star Line rather optimistically announced that the Queen Elizabeth would undertake her maiden voyage from Southampton to Cherbourg and New York on the 24th April 1940.

As the world's largest liner, while very obviously a Cunarder, the Queen Elizabeth would in some ways be much closer in feeling to the French Normandie than to her own fleetmate, Queen Mary. Her overall appearance would be more sleek and refined and with a much tidier profile. The two funnels would give her a much greater amount of deck and promenade space as well as allowing for an increase in passenger accommodation. Three anchors were provided, instead of the two on the Queen Mary, the additional one being placed in the centre of her stem. The bow itself, as

was apparent on the day of her launch, was shaped with a greater rake than the Queen Mary's. As a result, the Queen Elizabeth was thirteen feet longer than the older ship. Another new feature was the absence of the break in the forward part of the hull. The flush main deck produced a remarkably graceful line from the bow to the bridge.

The Queen Elizabeth was a quadruple-screw vessel, driven by four sets of Parsons single-reduction geared turbines capable of developing 160,000 horsepower. Each of her manganese-bronze propellers, machined from a single casting, weighed 32 tons and was driven by an independent set of machinery with a large gear wheel. Each of the gear wheels was 14 feet in diameter and the total weight of all four amounted to nearly 320 tons. Every one of the 257,000 individual blades on each of the eight turbines, one forward and one reverse on each shaft, was tested and fitted by hand. Two separate engine rooms were required for her propelling machinery. Steam was supplied to the sixteen turbines by twelve high-pressure water-tube boilers. These were the largest boilers ever constructed for a ship and contained 71,000 tubes. Oil fuel was distributed in about 40 bunkers, from which 4,000 feet of piping led to the furnaces.

The electrical services of the Queen Elizabeth were on a most elaborate scale. The four immense turbo-generators installed in her tremendous power station were capable of supplying sufficient electrical energy to meet the lighting and heating requirements of a town with a population of nearly 200,000. Four thousand miles of cable and approximately 30,000 lamps were installed.

In the three classes of accommodation - Cabin (it was envisaged that, like the Queen Mary, she would enter service with her principal accommodation categorised as Cabin Class rather than First Class), Tourist Class and Third Class - the Queen Elizabeth was to have twenty-nine public rooms, many of which were to have the latest system of air-conditioning. A specially equipped theatre and a Garden Lounge were to be included in the magnificent range of Cabin Class public rooms on the Promenade Deck. Another 'innovation' was to be the Restaurant Deck which, as its name implied, provided accommodation for all three impressive restaurants, as well as the spacious kitchens, service rooms and pantries. Also to be included were a gymnasium, squash racquets court, swimming pool and Turkish and electric ray baths for Cabin passengers. Tourist Class passengers were also to have their own gymnasium and swimming pool and a separate gymnasium was to be introduced for Third Class passengers. In addition, the Sports Deck, for all classes, and the wide terraced decks at the aft end of the ship would provide what were described as being 'magnificent open-air playing fields'.

The ship was to carry twenty-six motor lifeboats, most of them thirty-six feet long and each capable of carrying 145 people. The complete system of watertight doors was controlled hydraulically from the bridge, while

⚠ The hull has been safely launched and has been towed to the fitting out quay, where it is inspected by a crowd of guests.

the arrangements made for preventing, detecting and extinguishing fires was to be the most comprehensive ever installed afloat at that time. She was also to be fitted with gyro-pilot equipment for automatic steering, which, since it eliminated the human element, could increase the average speed of the ship by as much as four-tenths of a knot. A course-reading instrument would automatically register all alterations of course and the time of their occurrence. There was to be the usual echo-sounding apparatus for ascertaining the depth of water at the rate of fifty soundings a minute; electrical equipment on the bridge to operate the three deep-toned whistles, each weighing about a ton; an electrical appliance which instantly extinguished small lamps on the bridge if the navigation lights failed; and, of course, a complete service of loudspeakers and telephones throughout the ship.

For fourteen months after her launching the *Queen Elizabeth* sat alongside her fitting out berth. Despite the difficult political situation in mainland Europe, Cunard-White Star and John Brown & Co. were still working to their original schedule. Luckily, very little industrial unrest had been encountered at any time during the construction of the *Queen Elizabeth*. The only time that there had been a problem had been during the summer of 1939, when 350 plumbers walked out in protest at what they claimed was an encroachment on their area of work by coppersmiths. It was one of those silly issues, with the plumbers claiming that the copper piping being used by the coppersmiths actually came under their jurisdiction. The strike lasted two weeks.

The large windows that would flank her promenade decks and give panoramic views from her forward superstructure had been cut out and the large letters, each two and a half feet high, spelling out her name were affixed to her bow and at her stern with 'Liverpool' as her port of registry. Even before her funnels were fixed she was beginning to look like a ship ready to take to the sea but during the summer months of 1938, the first sections of these were lifted aboard.

Mr. George Gray Wornum, the influential architect and designer, was in overall charge of the interior decoration of the liner and therefore he had the responsibility of co-ordinating the artistic skills of the many people whose works would be incorporated into her. Gradually, as the months passed the bare steel spaces began to take on the recognisable forms of lounges, bars, restaurants and cabins. Rare and unusual timbers had been acquired to panel these rooms, particularly those in Cabin Class. From the Empire and beyond came Birch, Blistered and Bird's Eye Maples, Silky Oak, Bean Wood, Laurelwood, Coralwood, Sandalwood, Rosewood, Tulipwood, Beefwood and Olivewood. There were also Satina, Thuya, Mahogany, Zebrano, Purple Heart, Coromandel, Cherry, Almond, Sycamore, Acacia and Laburnum. The Captain's cabin was panelled in a veneer made from Wych Elm which had been used as pilings for Waterloo Bridge, built in 1811. When a new bridge was

built these pilings were removed and the wood was found to have been bleached an attractive grey by the waters of the Thames. Over 1,000 tons of Burma Teak was used to plank the decks and for other carpentry work on board.

On the 3rd September 1939, a little over a week after Cunard had announced the date of the maiden voyage of the *Queen Elizabeth*, war was declared between Great Britain and Germany. Everything suddenly changed, not least the work in the John Brown's shipyard. There were now other priorities and many of the workers were moved away from the almost completed liner to concentrate on naval vessels: while the fitting out work continued on the *Queen Elizabeth*, it was done at a less urgent pace. Would her voyage to New York take place as planned?

Indeed, the future not only of the *Queen Elizabeth* but also of the *Queen Mary* was suddenly called into question. The *Queen Mary* had arrived in New York the day after the declaration of war, having had aboard a record 2,332 passengers as well as a considerable cargo of gold bullion. Americans, either on holiday in Europe or even those who had been living there, fled in their many thousands and berths aboard all of the New York-bound liners were suddenly at a premium. On the 6th September Cunard-White Star announced that all sailings of the *Queen Mary* had been cancelled for the foreseeable future. Arrangements were made for those members of her crew who were part of the Royal Naval Reserve to be returned to Britain. Thus, within just a few days of her arrival in New York only a handful of her officers and crew remained on board. As there were countless rumours (though none of them ever confirmed) of German sympathisers active in New York, an agreement between British Intelligence and their American counterparts as well as the FBI and the New York Police Department ensured there was a protective cordon around Cunard's Pier 90. The sabotage of the *Queen Mary* would have made fine Nazi propaganda.

The future use of the two liners in the time of war was discussed in Parliament. They were seen as little more than vulnerable giants. It was suggested that as the *Queen Elizabeth* was totally untried she should be laid up in a remote Scottish loch. Alternatively, there were suggestions that she either be sold to America or even have her superstructure cut down and be converted into an aircraft carrier. The important thing was that the decision had to be made and made quickly as her fitting out berth would soon be needed for the 35,000 ton battleship *Duke of York*: work had progressed on that vessel and she was to be launched on the 16th September. While the debate continued, both in the Admiralty and in Parliament, regarding the future of what their critics had labelled 'the white elephants', the *Queen Mary* was given a change of livery to a light blue/grey, a colour that would make her more suited to a wartime role, whatever that might be.

Their Majesties the King and Queen journeyed up to Glasgow for the launching of the new battleship and it was at this time that the King was finally able to visit the almost completed liner. She was the very pride of the British merchant fleet, the largest liner the world had seen. Her overall length was 1,031 feet, she was 118 feet wide and had a draught of 39 feet: her gross tonnage was 83,673.

Mr. Winston Churchill, First Lord of the Admiralty, was very concerned for the safety of the *Queen Elizabeth*. He was anxious that she be completed as soon as possible and then moved from harm's way, away from the British Isles. As a consequence, on the 2nd November 1939 he issued orders to the Ministry of Shipping that the *Queen Elizabeth* should be made ready to go to sea. A special licence was granted for the supply of valuable steel and labour so that she could be completed to such a state that she could sail away to safety. Once again workers swarmed over the liner but now the work was focused just on what was essential to make the ship ready for sea, thus any further work on the fitting out of her passenger accommodation was brought to a halt. On the 16th November 1939 her boilers were lit for the very first time and on the 29th December her engines were turned under steam. This enabled various tests to be made while the ship was still alongside but it would still be another three months before she would be ready to leave the builders' yard and take to the sea. During this time she lost her glorious Cunard livery and instead was painted in a blue/grey all over, including her windows and portholes, and a degaussing coil was hastily fitted around the outside of her hull. This was rubber-coated copper cable which was electrically charged and had the effect of neutralising the magnetic field that would have

been created in the hull during the ship's construction. It was hoped that this would ensure that she was immune from the menace of magnetic mines. The *Queen Elizabeth* was one of the first ships to be fitted with such a device, so it was something of an experiment at that time.

During this period, at one of the meetings to plan *Queen Elizabeth*'s voyage away to safety, Sir Percy Bates asked his superintendent engineer: "Assuming we have got to do this extraordinary thing, break our contract with the builders, and send an untried ship across the Atlantic without thinking what we might meet on the way, what sort of speed do you think you could put up?" He replied: "I think about 25 knots." Then one of Sir Percy's colleagues asked: "Well, Mr. Austin, suppose there was a German submarine about, what would she do then?" The engineer answered: "Oh, not very much more than 32."

The *Queen Elizabeth* would be heading, they said, for Southampton, as that was the only British port with a dry dock large enough to take her. On board was Captain Duncan Cameron, the pilot who had taken the *Queen Mary* from her fitting out berth and down the River Clyde and he had been Cunard's choice to guide the *Queen Elizabeth* on that same journey. Although it had been his plan to leave the ship once she arrived at the Tail of the Bank, Cunard had apparently been keen for him to remain with her – for the start of her coastal journey down to Southampton. Thus this was all part of the plan to confuse people (and particularly any enemy agents) as to her destination.

The *Queen Elizabeth* is moved slowly away from the fitting out basin on her way to Tail of the Bank where final preparations will be made for her secret Atlantic crossing.

Chapter 4

QUEEN ELIZABETH AT WAR

During 1940 there were to be just two tides on the River Clyde that would be high enough to get the *Queen Elizabeth* safely away from the port area of Glasgow and allow her to anchor off Gourock. The first of these tides was on Monday the 26th February: this was the opportunity that had to be grasped. The quiet of the 'Phoney War' could not last for ever and, although waiting until the next suitable tide, in August, would have given John Brown's men the time they needed to finish so many partially completed tasks aboard the ship, it was not a risk that either Cunard or the Admiralty was willing to take. Every day waited was a day nearer to possible aerial attack from German bombers: the *Queen Elizabeth* had to be moved on the February tide.

With no announcement that the new liner would be moving down the Clyde on that day, there were few people to see her begin this momentous journey towards the sea. However, an 83,000 ton liner cannot be moved so far down a river without anyone noticing - particularly when she has become such a dominant part of the skyline, as well as a dominant part of people's lives, for over three years. With her attendant tugs sounding their sirens back and forth and an aircraft circling overhead, it became clear that something important was happening. The handful of people who had stopped to see the great ship moved, for the first time since she was launched, were gradually joined by others as the word began to spread: "The *Queen Elizabeth*, she's leaving!" Eventually, there were several hundred people lining the banks of the river at any handy vantage point.

The passage down the river took about five hours, fraught with tension. She anchored off the Tail of the Bank and after the brief handing over ceremony from John Brown's to Cunard-White Star Line the following afternoon, she began three and a half days of tests and compass adjustments. But these tests were all undertaken with the ship still at anchor. It was too great a risk to undertake any proper trials voyage. While standing at anchor she took up into her davits all but eight of her twenty lifeboats. All her boats had been off-loaded prior to her journey down the Clyde in order to make her lighter and therefore ride higher in the water, thus lessening the risk of her running aground.

At 7.30 am on the morning of Saturday the 2nd March the *Queen Elizabeth* weighed anchor and headed out into the early morning mist towards New York. She was not alone: four destroyers and several aircraft accompanied her as far as the coast of Northern Ireland. Then, as she gathered speed and the naval escort peeled away from her, the largest, newest and totally untried liner in the world really was on her own. The open Atlantic Ocean was before her and whatever threats that might hold.

It was the most curious of voyages for her 398 crew members. Some of their accommodations were still unfinished, with unsecured light fittings, unconnected electrical cables and bare steel decks that were a sharp reminder of the lack of heating. This was all in acute contrast to those passenger areas of the ship which had been completed with their luxurious wall coverings of tapestries, rich panelling and other fabrics and with deep-pile carpets underfoot. The furniture that had been delivered to the ship was covered in protective dust sheets which highlighted the ghostly effect of the almost empty liner.

Although radio silence was largely enforced, the speeding *Queen Elizabeth* did receive one message: it required that she change course in order to avoid being in the same area as a convoy. Other than that, she sailed in silence, blacked-out at night and maintaining a zigzagging course for the entire journey in an attempt to confuse any U-Boats which might have been encountered. The circumstances inevitably generated a special bond between those on board and the purser organised a club, 'The Unruffled Elizabethans'. Captain Townley was the club president while Captain Cameron, her unwitting passenger, was one of the club members. While there was work to be done during the crossing – tests and inspections of her untried machinery (for although she had been officially handed over to Cunard, some shipyard officials had remained on board to monitor the smooth running of the ship) – in the evenings members of The Unruffled Elizabethans would provide entertainment with stories, songs or musical recitals. Despite the odd circumstances of their being together and the strangeness of this 'maiden voyage', their aim was '… that true Twentieth-Century Elizabethans are able to remain under all conditions completely unruffled'.

The crew of the *Queen Elizabeth* were not fully able to live up to this tenet of The Unruffled Elizabethans, for although the voyage was completed under conditions of such secrecy almost all of New York seemed to be aware of their approach. The first sign of this was when a TransWorld airliner flew over the ship. Then a member of the crew heard on a radio

◁ Manhattan motorists have a grand view of the three mightiest liners in the world, together for the only time. From left to right:: *Normandie*, *Queen Mary* and *Queen Elizabeth*.

△ Still in her peacetime livery but with neutrality markings painted on her sides, the shapely Italian *Rex* is pulled by tugs from her berth alongside the *Queen Elizabeth* in Manhattan.

(which he was not actually supposed to have on board) a BBC broadcast which repeated the announcement from New York that the *Queen Elizabeth* was on her way. Their only encounter with another ship, after the destroyer escort had left, came as they neared New York and met the outbound sludge carrier *Coney Island* and the two ships saluted each other with blasts on their sirens as they passed.

When she reached New York, a small fleet of Moran tugs carefully eased the *Queen Elizabeth* into her berth and the three largest liners in the world were together: *Queen Elizabeth*, *Queen Mary* and *Normandie*. The New York Times was as enthused about her arrival as all the other newspapers: they called her the 'Empress Incognito' and referred to the '… unheralded arrival of the biggest and the fastest liner in the world'. Caught up in its own hyperbole, the report continued: "Any landlubber can see that the *Queen Elizabeth* is a fine ship, as sleek and graceful as a yacht; a credit to the British merchant marine". Indeed, it was safe to assume that under her all-encompassing coat of grey paint she was a fine ship and there was no doubt that she was a credit to the British merchant marine – but as graceful as a yacht? *The New York Times* also very rightly drew attention to the fact

that she was new in design, pointing out that the *Queen Mary* had been conceived before the crossing of the *Bremen*, the *Rex* or the *Normandie*. The report went on to say: "The *Queen Elizabeth* is the first super-liner to embody the lessons of these maritime pioneers of our streamlined era".

Whilst under those strange circumstances we cannot deny the *New York Times* reporter his excitement, it was, in fact, all too apparent that despite having sent a designer aboard *Normandie*, Cunard had still elected to steer a careful path when it came to the external design of the *Queen Elizabeth*. With the three ships together, comparisons could be made. While the *Queen Elizabeth*'s after decks were lacking in the clutter and awkward angles of those of the *Queen Mary*, they still had none of the exquisite grace of the elegantly tiered after decks of the *Normandie*. That ship, with her graceful and rakish lines, and despite her three large funnels, belied the fact that she was an 83,000 ton liner whereas, with her more upright appearance, the *Queen Elizabeth* looked every bit of her 83,000 tons.

After the days of enforced silence during the dash across the Atlantic one particularly important message was received aboard the *Queen Elizabeth*. It came from Her Majesty the

Queen: "I send you my heartfelt congratulations on the safe arrival in New York of the *Queen Elizabeth*. Ever since I launched her in the fateful days of 1938, I have watched her progress with interest and admiration. Please convey to Captain Townley my compliments on the safe conclusion of her hazardous maiden voyage. Elizabeth R."

Berthed along with the two Cunard 'Queens' and *Normandie* were Cunard's elderly *Aquitania*, the last four-funnelled liner in the world, and the virtually brand new *Mauretania*. Subsequently, in the late afternoon of the 11th April, almost three weeks after the *Queen Mary* had left this remarkable line up, the superb Italian liner *Rex* arrived, glorious in her full Italian Line livery. She tied up in the berth next to the *Queen Elizabeth*, her racy lines and sparkling livery in sharp contrast to the grey bulk of the huge Cunarder. The *Rex* would return to New York and tie up next to the *Queen Elizabeth* just one more time before the transatlantic services of the Italian Line ceased. The beautiful *Rex* and her running mate *Conte di Savoia* would be laid up - never to sail again.

The three British and French Atlantic giants had been together for just two weeks. In the afternoon of the 21st March the *Queen Mary* departed. Her war time career was

about to begin: it had been decided that she would be used as a troop-transport vessel. During the discussions between the Admiralty and Government, the vast size of the two 'Queens', and therefore their huge potential to carry far more troops than any other ship had done before, was acknowledged. The initial argument against this was that because of the sheer size of the two ships the Royal Navy would have to assign valuable vessels, cruisers or destroyers, to escort them – vessels that could be put to far better use elsewhere. It was also claimed that the fuel that each liner would burn every day would be better used by the Royal Navy ships. The argument in favour of the 'Queens' was simple: the vast capacity of the ships was their greatest asset; they could move an unprecedented number of troops to wherever they were needed, allowing for their most effective use. Built as potential transatlantic record breakers, their speed would ensure that they could outrun any U-boat or other warship, thus ensuring that there was no need for a naval escort wherever they went. The speed of the 'Queens' was their own defence. It was a compelling argument and it won the day. On the 6th March 1940 a message was sent from the Admiralty to the directors of Cunard-White Star informing them that the services of the *Queen Mary* were required by King and Country. The message further stated: "His Majesty's Government relies on the goodwill of yourselves, your staffs and agents in carrying out these instructions and preparing the ship for the King's service, especially as regards clearing cargo, fuelling, storing and manning."

On the 21st March 1940 the *Queen Mary* sailed from New York, bound for Sydney, Australia. It was there that work would be undertaken to fit her out as a troopship. In order to help ensure her a safe passage, no indication had been given of her intended voyage: first down to the Caribbean island of Trinidad and then across the Southern Atlantic to Cape Town. In fact, careful rumours were seeded in order to put the German navy off her scent. Even the newspapers reported, with some authority, that both the *Queen Mary* and *Mauretania* would be used to carry men and supplies between the west coast of Canada and Australia. The *Queen Mary* arrived in Sydney on the 13th April and, after conversion work, started her first voyage in her new role as a troopship on the 5th May 1940, sailing from Sydney to Scotland.

By now, with Britain well in the grip of the war, there was a major change: on the 10th May, Winston Churchill replaced Neville Chamberlain as Prime Minister.

With the *Queen Mary* gone, the *Queen Elizabeth* was then moved into the berth that she had vacated and this allowed even greater comparison between the *Queen Elizabeth* and *Normandie* which, had fate not been so unkind, would have been direct rivals. The majority of the men who had crossed aboard the *Queen Elizabeth* were returned to Britain, sailing back on the *Scythia* and leaving the 'Queen' with just a skeleton crew of 143 to maintain her. Under the Geneva Convention

Now fitted out as a troopship, *Queen Elizabeth* lies in Sydney harbour awaiting the embarkation of over 5,000 Australian servicemen whom she will carry to the battlefields of the Middle East.

it was only possible for maintenance or construction work of what was described as a 'non-belligerent nature' to be carried out. However, six weeks after the departure of the *Queen Mary*, the *Queen Elizabeth* was moved over to the Todd shipyard in Hoboken. This yard had been contracted to continue with the work on board that John Brown's workers had been unable to complete but none of this was of a military nature. To have done that would have compromised America's position as a neutral country. Thus, the decks were caulked and equipment which had been transported aboard the ship as cargo was unpacked and fitted. Whilst this was taking place much of what had been placed aboard for her role as a passenger liner, furniture and other fittings, was taken off and placed in storage.

The *Queen Elizabeth* remained at her berth for eight months. During early November her skeleton crew were joined by 322 further crew members (who had travelled to New York via Canada) bringing her compliment up to 465. There was speculation in the New York newspapers and along the waterfront that something was about to happen with some suggesting that she was to depart for Halifax, Nova Scotia, while others thought that she was just being moved to another berth. Those who had watched carefully would have realised that not only had the ship received additional crew

members but she had also taken on a full load of fuel and water. None of these things would be required for a change of berth and they were hardly even necessary for the short voyage up to Halifax. While the work had been going on to finish off the multitude of tasks aboard the *Queen Elizabeth*, a meeting had been held in New York between Cunard officials and representatives of the British government and they had decided that the ship should follow the *Queen Mary* and also take on the role of troop transport. There was, however, much to be done to her first, things that it had been impossible to undertake while she was alongside her Manhattan berth. She had been in the water for two years, so her hull needed to be cleaned and the remains of her launching gear also had to be removed. Therefore, she must be dry docked and the nearest such dock that was available to her was on the other side of the world – in Singapore. To have attempted to place her in the dry dock at Southampton would have exposed her again to the high risk of attack from German aircraft; and the naval dock at Bayonne, New Jersey was denied to her because of American neutrality. The only other dry dock large enough to accommodate her was on the West Coast of Canada and to reach that she would have had to trek round South America, a voyage that was even longer than that out to Singapore.

At 3.30 pm on the 13th November she slipped from her berth and again headed towards the Atlantic. This time she was on a southerly course. She was scheduled to make two stops during this voyage in order to take on both fuel and water. The first of these was a rendezvous with an oil tanker several miles off the island of Trinidad. Then she steamed across the South Atlantic to South Africa and anchored off the Simonstown naval base at Cape Town. Her arrival caused great interest and large crowds of people went along to see this huge new liner. She arrived in Singapore three weeks after having left New York. As soon as the *Queen Elizabeth* was secured in the dry dock, the first task was to rid her of her unwelcome passengers – the rats which had managed to get aboard the ship while she had been alongside in New York. Her conversion into a troopship would take seven weeks and it was hot and unpleasant work on a ship designed to operate in the chilly North Atlantic. Part of the conversion work on the *Queen Mary* had been undertaken at the same shipyard (as well as in Sydney), so the lessons learned helped in the transformation of the *Queen Elizabeth*. Her capacity was increased to enable her to accommodate 5,000 troops. Guns were fitted on her upper decks and her glass-panelled engine room skylights had covers welded over them. While affording her engine room crew some measure of protection in case of aerial attack, covering these skylights meant that the temperature in the engine rooms, particularly while in the tropics, would rise to an almost unbearable level. The

hull of the ship was once again returned to black but she retained her grey upper works.

While the *Queen Mary* had been refitting at Singapore some rougher elements of her crew, apparently not regular Cunard men, had caused a lot of disruption. The *Queen Elizabeth* had the misfortune to have a similar element aboard but after several unpleasant incidents they were taken off the ship, under armed escort, and were returned to the United Kingdom.

The arrival of the *Queen Elizabeth* in Sydney in February 1941 was little short of sensational: crowds lined the coast and harbour and the numbers of people on the famous harbour bridge brought the traffic to a standstill – with car drivers also getting out to gaze in awe at the huge liner. The local ferries, too, were crowded with people all anxious for a view. Further conversion work on the ship was undertaken at the Cockatoo Docks and Engineering Company – this included changing some of the things which had been done in Singapore because they were regarded as not of a good enough standard. In order to enable her to carry over 5,000 troops, hammocks and additional bunks were installed.

In April the two 'Queens' met for the first time since they had been in New York. However, Sydney harbour was not large enough to accommodate both ships together. Therefore, one of them would load her troops by tender while she lay at anchor in the harbor, with the other ship standing off, waiting. With 5,600 troops aboard the *Queen*

▽ Convoy US 10 with left to right: *Nieuw Amsterdam, Queen Mary, Queen Elizabeth* and *Mauretania* and *Ile de France* is out of shot. Taken in the Bass Strait.

Elizabeth and 6,000 aboard the *Queen Mary*, they were ready to make their first convoy voyage together. Amongst the various other famous liners in the convoy were the *Ile de France, Nieuw Amsterdam, Aquitania* and *Mauretania*. With the two mighty 'Queens' joining it, this was a most remarkable gathering of some of the most significant liners in the world. For the 'Queens', however, it was a relatively slow-moving voyage as they were limited by the speed of the slowest vessel in the convoy. Their journey was across the Indian Ocean and then up the Red Sea to Port Tewfik since the troops they were carrying were destined for the fighting in the Egyptian desert. The emphasis of the war had turned to this area after Mussolini had staged an invasion on Egypt, which at that time was a British protectorate. The ships returned to Australia carrying wounded and prisoners. On board both the 'Queens', as well as on other liners in the convoy that had been designed for service on the North Atlantic, it was an uncomfortable time voyaging between Australia and the Red Sea and the high temperatures on board the ships while in those tropic waters were the cause of several deaths. Almost a year was spent on this service and between them the 'Queens' transported nearly 80,000 troops to the Red Sea port.

By December 1941 the *Queen Elizabeth* was temporarily laid up in Sydney. Once the Japanese had attacked Pearl Harbour and therefore brought the United States into the war, the Pacific was an especially dangerous place for her to be. With the very real fear of a Japanese invasion of Australia, that country needed her remaining troops at home.

That same month, Churchill and his staff travelled to Washington for a joint strategic planning session. There it was decided that they had to adopt a strategy of 'Germany first' as Nazi Germany was perceived to be the greater threat. However, there was a very real need to not loose what control they had in the Pacific – Australia had to be held. It would be a lengthy business withdrawing the Australian troops from the North African desert, so in the meantime US troops would have to be sent to ensure Australia did not fall into Japanese hands.

During the conference it was decided that the Americans would be responsible for the operation of both the *Queen Elizabeth* and the *Queen Mary*. Their crews would remain Cunard employees but the costs of operating the two ships would be paid by the United States Government. This of course would mean that the ships would become subject to U.S. Naval regulations. The decision was also made to increase their troop-carrying capabilities so that they could each carry an entire division. Giving the ships this capability would probably enable the Allies to change the course of the war.

The *Queen Mary* had been returned to the Clyde and it was decided to send the *Queen Elizabeth* to Canada to be dry docked at Esquimalt, as using the Singapore dry dock was now out of the question. After a year in tropical waters she

had a large amount of growth on her hull which urgently needed removing as it was reducing her speed by as much as two knots. For the long haul across the Pacific the *Queen Elizabeth* needed two stops for refuelling and to take on additional water. The first stop was in New Zealand and the second was at the remote Nuku Hiva in the Marquesas Islands, where she was to meet up with an American tanker. But the tanker had had a difficult voyage and she was not at the appointed rendezvous and this caused some anxious minutes as a Japanese raider was known to be active in the area. The tanker appeared ten minutes late and then the refuelling began, taking eight hours to complete. Even having arrived at Vancouver Island, the problems of the voyage were far from over. Due to a miscalculation they missed the tide and had to steam around waiting for the next one. Then, as her crew manoeuvred her into the dry dock some chains knocked over some of the dock blocks, with the result that once again she had to steam around for 24 hours while the dock was pumped dry, the blocks reset and the dock reflooded. A considerable amount of work was done quite apart from the cleaning of her hull. The interiors were fumigated, more guns were fitted and some work was done on the degaussing coil towards making it rather more permanent.

The *Queen Elizabeth* then sailed from Vancouver to San Francisco for further work to be done on her. On her arrival she briefly ran aground near the Golden Gate Bridge. At a meeting on board the ship it was decided that she would in fact be able to carry far more than the 5,000 or so troops that she had been accommodating on her Sydney to Suez runs. So the Australian-installed hammocks and bunks would have to be removed and an altogether different form of sleeping accommodation would be installed in their place. It took five days to remove the Australian sleeping accommodation and in its place was fitted what were known as 'Standee' bunks: made of tubular steel and canvas, these could be erected so that they stood two, three, four or even five to a tier – and these were fitted into every available space. With her troop-carrying capacity now considerably increased, the *Queen Elizabeth* departed San Francisco in a small convoy on a voyage back to Sydney, again via the Marquesas, with 8,000 American troops on board to help with the defence of Australia until more Australian troops could be recalled. As the *Queen Elizabeth* approached Sydney Harbour she encountered the *Queen Mary*, outbound.

The *Queen Elizabeth* remained in Sydney for almost two weeks before leaving on the 19th April 1942 on a voyage that would take her to Cape Town, Rio de Janeiro and New York. Among the people on board were 180 American servicemen who had been wounded during the fighting in the Philippines. At Cape Town, German prisoners of war and their Polish guards were embarked: when the ship arrived at Rio she was the centre of considerable security, with searchlights continually sweeping the water around her and with armed

On the *Queen Elizabeth's* North Atlantic trooping voyages every available space was filled with bunks. Compare this view of the Observation Lounge with that on page 68.

guards in boats circling the anchored liner to ensure there was no attempt to escape.

The U.S. Army Chief of Staff, General George C. Marshall, had a very clear strategy for the invasion of Europe: directly across the English Channel into occupied France. Churchill on the other hand had envisaged an attack somewhere along the Mediterranean coastline. However, regardless of where the attack would take place, the most important thing was to build up the required force for the invasion. Even before the United States had been drawn into the war, their Navy Department had sent an 'observer' to London to prepare the groundwork for cooperation with the Royal Navy in case they should become involved. This foresight enabled the future planning to move quickly towards its goal and establish what was known as Operation Bolero. The aim of this operation was to transform Britain into what would ultimately be referred to as 'the greatest operating military base of all time' and it came into effect in April 1942. At the very heart of Operation Bolero were the Atlantic liners *Queen Elizabeth* and *Queen Mary*. They were however, far from the only vessels involved in this vast

operation; at its height, 6,900 ships brought more than five million tons of supplies to Great Britain as well as over one and half million men.

The *Queen Elizabeth* finally arrived in New York for employment along with the *Queen Mary* on what was to be known as the 'GI Shuttle.' But before this began it was decided that, even though the shipyard in San Francisco had fitted in as many Standee berths as they thought possible, her troop-carrying capacity could be increased even further – to 10,000. She sailed from New York for Gourock, packed with GIs, on the 5th June. After having arrived at Gourock she then made a voyage, via Freetown and Simonstown, to Suez with reinforcements for the British Eighth Army to help stem Rommel's advances towards the Suez Canal. She then sailed back to New York by way of Cape Town and Rio de Janeiro, arriving there on the 19th August.

Before she departed on her next GI Shuttle voyage, even more Standee bunks were fitted, giving her a capacity of 12,000 but special dispensation was granted to enable her to carry a further 3,500 men (during the summer months)

Watched by a U.S. Navy blimp, the *Queen Elizabeth* makes a summertime departure from New York. Note the degaussing strip along the ship's side, intended to reduce her attraction for magnetic mines.

However, not all the cabins were squeezed full of 'Standee' bunks: many of the officers carried were afforded the luxury of being berthed with just one or two others. Officers also had stewards to look after the cabins and maintain their kit but, as in peace time, cabin stewards had to be tipped!

The conversion of the 'Queens' to accommodate such enormous numbers of troops was not just a case of squeezing in the 'Standee' berths wherever possible. There were other considerations that had to be taken into account as well. An entire routine had to be worked out regarding the access to and use of each ship's facilities: several thousand men would not all be able to take a shower at the same time, eat at the same time or even move around on deck at the same time. The conversion of the *Queen Elizabeth* was a simpler task than that of the *Queen Mary*, basically because she had entered service in a far from finished state and the absence of most of her interior furnishings and décor meant that far greater use could be made of her public spaces. It was particularly easy to convert those decks which were dedicated to cabin accommodation. It took less than two weeks for the additional Standee bunks to be fitted along with the extra toilet and shower facilities which had to be created.

The decision was also made that each of the 'Queens' should have increased armament, giving them fire power equal to that of a light cruiser. Their handful of twenty-millimetre anti-aircraft guns was increased to twenty-four and ten forty-millimetre guns in five twin-mounts were also added. In addition, there were six three-inch guns in high-angle/low-angle mounts, two in front of the bridge and four on the after decks. The four-inch guns which had originally been fitted at the stern of each ship for defence against submarines were replaced by rather more effective six-inch weapons. It was weaponry enough to ensure that the 'Queens' were as well protected as possible against a surfaced U-boat, raider or other vessel as long as it was not a destroyer. However, their main means of defence remained their speed.

New York to Gourock, back and forth, that would now be the principal route for the *Queen Elizabeth* for the rest of the war, albeit with occasional diversions to Halifax, Nova Scotia. Gourock, at the mouth of the Clyde, had been chosen because it was regarded as being the safest terminal for the 'Queens', being somewhat beyond the range of most of the planes operated by the Luftwaffe. While war raged elsewhere in the world, what happened on the North Atlantic was the key: whoever lost the battle of the North Atlantic would lose the war and by 1942 it all hung in the balance. All indications were that the balance would fall in favour of Germany. By 1942 the German U-boats were sinking 500,000 tons of shipping in the Atlantic each month.

Immediately clear of the port the 'Queens' steamed at a steady speed of between 28 and 30 knots and they followed a very carefully worked out course in a zigzag pattern. This actually looked as though it was being done

when they could sleep on the open deck or else share a bunk on a rotational basis. Had the worst happened and it had been necessary to abandon the ship, ten thousand men could, possibly, have been carried in her complement of lifeboats and rafts but based upon the speed and reliability of the *Queen Elizabeth* it was considered worth taking the risk and packing several thousand more men aboard. Indeed, both the *Queen Elizabeth* and the *Queen Mary* were ultimately fitted to be able to carry as many as 15,000 men. The American conversion of both the ships has been described as 'sheer ruthlessness.' Nowhere on either ship, apart from the crew quarters and the engineering spaces, was considered sacrosanct. Standee bunks were squeezed in everywhere: cabins that had for example been designed to accommodate four passengers were fitted to take up to twenty-one GIs. There were even bunks, seven high, in the swimming pool.

Six troops relax on their bunks as best they can in a cabin which in peacetime would have accommodated no more than two passengers.

on a purely random basis but in fact it was calculated with such care as to ensure that each ship was making a constant and steady progress towards her destination. There was a whole variety of course combinations, each one being given a number. It was not until the ship was at sea that the captain was allowed to open the sealed orders that had been delivered to him shortly before sailing: then he would know which of the zigzag patterns was to be followed and what speed was to be maintained. Neither ship was allowed to follow the same course on two consecutive voyages. One such course required the ship to steam along her 'base course' for four minutes, then to alter her course twenty-five degrees to port and maintain that for eight minutes. Then, the ship would be turned to starboard fifty degrees and hold that course for eight minutes, then turned back twenty-five degrees to port once again – which would bring her back on her 'base course', again holding that for four minutes. This was followed by a twenty-five degree turn but this time to starboard and eight minutes later a fifty degree turn to port, then eight minutes after that a twenty-five degree turn to starboard and again she was back on her 'base course'. This pattern (or one of the others similar to it) was repeated every

forty minutes across the Atlantic. There was a special clock in the wheelhouse which chimed whenever it was time to make a course change. It would therefore, with a combination of high speed and such a course pattern, be all but impossible for a U-boat commander to work out a firing solution: the ship would not be in range long enough for him to make any corrections to his initial approach or even be able to line up for a second shot. However, the Germans did not need a crystal ball to work out the route on which the ships were employed, their great size meant that there were really at that time only two ports that they could use – New York to Gourock and return.

There were elaborate measures in force to ensure that only a very few people knew when the ships would sail: even their captains were only given twenty-four hours notice of their sailing time. A very select handful of naval officers, on both sides of the Atlantic, were also privy to the information. They were the men whose ships would provide the escort out from either New York or Gourock or be there in position in the Atlantic to escort them back into port. There was very careful screening, by American and British Intelligence, of their crews. Despite this, there were a few attempts to sabotage the liners (or maybe these were just stupid acts of vandalism): holes were found in lifeboats, or bottle caps in fire hoses. More seriously, in April 1943, during a routine inspection of the ship, two bombs were found in the machinery spaces aboard the *Queen Elizabeth*. They were defused and then thrown overboard.

The logistics of bringing up to 15,000 men on board the ship was a complicated affair fraught with untold difficulties, particularly when one considers that many of the young men had probably never even seen the sea, let alone a ship – particularly a ship as large as the *Queen Elizabeth*. But even the marginally more sophisticated of the GIs were bewildered by the *Queen Elizabeth* and the *Queen Mary*, convinced that any vessel as stupendously large would very naturally be American – despite the fact they had British crews. It was not unknown for them to accost a crew member and say: "How come you English can't build a boat like this?" Before boarding, the GIs would be gathered at Camp Kilmer in New Jersey for training and instruction on how to board the liners, how to find their allotted bunk and how to stow their kit: all of this done with the aid of giant mock-ups of part of the two ships. On boarding, each man was given either a red, white or blue disc: this indicated in which part of the ship he had to

remain during the entire voyage. To be found outside one's allotted area elicited a fine, which usually involved assisting the crew in their tasks. Another essential rule was that no man could ever be without his lifebelt.

Boarding the ship was done under cover of darkness and night time sailings were always arranged to avoid the full moon. As the ship sailed out of New York harbor, every man had to stand completely still until the ship was well out to sea. This was in order to avoid any great rush of men to one side of the ship or the other for a farewell look at the famous Manhattan skyline or the symbolic Statue of Liberty. Huge numbers of men moving rapidly to one side or the other would have had disastrous consequences. The normal draft of both the 'Queens' was 29 feet 6 inches but when they were packed with 15,000 troops this increased to approximately 44 feet, thus making it only just possible for the liners to clear the top of the Holland Tunnel as they sailed out of New York harbour – as long as everyone stayed perfectly still!

The other great logistical nightmare was feeding such an enormous number of men, not only the troops being carried but around 1,000 crew members as well. There were six sittings for each meal, 2,000 men at each, and each sitting lasted no longer than forty-five minutes. Just two meals were served, breakfast between 6.30 am and 11 am; and dinner

▽ Two thousand Canadian troops are crowded into the First Class Dining Room which has, however, not lost all of its intended peacetime splendour.

American GIs watch the *Queen Elizabeth* as she rests in the Clyde with one of the famous 'Puffers' (small Scottish coasters) lying alongside.

between 3 pm and 7.30 pm. As the men left breakfast they would be given a pack of sandwiches to ensure they had something to eat between then and dinner time. A remarkable quantity of food had to be loaded in New York for each voyage:

155,000 lb of meat and poultry
124,000 lb of potatoes
76,000 lb of flour and cereal
53,000 lb of butter, eggs and milk powder
31,400 lb of tea, coffee and sugar
31,000 lb of canned fruit
29,000 lb of fresh fruit
20,000 lb of bacon and ham
18,000 lb of jam
4,600 lb of cheese

What had been planned as the opulent First Class Dining Room was converted into a cafeteria-style mess hall for the enlisted men. The Officers' Mess had been designed to be the Tourist Class Lounge. Here there remained some vestige of Cunard service. Unlike the enlisted men, the officers were not required to line up for their food. Instead, they had the luxury of sitting at proper tables with linen and silverware and with a steward to bring their meals to them. These stewards, like their cabin stewards, had to be tipped at the end of the voyage.

During the five day voyage the troops would keep themselves amused in several ways, the favoured entertainments being cards and dice. The games seemed never-ending: when one man would step away, his place was immediately taken by another. The fact that these games were strictly forbidden added to their appeal and a watchful eye had to be maintained for the patrolling Military Police. Chewing gum was banned as the discarded pieces were difficult to remove from the decks. It was the one thing that was not sold in any of the

This photograph, taken from a crowded troop tender, gives a fine view of the liner's side with its degaussing strip and a myriad of rivets.

nine canteens that had been set up around the ships. In each of these the GIs could buy soft drinks, cigarettes, what they referred to as 'candy,' razor blades and other toiletries. While the time was in part whiled away with games of cards or dice, the men were required to attend lectures on a whole variety of subjects: tactics, equipment, personal hygiene and on how to get along with the British. For the great majority of them this was their very first journey beyond the shores of America – and perhaps many of them, had the war not intervened, would never have left their home country. Every GI was issued with a leaflet that had been written by the U.S. Army Special Services Division: 'A Short Guide to Britain'. It contained what were perceived to be the most crucial dos and don'ts about everyday life in Britain along with generally very sound advice. Regardless of whether it was winter or summer the voyage across from New York to Gourock was cramped and unpleasant. Many of the young men, away from home for the first time, were fearful of what the future held. They could only hope that one day they would be making the return voyage in one piece.

In order to ensure that the gunnery crews were fully alert and ready in case of attack, daily drills were held. These drills did a great deal to uphold the morale of the troops on board for they were essentially helpless for the duration of the voyage. Apart from these daily drills, with the barking from the smaller guns and the thunder from the larger ones, the 'Queens' swept swiftly and silently back and forth across the Atlantic. It was not unknown for a lone trawler or patrol vessel to suddenly become aware of the fast approaching bulk of one of the grey-painted 'Queens' – a fact that earned them the appropriate nicknames 'the Grey Ghosts'.

While both the 'Queens' were forbidden to stop while at sea, sometimes the forces of nature intervened. On one particular westbound voyage the *Queen Elizabeth* encountered a storm of such ferocity that she was forced to hove-to for two days, barely making 10 knots. During this storm, having met one particularly enormous wave, the bows of the liner seemed to be disappearing down into the depths of the ocean; then another wave hit, smashing windows on the bridge and sending her quartermaster flying from the wheelhouse and into the bridge wing. Vibration was felt throughout the ship as the propellers raced as her stern was lifted clear of the sea. Slowly, the *Queen Elizabeth* righted herself but her fore-deck was damaged, the forward capstans were out of commission and the anchors were jammed. The Staff Captain's cabin window was also smashed and the Staff Captain suffered some injury. Luckily, there were no other casualties but this had not been the case on another occasion. Then, caught between the crests of some 40-foot waves, the *Queen Elizabeth* dropped into the trough: those manning the guns on the upper deck fell to their deaths while many of the soldiers who were unfortunate enough to be in the top berths of the five-high Standee bunks were thrown to the deck and were seriously injured. Such an encounter with a sea of this nature was, however, unusual. Nevertheless, the Atlantic could indeed be very rough at any time of the year and for some poor mid-westerner who had never even seen the ocean this was a terrifying experience indeed. Even for those who were not unduly affected by sea sickness, the results of their fellow men who were could be enough to make them ill as well. Thus there were many meals that, having been consumed, were soon disgorged onto the decks. This was a factor that the conversion of the 'Queens' into vast troop-carriers had not been able to address. As a result, the ventilation systems that had been designed to cope with the demands of a maximum of around 3,000 people could barely cope - particularly so if it was a crossing of entirely rough seas, when the men were unable to get out onto the decks.

Even before the naval escorts, usually about six destroyers and generally a light cruiser, made their rendezvous with either the *Queen Elizabeth* or the *Queen Mary* as she approached Scotland, the ship would be met by a Sunderland flying boat from the RAF's Coastal Command at about 600 miles out from the coast. The sight of the aircraft would generate a feeling of relief throughout the ships even though there was some way still to go – it meant that they were no longer on their own. The naval escort would be met off the north coast of Ireland and the destroyers would take up position ahead of the 'Queen' so that they could use their listening devices, asdic or sonar, to scour the waters for any sounds of prowling U-boats. Meanwhile, the cruiser would stay close to the liner to give protection from any enemy aircraft. With the first sight of land as many men as possible would try to get out onto the deck: for most of them it would be the first time they had seen a foreign country.

When the ship arrived at her anchorage off Gourock, the GIs would be disembarked into a variety of vessels to be taken ashore and then onward to military bases throughout the British Isles. (When the 'Queens' began service as troop-carriers on the North Atlantic, the dock at Gourock had not been completed so they anchored off and the troops were disembarked into tenders. By the middle of 1943 construction of the dock was completed.) Every convoy that crossed the Atlantic (the 'Queens' were not alone in transporting GIs from the United States to Britain but they were each regarded as being a convoy in their own right) had to be coordinated with every other Allied troop movement and with Allied shipping. This was to ensure a minimum of confusion at the ports of embarkation and disembarkation. The overall responsibility for this lay with the Admiralty and they worked in conjunction with the Board of Trade, which had ultimate charge over all British-flagged merchant ships; the Operational Intelligence Centre, which watched the movements of U-boats and surface ships; and the Naval Control Service that kept track of all non-British shipping. Escort assignments on each side of the Atlantic were co-ordinated with the British Home Fleet and the Western Approaches Command, also the U.S. Navy's Atlantic Fleet and the Royal Canadian Navy. It was rather ironic that a lot of the planning of the eastbound voyages was done in at the Allied Combined Shipping Operations Office in New York, which before the war had been the German Consulate.

Then, quite apart from ensuring the smooth operation of everything at sea, the transportation of the troops both to and from the ships had to be worked out and this was a process that had to be equally finely tuned, ensuring that road, rail and air transport all linked so that the 'Queens' with their precious cargo of GIs sailed on time. Once the troops had arrived in Britain, they were moved efficiently onward to wherever their unit was to be based. After they had disembarked, another army would come aboard the liners – cleaning ladies, about 120 of them. Like everything else that went on aboard the 'Queens', their work was done under the ever-watchful eyes of the Military Police. While they went about their duties, the fuel – about 8,000 tons of it - and stores would be replenished and the vessel made ready for her voyage back to New York. The time the 'Queens' spent at Gourock had to be minimal: they were still vulnerable to attack while they were there. Thus, unless any repairs or other work had to be undertaken, the ship would

be ready for her return voyage to New York within four or five days. There would be a lesser number of people on these westward voyages: the injured as well as prisoners of war and civil and military passengers. Just how many people were to be carried aboard the 'Queens' dictated how many crew they would carry and this would vary between 850 and 1,000 men: they were divided into four departments: engineering; catering; deck; and then the permanent military staff. The latter group was made up of a combination of British, American and Canadians, officers and enlisted men, 120 of them in all. Their role was to act as liaisons between the officers and senior NCOs of the units that had been embarked and the senior staff of the crew. The senior officer of the permanent military staff had charge of the gunnery and ordnance specialists (who were responsible for the anti-aircraft and deck guns), the medical personnel working in the infirmary, the Military Police detachment and a handful of Red Cross workers.

From the very outset of their Atlantic crossings, the *Queen Elizabeth* and *Queen Mary* proved the wisdom of the decisions that had been made by Churchill and Marshall and it was claimed that together they were equal to a fleet of twenty normal troopships. That calculation takes into account not only their size but also their high speed which enabled them to make more voyages in a given time than other liners could have done. Their value as troop-carriers and therefore their immense contribution to the war effort, while highly appreciated on both sides of the Atlantic, was not lost on Hitler either. As a consequence, he offered a reward of one million Reich Marks to the U-boat commander who sank either one of them. To 'bag' either the *Queen Elizabeth* or the *Queen Mary* became the ultimate prize.

On the 9th November 1942 a report reached New York indicating that the *Queen Elizabeth* had been sunk and with considerable loss of life. Germany's Information Minister, Joseph Goebbels had been heard announcing that *U-704* had sighted her while she was about two hundred miles off the coast of Ireland, on her way to New York. (On this particular voyage the *Queen Elizabeth* had been carrying government and military officials who were heading for a strategy conference as well as several thousand women and children who were being evacuated.) The commander of *U-704*, Capt.-Lt. Horst Kessler had claimed that he had fired a spread of four torpedoes at the liner and one of them had hit her. At the time, the *Queen Mary* was alongside her New York berth and this news was received with considerable sadness. Staff Captain Harry Grattidge was entertaining a group of people to a pre-lunchtime drink and the meal followed in a gloomy silence. As lunch came to an end a call was received from Cunard in Liverpool: for a few moments there was some confusion between Grattidge and the caller and then it was established that, far from lying at the bottom of the Atlantic, the *Queen Elizabeth* had arrived safely and was at anchor at Quarantine. Grattidge turned to his luncheon companions

Returning Canadian WACs are crowded in their cabin as they cross the North Atlantic en route for New York – and then home. Space and privacy were at a premium.

and gave them the news, at which a toast was proposed: "To the two great ladies of the Atlantic – the 'Queens'".

It appears that it is very likely that three of the torpedoes from *U-704* ran too deep and as a result missed the liner entirely. The fourth seems to have perhaps run too high and slammed into a wave with enough force to cause it to detonate. The crew of the *Queen Elizabeth* did report hearing an explosion on that day but no submarine was actually sighted. It seems as though on that occasion Hitler's reward came perilously close to being claimed and the whole course of the war changed. (Alan Turing, the cryptographic genius was one of those travelling aboard the liner at the time to attend a conference.)

There was one other occasion when it seemed that the *Queen Elizabeth* might be facing the threat of attack by several submarines. In the last days of the war, in March 1945, when she was on one of her final voyages carrying GIs to Europe, she had just picked up her naval escorts when they flashed a message across to her that two of the destroyers had picked up the sounds of submarines lying across her course. The escort vessels immediately went over to attack. With depth charges exploding all around, the *Queen Elizabeth*'s master, Captain C.M. Ford, ordered Full Ahead with no course change. In the event, no submarines were actually sighted and the liner arrived in Gourock unscathed.

While both of the 'Queens' were blessed with good luck during their wartime careers, it was the *Queen Elizabeth* which was certainly the luckier of the two, as those were really the only incidents of any consequence to have affected her. The *Queen Mary* on the other hand seemed often to encounter such events, with her tragic collision with the cruiser *Curacoa* being the most unfortunate.

From early 1942 both the *Queen Elizabeth* and the *Queen Mary* were regularly used on their westward return voyages to transport German and Italian prisoners of war to detention camps in America and in Canada. Each of the liners, having already been divided into three sections to enable easier movement of the GIs aboard, was thus well-suited to this additional role. For the POW voyages barricades were placed at the partitions which separated each section, electric alarms were installed and there were armed guards at each barricade. By the end of 1943 the two ships had transported almost

These American GIs are given the opportunity to visit the bridge. Some of them may have been surprised to learn that the *Queen Elizabeth* was a British ship.

170,000 prisoners across to the United States and following the D-Day invasion the numbers grew to such an extent that in September 1944 alone 55,000 German prisoners were transported across the Atlantic by the 'Queens' and other liners. By the end of that year, the 'Queens' were carrying an average of 5,000 prisoners on each voyage. There is a story, though one wonders just how true it may be, that as the POWs aboard either the *Queen Elizabeth* or *Queen Mary* got their first sight of the fabled Manhattan skyline they would look aghast. Nazi propaganda, apparently, was leading Germany to believe that New York lay in ruins.

One may also speculate on the idea that as the German Naval High Command were well aware that the 'Queens' were being used to transport vast numbers of German prisoners across the Atlantic the liners actually had an immunity from U-boat attack – at least on their westbound voyages. However, that appears to be very unlikely as it contradicts the standing operational orders of the U-boat service – and no U-boat commander, once having got one of the 'Queens' in his sights, was likely to pass up the opportunity of acquiring Hitler's one million Reich Marks!

The propaganda value of the loss to the Allies of either one of the 'Queens' would have been worth the price of a few thousand prisoners: whether on the field of battle or on the high seas their lives would have been sacrificed for the ultimate glory of the Fatherland. In March 1943 the U-boats in the Atlantic reached their very peak of success, sinking 625,000 tons of shipping. However, just two months later the tables began to turn and Admiral Dönitz lost 43 of his U-boats. As a result, the rest of the fleet was withdrawn from the North Atlantic until the autumn. Although the U-boat threat was now lessened, that did not mean that the 'Queens' were in any way out of danger. They remained probably the ultimate goal of every U-boat commander.

The 6th June 1944 was when Operation Overlord was launched: 175,000 soldiers and 50,000 vehicles were landed upon the Normandy shores of Northern France. They were backed up by a naval force of over 5,000 ships and approximately 11,000 aircraft. It was not however, until August that the Allied forces were really able to begin the move across Europe that they had envisaged. With this move, Luftwaffe airbases fell to the advancing troops and the port

The pipe band of the Canadian Irish Regiment exercise on the open spaces of the Sun Deck on the final day of their homeward voyage.

of Southampton, now less vulnerable to attack, could be opened up in the Autumn of that year to troopships other than the 'Queens' – there was the general feeling that to move their terminal to the Hampshire port would be tempting fate. But while the German army was in retreat the Allied armies advanced across France at such a rate that they began to outrun their lines of supply and this had the effect of slowing their advance. The German army was then able to stand its ground and fight back. The role of the 'Queens' became ever more necessary and between May 1944 and April 1945 they carried more than a quarter of a million soldiers. Such was the urgent demand for troops that on one voyage the *Queen Mary* actually transported 15,740 men – combined with her crew (of 943) this was the greatest number of people ever embarked aboard a ship at one time. While the *Queen Elizabeth* usually carried about the same numbers as the *Queen Mary*, she never equalled that extraordinary number.

As 1944 progressed, it became very apparent that there was a dire need for vessels to be used as medical transports to deal with the ever-increasing numbers of wounded men. Some attempts had been made to convert the cargo holds of Liberty ships into wards but the very basic nature of these ships meant that they were far from ideal for this role. With the need for medical transport becoming ever more urgent, it was decided that once again the *Queen Elizabeth* and *Queen Mary* would be the ideal ships and in October 1944

they were surveyed in New York. Together, the Ministry of War Transport, the U.S. Surgeon General's office and the U.S. Army's Transportation Corps drew up plans for 1,700 wounded men to be accommodated on board each ship – a thousand of them being stretcher cases. Once again the work took less than two weeks to complete. Some of the public rooms were transformed into wards, laboratories were added and some of the larger cabins were turned into spaces where the patients could be given physical therapy or receive other attention. The permanent medical staff on each of the ships was increased from just thirty five to over three hundred. Later that month, they began carrying the seriously wounded GIs and Canadian troops back to New York. Just three months later, the medical facilities aboard each of the 'Queens' were further increased to enable them to accommodate two thousand stretcher cases and one thousand other injured. The timing of this further expansion of the medical facilities aboard the ships could not have been more opportune as the months that followed saw the Allies suffer their heaviest casualties of the entire Western European campaign. By the end of January 1945 almost 80,000 American soldiers had suffered from either enemy fire or from the intense cold – or both. At that time, the additional troops brought over to Europe were essential: the role of the 'Queens' was as important as ever it had been before.

Then, suddenly, it came to an end. It was in March of that year that both the *Queen Elizabeth* and the *Queen Mary* made their last voyages to Gourock with troops on board. The Third Reich was in collapse and the war in Europe was almost over. The 'Queens', though, continued their shuttle-service to New York carrying the wounded men, these voyages continuing until June. Meanwhile, further plans were being drawn up for the future use of the two hard-worked liners. This time it was for the transportation of the GIs back across the Atlantic so that they could be made ready to head out to the Pacific and face the Japanese. The *Queen Mary* was the first to return GIs to America, 14,777 of them, arriving in New York to an incredible welcome on the 20th June. When the *Queen Elizabeth* arrived later in the month with an equally large number of men aboard the tumultuous scenes were repeated, with ships in the harbour sounding their sirens, thousands of people lining the waterfront, helicopters and blimps overhead and a brass band on the dockside. On their eastbound voyages the 'Queens' carried thousands of Britons who had been evacuated during the early days of the war. So again an enthusiastic welcome greeted the ships as they arrived home.

On the 7th August 1945, the *Queen Elizabeth* sailed from Gourock for the final time as a troopship. As she departed the port that had been her home for so long she sent the signal: 'Thank you, Gourock!. For 27,000 GIs the 14th August was a particularly happy day. Twelve thousand had just disembarked from the *Queen Elizabeth* and a further fifteen thousand were mid Atlantic aboard the *Queen Mary*.

All of them were probably assuming that after some period of rest and then retraining they would be shipped off to the Pacific. Instead, on that day came the news of the Japanese surrender. The war was at an end.

However, the *Queen Elizabeth's* role as a troopship was far from over, even though she had bad farewell to Gourock. On Monday 20th August 1945 she arrived at last in Southampton. It was a dull grey and wet day and her welcome to the port was quiet and low-key: not at all like the exuberance she had experienced when arriving in New York. The Southampton Borough Police Band played as she slipped into her berth shortly before noon. A small crowd of spectators had gathered to watch as the tugs brought her alongside. The band played the national anthems of both Britain and America – and that was it. Quietly and without fuss, the *Queen Elizabeth*

was home. The Mayor of Southampton along with other civic dignitaries went aboard and speeches of welcome were made during which, rather curiously, she was described as being 'Southampton's Baby'.

Captain Townley, who had been the first to command the *Queen Elizabeth*, had been succeeded by Captain E.M. Fall and it was he who had had command of the ship for most of her wartime career. Having brought the *Queen Elizabeth* home, it was time for Captain Fall to retire. Commodore Sir James Bissett now took command. He had very recently received his knighthood, having been in command of the *Queen Mary* since 1942.

A few days after her quiet arrival, having embarked almost 15,000 GIs, the *Queen Elizabeth* departed from Southampton in fine style. There was a greater crowd of

In August, 1945, with the war ended, *Queen Elizabeth* made her first visit to her homeport of Southampton and embarked 15,000 American servicemen who were returning home.

people and a salute provided by eight Meteor jets flying overhead. Amongst the GIs aboard was Colonel James Stewart of the USAF – formerly of Hollywood. Three similar troop-carrying voyages were made from Southampton and it was on the 24th September, while the ship was in New York at the end of her second crossing, that Commodore Bissett had the funnels of the *Queen Elizabeth* restored to their proper Cunard livery. It was a fine symbolic gesture towards a world returning to some measure of normality. It was on the third of these voyages that the *Queen Elizabeth* carried what was believed to be the largest number she had ever had aboard: 15,077 GIs and other passengers and 855 crew members.

Throughout the years that she operated the GI Shuttle along with the *Queen Mary*, the *Queen Elizabeth* made thirty-five crossings of the Atlantic. By the end of May 1945 the 'Queens' had between them carried 1,243,538 'passengers'. On the North Atlantic alone a total of 869,694 people had been carried eastwards and 213,008 had been transported westward between Gourock and New York. Between April 1941 and March 1945 the *Queen Elizabeth* had steamed 492,635 miles and had carried 811,324 people. These were remarkable facts when one considers that there were those in 1939 who had felt that there was no use for such vast vessels during the time of war. They had suggested that such symbols of peacetime luxury should just be laid up

It was a tribute to the engineers and workmen, both at John Brown's shipyard and aboard the *Queen Elizabeth*, that during the six years of war and almost a million miles of steaming she never suffered a serious breakdown or failure of any kind. This was a remarkable fact when one considers that the ship was all but immediately pressed into service, very hard service, without so much as a single mile steamed to test her engines. Likewise, already well-tested with several years of service behind her, the *Queen Mary* also steamed flawlessly through those years of conflict.

By October 1945 the 'Queens' had returned almost 150,000 GIs back to America. Although this was a fact that filled the American public with relief and happiness, it did not much please the British. While no one questioned the contribution the two liners made to the war effort and their remaining under American control during the war, questions were being asked in Parliament and in the press why both the 'Queens', along with their fleetmate *Aquitania*, were being used to ferry home GIs from Europe while many British soldiers remained out in the Far East.

Britain's new Prime Minister, Mr. Clement Atlee, cabled President Truman: "With so many of our troops overseas awaiting repatriation after nearly six years of war and separation from their families, I cannot justify to the British public the use of our three biggest ships in the American service." While not exactly making an outright demand for the immediate return of the three ships, Mr. Atlee was blunt in his expectation that the United States would make a sufficient number of other ships available, equal to the capacity of the *Aquitania* and the 'Queens'. The original plan of the U.S. Army Transport Command had been to have all the GIs who were eligible for return to the United States back home by the end of January 1946. However, President Truman ordered the Army Transport Corps to work out a reasonable arrangement with the Ministry of War Transport and within less than a week of the cable being sent the *Queen Elizabeth* and the *Aquitania* were immediately returned to British control, thereby putting the carefully worked out plans awry. Meanwhile, the *Queen Mary* remained under American control in order to continue the repatriation of GIs from Europe; and in order that they might stick to the original plan there had to be a great deal of reorganising and rerouting of other liners to get 'their boys' home when promised.

The work that this involved was a fact totally lost on the American public, who could only see two of the largest troopships suddenly being taken out of their service and 'given' to the British – quite ignoring the fact that they were British liners in the first place. Newspapers across America echoed the cry of the unfair way in which they were being treated and that the British were being given preferential treatment. It was unfortunate behaviour, on both sides of the Atlantic, but perhaps understandable when one considers the stress of the previous several years. Now the *Queen Elizabeth* was returning Canadian troops home from Europe. She made her first arrival at the port of Halifax, Nova Scotia on the 26th October with 12,517 troops aboard. Commodore Bissett, however, was less than pleased with the berth, feeling that it was too exposed to the wind and he feared that under certain circumstances the *Queen Elizabeth* could end up causing damage to the quay or indeed herself. He therefore requested that all future such voyages should be into either New York or Boston: the Canadian authorities were not pleased as they felt that it was important for their returning service men to immediately set foot on home soil. However, the Commodore was adamant and his first concern was for the safety of his ship. On the return voyage the *Queen Elizabeth* carried men who had been interned in prison camps in South East Asia. They had been shipped across the Pacific to Vancouver and then placed aboard trains to journey across Canada. On her return to Southampton on the 5th November, after that first voyage across to Halifax, there was an air of excitement aboard amongst the men who for so long had suffered the torture of the Japanese camps. But they were denied any tantalising glimpses of England as the liner made her way past the Isle of Wight and up Southampton Water – it was all shrouded in a thick fog.

Once disembarkation was complete, the ship entered the King George V graving dock for her first dry-docking in Britain.

In January 1946 both the 'Queens' made their last troop-carrying voyages. On her first voyage of that year the *Queen Elizabeth* had a very distinguished passenger, Winston Churchill. It was the first time that he had

Eight Meteor jets of the RAF salute the *Queen Elizabeth* on her first departure from Southampton, her originally intended homeport, on the 26th August, 1945.

travelled aboard the ship, though he had sailed over to America aboard the *Queen Mary* on several occasions during the war. He was now no longer the Prime Minister and he and his wife were on their way to a holiday in Florida. Later, in a tribute to the ships he would say: "Built for the arts of peace and to link the Old World with the New, the 'Queens' challenged the fury of Hitlerism in the Battle of the Atlantic. Without their aid the day of final victory must unquestionably have been postponed." Before her return to Southampton a most precious item was loaded aboard: a copy of the Magna Carta, which was normally housed in Lincoln Cathedral but had been sent to America for safe keeping. Packed in a copper-lined metal case, it was too large to be stored in the strong room and therefore made the voyage under the Commodore's bed.

With the GIs back home, and following the Japanese surrender, the governments of both the United States and Canada were facing a new problem. Many servicemen during their time in Britain had met and married young women, many of whom were now parents to young children. Their American and Canadian husbands

wanted them to be brought across to join them. It was an unprecedented situation and in fact would involve 60,000 war brides and children. Initially there was some resistance from the British government to the idea of using either of the 'Queens' for this duty as they were anxious to have them restored to full passenger service as soon as possible. But the Americans were insistent and ultimately a compromise was reached. It was agreed that the *Queen Mary* would remain under American control for a further six months to make these voyages, reuniting these young men with their brides. The *Queen Elizabeth* would return home to be completed for commercial service – at last.

On the 6th March 1946, when the *Queen Elizabeth* arrived in Southampton, the Ministry of War Transport made the announcement that she would be the first ocean-going passenger ship to be released from His Majesty's Government service. She would become a symbol, to Britain and to the world, of recovery from the war - in the same way that the *Queen Mary* had been symbolic of an end to the Depression.

R.M.S. QUEEN ELIZABETH

Chapter 5

AN ICON OF PEACE

In preparation for the restoration work to come, the Standee bunks and huge numbers of lifejackets were removed from the *Queen Elizabeth* while she was in New York. In the months following the end of the war, Cunard had been discussing with John Brown's their plans for the conversion of the ship into the liner which had been planned to enter service six years earlier. However, it was impossible for her to return all the way up the Clyde to the John Brown yard for this work to be undertaken. Instead, a tentative plan was made for her to spend twelve weeks back at Gourock for the first stage of the work and then a further ten weeks at Southampton, alongside Berth 101 – a little over five months of work not only to recreate what had been in place when she made her secret dash across the Atlantic in March 1940 but also to continue with what had been left unfinished at that time, as well as repair the wear and tear of her war work. It was, under the circumstances, a remarkably short time scale.

Approximately four hundred of her crew were paid off, while a further four hundred or so remained. They would be the men who would return her to the Clyde and in the meantime they would begin some of the essential maintenance work. They were joined by three hundred men from John Brown's and in the next few weeks they removed more of her wartime fittings, all in preparation for her voyage up to Scotland and the major work that would follow.

Then, just two days before she was officially demobilised, it seemed that she might not actually make it into service after all. A fire was discovered on the morning of the 8th March, coming from what had at one time been the isolation hospital. More recently, this space had been used as a store room for medical supplies and it contained some highly inflammable liquids. For some reason, it had not been fitted with automatic sprinklers. Before it was possible to shut off the fans, the smoke found its way into the ventilation system and began to spread through the ship. Although the crew tried to fight the fire with hoses that were connected to deck hydrants, the smoke proved to be too dense to allow them near the centre of the blaze. Fire brigades from Southampton and several other Hampshire towns rushed to the docks to help. The ship which had been poised to become a symbol of recovery seemed likely to become a disaster. Could she have evaded Hitler's U-boats for six years only to fall victim to a fire while alongside in her home port? The firefighters were hampered by the fact that their telescopic ladders were not long enough to allow them to direct their hoses onto the heart of the fire. However, Commodore Bissett suggested lowering the ship's boats: the firemen got into them and the boats were hoisted up to Promenade Deck level and it was from there that they were able to effectively fight the fire. In all, it took three hours for the blaze to be extinguished.

Steel work and the beams that supported the Boat Deck were badly damaged. Elsewhere there was both smoke and water damage. Sabotage was the word on everyone's lips. However, in the end it seemed that it was nothing more than a simple accident. An expert in fire damage was asked to undertake an investigation. His conclusion was that it had 'probably' been caused by a workman who had gone into the former isolation hospital for a quiet smoke but had been unaware of the fumes from a broken bottle of highly inflammable medical spirit.

On the 30th March the *Queen Elizabeth* sailed from Southampton for Gourock and arrived there on the following day. She was to anchor off the Tail of the Bank and more workers from John Brown's would be ferried out to her each day. While it would have appeared to have been more logical for her to be tied alongside at Gareloch, which would in the eyes of the shipyard manager, William MacFarlane, have made the whole job much easier, Cunard were unhappy with the idea. Tied to the berth, she would have been exposed to danger if a strong wind blew from a particular quarter. On the other hand, there was concern from the engineering department about the length of time the ship would be at anchor, as she would need to have her engines running all the time. This would enable her to be manoeuvred if necessary but it would also put a great strain on her.

The work schedule was changed and, instead, Cunard gave John Brown's just ten weeks to complete the work while the ship lay at anchor. They were far from happy about this and made a plea for additional time but nevertheless it was done. It was estimated that her war service was in fact the equivalent of 25 years of normal service because she had not had proper overhaul and refitting work during that time. It was agreed that the Ministry of War Transport would pay the cost of repairing the wear and tear brought about by war work and bringing her back to pre-war condition, while John Brown's undertook to finish off those jobs that had been interrupted by her sudden dash to New York. Cunard would pay for any

◁ In peacetime livery at last, *Queen Elizabeth* makes a wonderful sight as she runs her speed trials in the Firth of Clyde in October, 1946.

With Cunard colours already restored to her funnels, *Queen Elizabeth's* hull and superstructure gradually shed their wartime grey as the former troopship lies in the Clyde.

Work proceeding on one of the *Queen Elizabeth's* funnels while she lies in Southampton.

extra work required that was in addition to their original specification.

One of the first jobs to be done, and one that would make an immediate difference to the appearance of the ship, was the removal of the degaussing coil and its protective steel housing. The hull was then readied for the removal of her grey paint and the restoration of her short-lived Cunard livery. Her teak decking was also restored, with some of it being replaced where necessary. Internal panelling was repaired and restored and her public rooms and cabins began to resume a suggestion of their earlier splendour. The galleys and store rooms were again returned to their proper form. Two thousand portholes were scraped clean of grey paint. Four thousand miles of electrical cable was checked and replaced where required, fire bricks were replaced in the boilers and each of her thousands of turbine blades was checked. In all it was the work of two thousand men – each one of them, along with the materials, ferried out to the ship each day. It was no wonder that the shipyard manager had pressed for all this to be done with the ship alongside.

Although the work was completed within the agreed time scale it was not without its labour troubles. The final fitting out was to be completed while the ship was back in Southampton. The Scottish joiners decided that they should be paid at the same rate as the workers there. However, Cunard resisted the idea, expecting that the other unions would then demand similar treatment and this would ultimately have a detrimental effect on future new buildings.

As there was an acute shortage of labour it was agreed that one thousand men from Clydeside would travel south to help with the continued restoration of the *Queen Elizabeth*. She arrived back in Southampton on the 16th June, at last resplendent in her full Cunard-White Star Line livery. Along with the thousand workers from the Clyde, a further thousand were also employed on the final stages of the work to complete the ship. During their stay in Hampshire the Clyde men were accommodated at Velmore Camp at Chandlers Ford and each day they were transported in a fleet of buses to and from the ship. Amongst the team of workers were 120 women, experienced French polishers, who were employed to help restore the paneling of exotic woods to lustrous splendour. They, however, were accommodated near the city centre.

Although the restoration of the *Queen Elizabeth* was being hailed as a symbol of the new peace, there were inevitably some dissenting voices, forceful but basically uninformed or at best with only a little knowledge. They were loud in decrying the work to return the liner to peacetime condition and service — these precious resources would be far better used on more essential work than wasted on a ship that only the rich would benefit from. It was *The Times* which sprang to the *Queen Elizabeth*'s defence (which was all very well but would those dissenters actually have been readers of *The Times*?) The newspaper reprinted its pre-war 'special' about the liner, which showed that most of the items and materials being used were those which had been in existence since

Externally restored but still needing much internal work, the *Queen Elizabeth* arrives in Southampton assisted by a Red Funnel Line tug/tender in June, 1946.

before the war and had in fact been destined to be fitted into the liner in the first place. Any new material that was being used, and inevitably there would have to be some, was being kept to a minimum. Thirty tons of paint was needed for her exterior and the *Queen Elizabeth* would sail with a very poignant reminder of her role as a troop-carrying vessel: some of the wooden rails of her Boat Deck, cut with the thousands of initials of some of the GIs that she carried, remained in place.

The *Queen Elizabeth* had undergone various conversion works during the years of war, in Singapore, Sydney, San Francisco and New York. During each conversion more and more items deemed to be unnecessary, unessential or just in the way were removed and placed in storage ashore. Thus many of her furnishings, fixtures and fittings were scattered the world over. It was a major task, at a time when most of the world was pulling itself together after the rigours of war and with perhaps other priorities, to get these items organised, out of storage and shipped back to Britain. Those that had been stored in the United States were placed aboard *Aquitania* on one of her voyages back to Southampton. Things that had been stored in Sydney were returned to the United Kingdom via Liverpool, where they were kept for a time at Pilsworth in Lancashire. Then there were the items destined for the new liner that had, in those

early days of 1940, never actually made it on board. These were subsequently stored in places such as Brockenhurst, Lymington and Woolston during the war. While the *Queen Elizabeth* was undergoing restoration, Cunard rented two hangars at Eastleigh and it was to these that all the fixtures, furnishings and other fittings were brought. There were over 21,000 pieces of furniture including 4,500 settees, chairs and tables; 4,000 mattresses; 50,000 items of bed and table linen; 6,000 curtains (which apparently represented three miles of fabric); and 2,000 carpets and rugs. The works of art aboard the ship were renovated by the artists. Unfortunately, there were those items that disappeared (one way or another) during her trooping days – and where are they now? These were replaced by other works.

On the 7th August the *Queen Elizabeth* was manoeuvred into the King George V dry dock. This had to be delayed by twelve hours due to high winds. Once she was inside the dry dock her rudder was inspected, inside and out; her screws were removed and cleaned; the underwater hull was also cleaned and painted; the anchors were tested and each link of the anchor chains was tested and painted.

As the restoration work gathered momentum, so the ship became more and more the symbol of recovery. Further press coverage of the work was such that after a while she was being hailed as 'The Wonder Ship' and inevitably she took on the

The great liner being eased into the King George V dry dock at Southampton. Although she has seen six years of service and has steamed about half a million miles, she has yet to undergo her sea trials.

⚠ With the famous Southampton cranes in the background, the *Queen Elizabeth* attracts attention as she makes for her berth after leaving the King George V dry dock.

mantle of being the Ship of State, not only the flagship of the Cunard-White Star Line but the flagship of the entire British nation. On Monday 30th September readers of *The Daily Graphic* newspaper were given the remarkable spectacle of the liner in the Thames, in an attempt to compare her to the size of the Houses of Parliament. "Pictures show you how the world's largest liner would make London landmarks look small – if the *Queen Elizabeth* could sail up to Westminster." Beneath the picture it stated: "On October 16th next the *Queen Elizabeth*, reconditioned after war service, starts her maiden voyage as a passenger liner to New York. The vast dimensions of this ocean queen cannot well be visualised from figures. In this comparison picture her length (1,031 ft) extends beyond that of the river frontage of the Houses of Parliament (940 ft) and is more than three times the height of the Victoria Tower (336 ft). Compare the liner's height (waterline to top of forward funnel 141 ft) with Big Ben (300 ft)." The other pictures compared the ship with the art deco-style tower of the London University building in Malet Street, pointing out that from her keel to the top of her masts she was 234 feet high and therefore her masts would rise 24

feet above the tower and noted that she was also higher than Nelson's Column in Trafalgar Square.

On the 6th October, with the restoration now all but completed (at a cost of £1 million), the *Queen Elizabeth* was made ready for a return voyage to the mouth of the Clyde to undertake the proper speed and other trials that had been denied her years before. Prior to her departure, Sir Percy Bates, Chairman of the line, visited the ship and Commodore Bissett. He brought the news that Her Majesty the Queen and the Princesses Elizabeth and Margaret would go aboard the ship once she reached the Tail of the Bank and would remain on board for the speed trials along the measured mile. He requested that there be no attempt at speed records, either during the trials or the maiden voyage. The company was content that the *Queen Mary* should hold the record for the fastest Atlantic crossing and it was enough that the *Queen Elizabeth* should be the largest liner in the world. Crossings in four and half days, dependent upon the weather, were all that the company was aiming for. A safe, reliable and regular two-ship service: for the pair to race against each other made no commercial sense and was wasteful of fuel.

▽ Still a record-breaker after years of war service, the *Queen Mary* arrives in Southampton after a particularly fast passage from Halifax, her last voyage as a troopship. She is greeted by her consort *Queen Elizabeth*.

The *Queen Elizabeth*'s arrival in the Firth of Clyde on the following day was delayed because of fog. After having achieved a speed in excess of 30 knots, without effort, on the measured mile, the ship anchored off Gourock and embarked a party of distinguished guests. There were Sir Percy Bates and his wife and several other Cunard Directors, also accompanied by their wives; there was the Right Honourable Alfred Barnes, Minister of Transport and his wife; and Lord Aberconway, the Chairman of John Brown Ltd., along with Lady Aberconway. There were also several senior officers and department heads from the Cunard-White Star Line, including the naval architect Mr. G.M. Paterson, Captain B.H. Davies the Chief Marine Superintendent and Mr. J. Austin the Superintendent Engineer (who in the meeting prior to the secret voyage over to America had given broad hints at the capabilities of the *Queen Elizabeth*'s machinery, if really pushed). The guests toured the public rooms and saw some of the cabins, doubtless marveling at the transformation. The Royal Party were to embark on the following day, the 8th October.

▷ A craftsman works on one of the rooms of the suite which will be used by the Royal princesses during the *Queen Elizabeth's* speed trials.

▽ The Royal party on board the liner during her trials. With them is Sir Percy Bates, the Cunard chairman, who died a few days later.

The *Queen Elizabeth* was big news. An early edition of the *London Evening News* on the 8th had a story headed "*Queen Elizabeth* is making her test run today" and followed with the report: "The liner *Queen Elizabeth* spent last night in 'The Hole' off the Tail of the Bank, where she often lay after her war-time runs across the Atlantic into the Clyde. 'The Hole' is the deepest and safest anchorage in these waters. It is safe even in bad weather because, as it was explained to me, even if a gale sprang up, the ship would have to drag her anchor up hill. But the weather today for the visit of the Queen and the two Princesses to the ship for her final testing run over the measured mile is good. Special arrangements had been made in case of fog. The *Queen Mary II*, the tender which will take the Royal Party to the *Queen Elizabeth*, was brought into Greenock last night and before she tied up alongside, bearings were taken which would enable her to find the liner, lying more than a mile away."

Another newspaper began its report in quite lyrical terms: "To Clydesiders the *Queen Elizabeth* emerges almost as a new ship. They were familiar with the massive grey-painted vessel that came and went at frequent intervals during the war, but they find it hard to believe that they are looking on the same ship now. The vivid whiteness of her upper works slashing across the dark painted hull in an unbroken line from stem to stern reveals her full beauty for the first time." It went on to report the upcoming event of the Royal visit and the trials voyage. "The Queen and her two daughters left Balmoral last night, and spent the night in the Royal Train, and all will go aboard the *Queen Elizabeth* over a small gangway slung between the small tender and the largest ship in the world. The Queen's standard will fly first from the little *Queen Mary II* and then from the *Queen Elizabeth*. Although the speed trials are two runs of two miles each, the Queen and Princesses will travel between 50 and 60 miles in the liner, which is scheduled to make two wide circuits in the Firth of Clyde. The ship will cross the Firth almost to the Isle of Arran and turn on to a third leg of a triangular course after passing over the two measured miles."

▽ Number Three boiler room receiving attention from shipyard workmen. The enormous task of making the ship ready for her peacetime career had to be completed to a particularly tight schedule.

The Royal Train arrived at Greenock station at 10.30 am. Sir Percy Bates was there to greet the Royal Party, Her Majesty the Queen and the two Princesses, as they were taken aboard the Clyde steamer *Queen Mary II*, which was alongside Prince's Pier. A crowd of spectators had gathered to watch their arrival. Before the Royal party was taken aboard the glistening liner, which naturally was dressed overall, the tender circled around it so that they could view it from almost every angle.

Once on board the liner, the Queen and the Princesses were introduced to Commodore Bissett and then he in turn presented his senior officers; they were then introduced to the Cunard directors and the other guests. A tour of the main public rooms was then undertaken. Meanwhile, on the bridge the Commodore and officers were making ready for the liner to continue with her trials; they weighed anchor at 11.15 am. As the *Queen Elizabeth* made her way along the Firth of Clyde the Staff Captain, Captain Wood, introduced the Queen to some members of the crew. Later, as luncheon was being served the liner was passing the southern tip of the Isle of Arran, all the time her speed being gradually increased. Shortly after lunch, while the Royal party were being given a tour of the galley, the speed had been worked up to almost 30 knots. Shortly before 3 pm they were escorted up to the bridge where each of the Princesses was given a stopwatch to time the liner's speed over the measured course.

The *Queen Elizabeth* made a splendid sight as she sped up the Firth of Clyde in the brilliant autumn sunshine. The Commodore had explained that one of the main aims of the trials was to ascertain what speed the liner could achieve at 175,000 horse power, rather than just establish her top speed. The first mile was covered in 2 minutes 1.3 seconds, which gave a speed of 29.71 knots. The next mile marker was reached in 2 minutes 1.0 seconds, a speed of 29.75 knots.

The following day a newspaper reported, under the headline "The Queen at the helm of giant liner": "The Queen took the helm of the 83,000-ton *Queen Elizabeth* at 30 knots off the coast of Arran in the Firth of Clyde yesterday.

▽ More work in progress, this time in the engine room while the *Queen Elizabeth* was being prepared for her trials. There was speculation whether she was a slightly faster ship than the record-holder *Queen Mary*.

Obeying the navigator's orders, the Queen changed course four points and then steadied the giant vessel. Afterwards she turned to the captain, Commodore Sir James Bissett, and said: 'How remarkably easy the wheel is.' The Master replied: 'All the more remarkable, Your Majesty, when you think that you are moving a rudder which weighs 140 tons.' Princess Elizabeth and Princess Margaret stood with a group of the ship's officers delightedly watching their mother take charge of the ship. It was on the third measured mile that the *Queen Elizabeth* achieved a speed of exactly 30 knots. Sir James explained afterwards that the ship was not out to establish a speed record. He added: 'We had some more up our sleeve.' On board the *Queen Elizabeth* were many of the underwriters who bear the burden of her £6,000,000 insurance on which the Cunard-White Star pay an annual premium of £75,000."

◁ Commodore Bissett looks on as Her Majesty the Queen takes the wheel during the vessel's speed trials.

▽ It was during those trials that this classic view of the ship was taken; as her last skipper, Commodore Geoffrey T. Marr said, "the dignity, beauty and symmetry of her lines when seen from the beam have never been surpassed."

On handing back the wheel of the liner to the Quartermaster, Arthur Campbell, the Queen joked that she hoped that she was returning the ship back to his control in good condition. She and the Princesses then left the bridge, the Queen continuing with her tour of some of the public rooms and sports facilities such as the squash courts, gymnasium and swimming pool, while Princess Elizabeth and Princess Margaret, having been given protective coats, were given a tour of the engine room.

The trials at an end, the *Queen Elizabeth* steamed at a more sedate speed back towards the Clyde. She was back at her anchorage at 5 pm and thirty minutes later the Royal party disembarked to return to Balmoral.

The following day four hundred specially invited guests of the company embarked for what was in effect a celebratory voyage back to Southampton. At 8 pm, with booming

▷ Restoration of the splendid marquetry panel, The Canterbury Pilgrims, designed by George Ramon. It contained 150 different types of wood and over 400 pieces of mother of pearl.

▽ The First Class Library. As in many of the public rooms, the obsession of the designer, George Grey Wornum, with rectangular shapes is very evident.

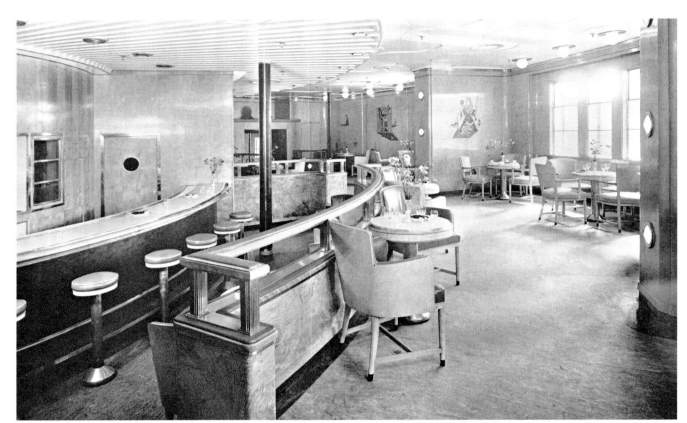

◁ The First Class Observation Lounge's cocktail bar and the First Class Restaurant. For British and European passengers in the late 1940s, a transatlantic crossing in First Class on one of the Cunard-White Star express liners was a return to the sophistication and luxury of pre-War days.

△ This nautically-themed tapestry by E. Esmonde-White provided a striking focal point in the very grand First Class Restaurant.

blasts from her siren, the *Queen Elizabeth* bade farewell to the Clyde and headed south. Floodlit, she arrived at 11 pm on the 10th October in what was still very obviously war-damaged Southampton: ready to begin earning dollars for war-ravaged Britain.

The following day Sir Percy Bates and Commodore Sir James Bissett entertained many members of both Houses of Parliament, including the Lord Chancellor and the Speaker of the House of Commons, to a luncheon on board. One of the M.Ps in the party was the writer and poet A.P. Herbert – he was in fact booked to sail on the maiden voyage – and he had written a poem to mark the occasion.

One of the changes that had been made to the *Queen Elizabeth* was that had she actually entered service in 1940 her highest grade of accommodation would have been classified as Cabin Class whereas Cunard had since decided to revert to the more appropriate First Class, with the other two categories being called Cabin and Tourist.

The First Class public rooms were located on Boat and Promenade Decks. Forward of the main hall, on Promenade Deck, was the semi-circular Observation Lounge. This was terraced, with the bar being at the lowest – entry – level of the room. In a contemporary publication ('The *Queen Elizabeth*' by D.S Watt and Raymond Birt and edited by Clarence Winchester, which was published at the time of the maiden voyage) it was described as being "… one of the gayest of rooms. The sweeping curves of the design give an exhilarating sense of movement. Its walls are of sycamore dyed to a lobster-shell colour into which are inlaid enchanting scenes of circus life." This was perhaps the most exciting room aboard the ship, with its broad sweep of windows giving a panoramic view forward over the bows. It was largely similar to the equivalent space aboard the *Queen Mary*, though perhaps styled with a lighter and more sophisticated touch. Aft of the main hall was the huge Lounge. Once again it bore considerable resemblance to its

The splendidly veneered sitting room of one of the First Class suites. Note the ventilating fan and the Bakelite telephone. (On page 63 there is a picture of this room being restored.) Another room in a First Class suite; this time, a bedroom.

counterpart aboard *Queen Mary* but it was somewhat simpler with less of the very obvious Art Deco embellishments. It was panelled in Canadian maple-burr, which was of an almost pinkish shade. In a central position on the aft wall was one of the most talked about works of art on the ship: a marquetry panel that had been designed by George Ramon, its theme being Chaucer's Canterbury Tales. In between the Lounge and the next large public room was a writing room. The next room was the Salon: its walls were covered in quilted satin, there were gilded ceiling mirrors and facing the orchestra platform was a deep recess into which was built a wide glass panel on which an exotic jungle scene was shown, complete with monkeys and fantastic birds. The furniture was veneered with a pale cream finish and was all arranged around a central dance floor. Aft of this was the Smoke Room: a giant chestnut tree that had grown on the Isle of Wight provided the veneers for this room, which was regarded as being as masculine as the Salon was feminine. Indeed, the room, while richly panelled, was very plain and sober with a mainly brown colour scheme that was slightly relieved with a light blue/grey. The Smoke Room contained a decorative map of the Atlantic and on this were models of both the *Queen Elizabeth* and the *Queen Mary*, enabling passengers to monitor the passage of the two ships as they crossed the ocean. On either side of the Smoke Room were the raised terraces of the Garden Lounge, furnished with cane chairs and flower boxes.

The First Class Restaurant was located on R Deck and it was approached from the forward foyer. This entrance space was panelled in a combination of English olive and ash burr and was dominated by a carving in lime wood of the Arms of Her Majesty the Queen, the work of Bainbridge Copnall. The lofty Restaurant was a full two decks in height and it was a square, at 111 feet extending the full width of the ship and being 111 feet in length. This huge room was panelled in London plane tree burr. There were three more carvings by Bainbridge Copnall within the restaurant: a large clock which, instead of numbers had the signs of the zodiac; and two large sculptures entitled The Fisherman and The Huntress. The most dominant work of art in the room, however, was a magnificent tapestry that had been designed by two South African artists, Eleanor Esmonde-White and Leroux Smith-Leroux. For those passengers who required some privacy, or who wished to host a more intimate gathering, there were private dining rooms in three of the four corners of the room, each decorated in a different style. One was panelled in English elm, another in willow and brown leather and the third in white and claret-coloured leathers. In the fourth corner of the Restaurant was a tiny cocktail bar.

For the ultimate in sophisticated dining there was the Veranda Grill, which was located up on Sun Deck. This elegant room was designed not just for dining but also for dancing. Although flanked with windows on three sides and allowing for a spectacular view aft over the terraced decks and away to the wake, the focus of the room was most certainly inward and towards the centrally-placed dance floor. Once again it was a recreation of a similar room aboard the *Queen Mary* but in a much understated and refined manner. The walls of the room were covered in a pale ivory-coloured sycamore veneer, the curtains were of peach velvet and the chairs were covered in pale blue leather with white piping.

The *Queen Elizabeth* had accommodation for 850 passengers in First Class, all of whom were accommodated amidships on A and B Decks and the Main Deck and forward on Sun and Promenade Decks. With the exception of the special suites which consisted of a sitting room, bedroom and bathroom (and which could be opened up to accommodate several people), the cabins were for either one or two passengers. The great majority of the First Class accommodations were outside, with portholes or windows. All of them had telephones and most (but not all) had their own toilets and bathrooms. Thus, even in the rarefied atmosphere of First Class a trip to the bathroom could mean going down the hall in one's bathrobe and slippers! Even so, thirty-seven different designs were used to create these cabins. Once again to quote Mr. Watt and Mr. Birt: "They are lovely rooms. Each is a perfect example of the art of the interior decorator, each is equipped for smooth and comfortable and gracious living."

For the 720 Cabin Class passengers there was an equally interesting array of public rooms. The Lounge was located on Main Deck. Apparently it could comfortably accommodate 200 people, which for the principal social centre for 720 seems somewhat limiting. However, the room had an airiness about it – due in part to the wide curving windows at its aft end. The after part of the room was a raised terrace with a balustrade of silver-bronze and glass. The walls were covered in pale vellum hide with bands of silver-bronze. Particularly attractive decorative features were two deeply engraved maps of moulded glass, showing the Northern and Southern Hemispheres. Messrs. Watt and Birt became positively lyrical in their description of this room: "The impression is one so cool, so light and airy that it induces a sense of almost insubstantiality; but the room is substantial enough. That deep rich carpet is laid in squares. At need they may be lifted to reveal a parquet floor for dancing." One deck higher, on Promenade Deck, were the Cabin Class Smoking Room, Cocktail Bar, Drawing Room and Library. The Smoking Room was certainly one of the most striking and attractive rooms aboard the ship with much more of the late Art Deco feel in its styling, whereas most of the ship seemed to be neither Art Deco nor the then more fashionable Art Moderne style. The decorative theme of the Cabin Class Smoking Room was tan, blue and cream and the focus of the room was towards the apse-like fireplace, surrounded by Maltese marble. Above this was a large panel of nine bas-reliefs designed by Norman Forest. He had taken the nine principal materials used in the construction of the ship –

The design of this light and airy Cabin Class Lounge may have been inspired by the décor of the pre-War Orient liner, *Orion*.
The *Queen Elizabeth*'s Cabin Class Restaurant may not have been as grand as the equivalent room in First Class but it had a very sophisticated Art Deco style.

steel, wood, copper, bronze, aluminium, lead, white metal, rubber and glass. Of each material he created a bas-relief that expressed the quality of the material and its usage. The Cabin Class Cocktail Bar was located behind the Smoking Room and had windows looking out over the after decks. It was a bright room and this was emphasised by the off-white furniture with upholstery in pale yellow hide. The bar itself was decorated with two paintings by Margot Gilbert entitled Wine and Beer. Forward of the Smoking Room were the Library and the Drawing Room, the latter having the facility to be turned into a chapel when required.

The Cabin Class Restaurant was also located on R Deck, aft of the galley that separated it from the First Class Restaurant. Unlike its First Class counterpart, it did not extend the full width of the ship and thus it was a room without windows or portholes. Instead, in each of the ten bays that flanked the room was placed a large glass disc etched with a flower design. With the aid of clever lighting and with each bay finished in silvered metal, the light that radiated was more brilliant than had there been just normal ports.

This was, in fact, a very smart-looking room with mahogany furniture upholstered with coral-coloured hide. On the walls hung two mirrors etched with designs by Margot Gilbert representing summer and winter carnivals.

The staircase that led up through the Cabin Class accommodation was the largest in the ship. On its flights and companionways ran a dado of elm burr which was edged with Australian walnut and then a frieze of bleached Queensland silky oak. In each half landing were set two niches faced with a gleaming black material and containing a green Poole pottery vase, floodlit from above. The effect was dramatic.

The cabins for the passengers travelling Cabin Class were spread over several decks. There was accommodation for 72 aft on D Deck and rather more were in cabins along the port side of C Deck (with just a small group on the starboard side). There were more cabins to either side of the restaurant and also aft of it and more were on A and B Decks, aft of the First Class accommodation. All were equipped with private toilet facilities and with a wash basin. In many instances the

▲ One of the most modernistic public rooms was the Cabin Class Smoke Room. The nine decorative panels over the fireplace represented various materials used in the construction of the ship.

cabins were also fitted with full private bathrooms, and those located on A and B Decks were quite as luxuriously fitted as similar accommodations in First Class. Four colour schemes were used to decorate the Cabin Class accommodations: blue, salmon, green and brown. In all, the cabin accommodation and public rooms of this class were exceptionally attractive and stylish but avoided the overt grandeur of First Class.

The Tourist Class accommodation was mostly amidships, on D Deck, and forward on the four decks above. Approximately 745 passengers could be carried in this class and once again Watt and Birt were fulsome in their praise of the not unattractive but rather simple appointments for this class. The staircases were 'as spacious as those of a sprawling country mansion and their dignity is enriched by the warm oak veneers of their panelling.' The Tourist Lounge was on B Deck and was panelled in walnut veneer. This room doubled as the library, as along one wall was a large bookcase. Facing the entrance was a marquetry panel, a landscape scene by George Ramon. The Smoking Room was on the deck above and extended the full width of the ship. This room was panelled with a pale straight-grained elm with marquetry inlays. At the aft end of the room was a small cocktail bar. On Main Deck was the forward-facing, semi-circular Winter Garden. At its entrance was a large glass screen which stood in mullions of bronze and carried an etched design by Ralph Cowan entitled 'The Birth of Life'. As one would expect, this room contained bowls and jardinières for plants and flowers which were grouped below the glass screen and round glass columns in the centre of the room.

Over 400 passengers could be accommodated in the Tourist Class restaurant, which was located forward on R Deck. It was a room of modest decoration and Watt and Birt gave it scant mention in their review of the liner's accommodation, merely referring to the fact that it stretched the width of the ship (albeit in a tapered shape due to its location in the hull) and the fact that on one wall hung a large decorated panel of glass on which was superimposed an electric clock with a glass dial. This, like all of the other clocks on board the *Queen Elizabeth* (and the *Queen Mary*), had been provided by Thomas Mercer, Ltd. of St Albans, the well-known marine chronometer makers who also provided clock systems for ships. Two of Mercers' 8-day chronometers were on the bridge of the *Queen Elizabeth*. The fact that they were 8-day chronometers was something of a rarity, since the vast majority were of the 2-day type. On both the 'Queens' one of these chronometers was fitted with electrical contacts which gave an impulse every half-minute. This was transmitted to a master clock, which sent out a more powerful impulse around the ship to 'slave' clocks which consequently all moved on together. Thus the time indicated throughout the ship was governed by the chronometer. Most of the 'slave' clocks had an impulse movement involving a 'click and pawl' arrangement and each impulse that they

received would result in a 'click' being heard as the hand jumped on a further half-minute. However, for the 'quiet rooms' Mercers developed a silent slave movement. Such was the concern that Cunard had for their passengers that they would not want them to be disturbed even by the gentle ticking of a clock. The Tourist Class cabins were located forward on C and D Decks, aft of the lounge on B Deck and aft of the Smoking Room on A Deck.

There were two indoor swimming pools aboard the *Queen Elizabeth*: one for First Class and one for Cabin Class. The First Class pool was down on C Deck and adjacent to it was what was referred to as the Turkish Bath. Rather curiously, the gymnasium and the Squash Court were several decks away up on Sun Deck. While Cabin Class passengers were denied the luxury of the Turkish Bath they did have the more logical arrangement - on E Deck - of their gymnasium being close by the pool: the pool itself being particularly attractive and larger than the one in First Class. It was lined with golden quartzite to give the water a glow as though lit by sunlight. The walls of the pool area were covered with a mother of pearl-like compound into which were placed a series of medallion designs that resembled cloisonné, while the columns surrounding the pool were faced with mosaic in shades ranging from deep ultramarine to emerald green.

There were two cinemas: one was located on Promenade Deck and was for First Class and Cabin Class passengers, with the First Class passengers entering through two sets of doors at the back of the room while the Cabin Class passengers entered through doors placed either side of the screen. It could seat 338 people and was adaptable so that concerts or recitals could also be staged there. It was a most attractive space and more than made up for the fact that the *Queen Mary* had been designed without such a facility. The Tourist Class cinema was a far more modest affair, located on the opposite side of the ship to the Tourist Lounge. There was seating for 130 passengers and a stage was also provided for other performances.

There was a complete hospital, on the starboard side of C Deck. It had wards for men and women, dispensaries, dressing and inspection rooms and an operating theatre. It also contained a complete dental surgery as well as an x-ray unit. Separately, in the after part of the ship there was also an isolation hospital for the treatment of any passenger who might be suspected of suffering from an infectious disease.

Even in those days when it was a commonly held view that 'children should be seen but not heard', fully-equipped playrooms were provided for them in each class. There was considerable deck space, both open and enclosed, for the passengers to take the bracing mid-Atlantic air, play deck games or just enjoy promenading.

The *Queen Elizabeth* was ready! For a voyage of a little less than a week, she could offer her passengers more or less all that they could desire. Indeed, with the harsh memories of the war still so fresh, this symbol of recovery, this icon of peace, represented more than an escape from ravaged and war-torn Europe: she was for many their way to a new world and a new life. For those in America she would represent, after so many years, real contact with family, with friends and with what had once been home.

Britain Can Make It. This was the optimistic name given to a trade and manufacturing exhibition aimed at showing to the world that, having won the war, Britain could now win the peace. Her major cities were, however, deeply scarred with the ruins of bombing raids and her people were tired. A long struggle of recovery lay ahead. The *Queen Elizabeth*, resplendent in fresh paint and stocked with food and other luxuries long unavailable in Britain and brought over from America aboard the *Aquitania*, was in effect proof that Britain could and would make it but the country was still to endure several more years of deprivation, hardship and rationing.

While A.P. Herbert's poem might have struck some patriotic chord, igniting a sense of pride and a feeling of understanding of the reason for the urgency to get the *Queen Elizabeth* into commercial service, another writer seemed almost to ignore these feelings, probably quite unintentionally. His tone, though, was virtually flippant in the light of the hardships being faced and still to be faced by the country: "…gleaming like a yacht, vast like a city, towering over the dockside in her enormous grace … where once she was grey and secret, now she is carnival with lights. Where once she was stark and stripped, now she is gay and opulent with the warm extravagance of luxury. She is the ultimate in liners, the greatest ship in the world!"

There were not too many Britons who would revel in the warm extravagance of luxury during the approaching winter months.

▽ On her maiden commercial voyage, the ship's stylish shops were thronged by passengers eager to purchase goods which were unobtainable in post-War Britain.

Chapter 6

MAIDEN VOYAGE

While the *Queen Elizabeth* was still in the early stages of refurbishment, Cunard announced that she would sail from Southampton for New York on her first commercial voyage on Wednesday the 16th October 1946. There was a huge demand for berths, even from some passengers who had intended to sail on her originally planned maiden voyage in April 1940.

Under the tantalising headline 'Food from Abroad', one newspaper reported just two days before the departure: "Among the 2,288 passengers who will leave for the United States in the *Queen Elizabeth*, the world's biggest liner, on Wednesday, are several who booked their passages before the vessel was launched. Two of the twelve best suites on the Main Deck amidships have been allotted to M. Molotov and M. Vyshinsky." (Vyacheslav Molotov was the Soviet Foreign Minister and Andrei Vyshinsky was the Soviet ambassador to the United Nations.) "Accommodation nearby has been given to members of their staffs. I understand that M. Molotov's cabin was occupied by Mr. Churchill when he crossed at the end of the war. Three other ambassadors are on the passenger list as well as an ex-Prime Minister, three newspaper proprietors, two Members of Parliament, four dance band leaders and several industrialists and businessmen. To feed the total complement of 3,538, the staff of Mr. B. Jones, the Chief Steward, will prepare, during the 4-day single voyage:

> 5 tons of flour
> 12½ tons of potatoes
> 10 tons of strawberries
> 13 tons of meat
> 25,000 eggs
> 10 cwt of tea
> 23,000lb of chicken, ducks and turkeys.

The only home-produced foodstuffs are boiling fish and potatoes. All other food is from the United States or Canada.

"The first passengers will embark tomorrow afternoon and the remainder on Wednesday morning. In the main vestibule on the embarkation deck they will find 12 smart 'bell hops'. A steward who had served in the liner during her trooping days was amazed at the transformation from war-time fittings to peace-time ornamentations. Passengers will be able to cash cheques and transact almost every form of banking business while the ship is at sea. Three offices of the Midland Bank will provide this service. There will also be radio telephone service facilities. Four special Southern Railway boat trains will leave Waterloo tomorrow with passengers for the *Queen Elizabeth*. The all Pullman-car trains will leave at 10.15 am."

What a changed world the *Queen Elizabeth* was sailing into. And what a supreme irony that the Foreign Minister of the country that Winston Churchill had probably feared even more than Hitler's Germany, the Soviet Union, was sailing to the United States on this British ship, in First Class no less – this champion of socialist equality – and in the very cabin that only months previously had cocooned Churchill himself! What had the world come to?

It was indeed a different world that the *Queen Elizabeth* was being prepared to face and an ocean denuded of the best liners that she had been designed to compete against. Of the great ships which had raced across the Atlantic during those latter days of the 1930s in a world suddenly startled out of the gloom of the Depression, few were left. So many had fallen victim of the war: *Bremen, Normandie, Rex, Conte Di Savoia*, each of them needlessly and stupidly destroyed. Among other important losses were the *Empress of Britain, Oslofjord, Pilsudski and Stockholm* along with many more, smaller but no less significant liners. It was a new beginning. *Queen Elizabeth* was but the spearhead. It would be more than a decade before the North Atlantic run would again achieve such a glittering height – but by then it would all be too late.

However, in mid-October 1946 all attention was on the preparations for the maiden voyage departure of the *Queen Elizabeth* and most of the newspaper reports focused on the fact that Molotov and Vishinsky were to be amongst the elite 2,288 passengers. However, Cunard-White Star were the very model of discretion and when the reporter F.G. Prince-White tried to extract more information about the Soviet officials travelling on the maiden voyage he was met with nothing more than: "It has been intimated to us that Mr. Molotov and Mr. Vishinsky will be sailing in the *Queen Elizabeth*." Any attempt to find out about any special arrangements which had been made for them encountered a veil of secrecy. Prince-White reported that: "When I asked at the Purser's office for the number of Mr. Molotov's suite I was met with lifted eyebrows and a rather constrained air of innocence. 'We have had no allocation for Mr. Molotov

◁ Typical Cunard stewards, many of whom hailed from Southampton, serve tea to passengers on one of the promenades.

Before the War, it would have been unthinkable to have women assistant pursers. Miss Elizabeth Sayers (later the Social Directress), Miss Margaret Morton, Mrs. Phyllis Davis and Miss Mary Marchant.

or Mr. Vishinsky so far. We don't know what is happening.' However, everybody on board today seemed to be expecting the Soviet diplomats to cross in this ship for the Big Four conference (in America) – and I was shown a very luxurious combination of connecting bedrooms and private dining room and sitting room which, it is understood, they are likely to use. The colour scheme of this suite is blue and gold and grey, with hangings and bedspreads of heavy blue-grey satin. The cost of the suite for the single voyage is 400 guineas." Commodore Bisset was apparently amused by all the media attention which the Soviet diplomats were generating. "They say he's coming with us do they? Well, we must certainly get together – and we must make sure there's some vodka available!"

For the first time in his career Commodore Bisset was to have women officers on his ship. They were four former WRNS officers who had been signed on as assistant pursers: Mrs. P. Davies, Miss M. Marchant, Miss Margaret Morton and Miss E. Sayers. All four of them were used to sea travel and during the war Mrs. Davies had crossed the Atlantic twenty-one times. The Commodore said: "I'm glad to have them – but only as assistant pursers mind! I never dreamed that I should one day be sailing with women officers; though in these days of conscription, when so many young men are called up for the Services, it seems we shall have to have girls for more and more jobs in ships." When questioned about perhaps trying to better the *Queen Mary's* speed of 31.69 knots he responded with caution: "We shall maintain a moderate average speed of about 29½ knots."

The *Daily Mail's* correspondent Rhona Churchill was to be one of several reporters on board the liner for the maiden voyage. She wrote that amongst the glittering array of passengers in First Class, would be the motor racing ace Woolf Barnato, the thriller writer Valentine Williams, the dance band kings Bert Ambrose, Jack Hylton and Geraldo and apparently 'at least fifty millionaires'. Miss Churchill had also covered the maiden voyage of the *Queen Mary* and found that she now encountered several crew members she remembered from that ship. Among them were Miss Hodgkins, Miss Kilburn and Miss O'Kane, each of whom had been a stewardess aboard the *Queen Mary*. One suspects that they were well and truly fed up with the ladies and gentlemen of the press asking questions about Molotov and Vishinsky. She reported: "'Do you want to see where we're putting the Russians?' one of them had whispered, and took me down the main stateroom deck into a luxurious treble-roomed suite with green satin bedspreads, maple-wood panels and a sitting room fitted with pink armchairs." (One wonders whether each reporter was not shown a different suite so that no one really knew where the diplomats would be accommodated.)

It was perhaps wholly understandable that the newspapers should have worked themselves into a frenzy over the preparations for the maiden voyage departure. For six long years they had reported the war, the battles, the bombings and the losses. While there ultimately came the jubilation of victory to report, the *Queen Elizabeth* was nevertheless the most brilliant and spectacular thing to happen to Britain for a very long time. The announcement of the keel-laying of the 34,000-ton *Caronia* in February had not achieved that same level of glamour at this stage. So, no matter how trivial, if it pertained to the *Queen Elizabeth* it was news!

Police precautions on an unprecedented scale for peace time were in operation both in and around the *Queen Elizabeth* in order to guard against stowaways or any attempt at last-minute sabotage or anything that might cause the smallest delay in her departure. Under the glare of arc lights on the quay, special police kept watch and guards extended far beyond the jetty. In the hotels where some passengers were staying on the night before embarkation, police were watching for confidence men or thieves. Meanwhile, Southern Railway dockyard police and detectives kept a strict watch on all the dock gates. It was reported that at least one special branch officer from Scotland Yard, a detective with a 'photographic brain' for faces, had been on duty for some days. Several names on the passenger list concealed the identities of C.I.D. men who between them knew nearly every criminal specialising in work on board the great liners - confidence men, card sharps and jewel thieves and others. It seemed as though the heady days of the trans-Atlantic service had really returned.

On Tuesday the 15th October, Boat Trains left Waterloo for Southampton carrying the Tourist Class passengers who were embarked later that day. On the following morning, further Boat Trains steamed out of Waterloo carrying those passengers who would be travelling Cabin Class and First Class. The locomotive hauling the all-Pullman carriages for First Class passengers was a 'Merchant Navy' Class engine appropriately named *Cunard-White Star* and a special headboard had been made that spelled out *R.M.S. Queen Elizabeth*. It had been planned for the chairman of the line, Sir Percy Bates, to see the departure of this train. Sadly however, he had collapsed in his office in Liverpool on the previous day. He had suffered a heart attack and had died.

It was such a cruel twist of fate: for so long he had worked to realise the dream of the two 'Queens' operating together across the Atlantic. War had stolen this from him once and now with the splendid new flagship glittering and fresh, the focus of so much attention on both sides of the Atlantic, he died knowing that his dream was about to become a reality but to experience it was denied him. The news of his death cast a pall over the officers and crew, which contrasted sharply with the celebratory air that otherwise pervaded the ship. Although the flags of shipping offices in Southampton and on many vessels were at half mast, those of the *Queen Elizabeth* were not and she remained dressed overall for the departure, as were the tugs that attended her. "Percy would have wished it that way," said Commodore Bisset. "We shall pay tribute to him on the day of the funeral in an appropriate manner." Out of respect for Sir Percy, the Southern Railway Docks and Marine Band, which was to have played the *Queen Elizabeth* out from her berth, did not do so.

By the death of Sir Percy Bates, at just 67, not only had the British shipping world lost one of its greatest personalities but the Merchant Navy one of its greatest friends. Sir Percy had been the chairman of the Cunard-White Star Line since the merger of the two companies in 1934. It was he who foresaw and urged the development of the *Queen Mary* and the *Queen Elizabeth*, enabling Britain to recapture the Blue Ribbon for the speediest Atlantic crossings. Sir James Lithgow, the shipbuilder, in a tribute, said: "Percy Bates was typical of the men to whom British industry and commerce owe their high reputation throughout the world. He had the vision, courage and judgement to initiate, great enterprise with integrity. His loss is a national calamity." Sir Percy's brother, Frederick Bates, succeeded him as chairman of the line.

At 10 am on the morning of the 16th Mr. Molotov and Mr. Vishinsky, along with their party, arrived from Paris in a specially chartered aeroplane at Eastleigh Airport. In an interview on board, the Soviet Foreign Minister referred to the British offer to place the cruiser *Dido* at his disposal for the trip from France but explained that there had been much work to finish. "We are very grateful for the courtesy shown to the Soviet delegation," he said. Two passengers, Mr. Cox and Mr. Elliott, wealthy businessmen, were transferred before the sailing and became neighbours of Mr. Molotov. The suites they occupied had been reserved for Sir Percy and Lady Bates, whose baggage remained aboard until the ship returned to Southampton.

Thousands of people had turned out to see the *Queen Elizabeth*, the pride of Britain, depart on this very special voyage. At the stroke of 2 pm the first mooring ropes were loosened and the Mayor of Southampton shouted: "Three cheers for the *Queen Elizabeth*!" and with the dockers, porters, passengers and onlookers cheering themselves hoarse the 83,000-ton liner, with flags and bunting flying and with the aid of eight tugs, began to move. By 2.26 pm the final hawser had been slipped and she was away from her berth. Seven times her sirens sounded and the twenty large ships in Southampton's docks that day answered in salute. One louder than all the others was that of the *Queen Mary*. This was a rare occasion on which the two ships would be in port together. Her wartime career now over, the *Queen Mary* too was being readied for a return to her pre-war splendour. Aircraft - bombers, helicopters even an airliner – flew over the *Queen Elizabeth* as she headed toward Southampton Water. Small craft - paddle steamers, motor launches, tugs and naval vessels - accompanied her. The skipper of a launch with 'Bye-bye Toots' painted on its roof signalled 'Bon Voyage' in semaphore with his hands, the captain of a naval craft wished 'God Speed and Good Luck' with his Aldiss lamp, and a saucy motor torpedo boat, keeping pace with the liner, suddenly shot ahead with a cheeky blast.

At first, the *Queen Elizabeth* maintained a steady 15 knots but as she headed out under grey skies into the Channel her speed was soon increased. Due to its still war-damaged state, no call was made at Cherbourg: instead it was a voyage directly to New York. (It was not, in fact, until 1948 that the *Queen Elizabeth* was able to include Cherbourg as part of her regular trans-Atlantic itinerary, with her first call at the French port being made on the 7th April of that year.)

Commodore Bisset was very moved by the whole occasion. "No other country in the world has brought into existence so wonderful a ship as this," he said. "I was to have retired from the seas, as I am in my 63rd year, but how could

I forgo the delight of such an experience as this? As a boy of 15 I went to sea but of all of the adventures I have had none compares with today."

One reporter, Paul Holt, captured the atmosphere of the departure perfectly: "The time is five o'clock and we are three hours on our way. Yet I will swear that many, perhaps 500, of our passengers have no idea that we have put to sea. No roar disturbs us, no thrum of engines, no shudder of keel against the swell. So serenely does this Queen ride that her masters and mistresses – 2,000 of us – ignore her, for we are busy. We are queueing.

"Since I came aboard, my fellow passengers have done little else. Do not think that half the time they know what they are queueing for. They see a queue and join it. Boat drill does not disturb them. Announcements over the loudspeaker they simply do not hear. They queue. So low has the war brought my countrymen.

"Mind you, there is no need for them to do this; it is a habit. I cannot say I blame them. I cannot say that the sight of 50 millionaires standing in a queue distresses me – although it makes me laugh a little. And yet, I think they might have been better employed. For this has been an emotional afternoon.

"Before we sailed there was nothing. Efficiency, yes. And a great promise of luxury. Flowers and chunk jewellery and women walking stiffly with pride. But there was no heart to it. Nothing really came alive until during the first hour of the soft cat-like tread of this great voyage of luxury. Two little paddle steamers, smutty and frothy and slow, were listing

Dressed overall, the *Queen Elizabeth* leaves Southampton on her maiden commercial voyage. The occasion was seen by many as a welcome sign of the restoration of peacetime normality.

△ Another view of the maiden departure. The tugs, too, are dressed overall and *Queen Elizabeth's* decks are lined with excited passengers.

visibly to port under the weight of their passengers, who flocked to the rail to cheer us.

"Neatly we passed them. And then the captain, Commodore Sir James Bisset, could stand it no longer. He sounded three deep, shuddering blasts on our great siren, and the little paddle steamers hooted and peeped wildly. I was standing on the Sun Deck with half a dozen engineer officers and they grinned a little and gripped the stems of their pipes hard between their teeth.

"So it was, perfect. These little islanders down there; these brave little people looking so small from the towering majesty of 83,000 tons. Waving to us, cheering us in pride. Not envious. Not resentful of these rich and casual people who are aboard. Not grudging them their chance. But proud of a great ship, the greatest ship in the world, which sails for England.

"I wish there had been a full complement of all my friends on the Sun Deck to cheer them back. But alas, there were few. There were too many of us too busy with our stewards and our room service and the friends we shall not need to invite to a cocktail party.

"I met a man who talked to me of the lovely white roll he had with his lunch. I met a man who was worried what had won the Caesarewitch. And then they were queueing for dressing gowns, ties, dolls and a great moment in English history was slipping by them. They will probably never miss it.

"To be sure, it was a wonderful lunch. You had your choice – lobster and steak and roast pork, apple pie and gorgonzola cheese and whatever else you wanted. I was, in a way, pleased to see how many people chose simple dishes like cold roast beef and ham, followed by gorgonzola cheese and lager beer. I thought they showed good taste.

"Mr. Molotov, however, who had spent the morning giving a Press interview in the corridor outside his Main Deck cabin, was not so modest in his meal. Correct as always, he came down to the main dining room, sat among the general guests. With some relish he ate his way straight through the recommended luncheon of minestrone soup, lobster, steak, apple pie … at this point he paused and asked for a glass of boiled milk which had been allowed to cool … then he continued with ice cream.

"7.30 pm – It is night now, and still there is no movement in this ship. The queues are decreasing. People have gone to their cabins, determined to dress for dinner this first night on board – a thing unheard of before the war. So keen are they to enjoy this pleasure.

"I saw a middle-aged woman just now, hurrying to her cabin to change. She was lovely in a musquash, but her stockings were odd, of different colour. She will be curing that by now."

The lure of the on-board shops was indeed more than the passengers could resist. The added attraction was that clothing coupons were not required. Within just three minutes of opening the shops they had to close again, so great was the rush to get inside. Inspector Wilkinson, of Scotland Yard, Special Branch, who had always been on duty with Mr. Molotov when he was in London, had gone down to Eastleigh Airport and had accompanied the Soviet delegation aboard the ship. The inspector received, quite unexpectedly, instruction that he was to sail with the party. He was quite unprepared and therefore without any luggage: a sympathetic passenger loaned him things until the shops were again opened.

The Soviet delegation had garnered a great deal of attention from the press, even to the point of reporting Molotov's statement: "I intend to live as an ordinary passenger, eating in the main dining room and sharing in the ship's life. After all, why not? I am a very ordinary man." How many of his fellow comrades back in the Soviet Union would have accepted that? However, apart from this 'ordinary' Soviet diplomat there were many other well-known people who were also travelling in First Class: Pamela Countess of Aylesford, the Earl and Countess of Birkenhead, the Earl and Countess of Carrick, Viscount and Viscountess Camrose, Sir William and Lady Collins, Sir Hugo and Lady Cunliffe-Owen, Sir Andrew and Lady Duncan, Sir Ernest Fisk, Sir Alan Herbert M.P. (the writer A. P. Herbert who had already celebrated the occasion with a poem), Viscount Lambert, Lord Leathers, Sir Simon Marks, Admiral Sir Gordon Ramsey, Sir William and Lady Rootes, Sir Reginald and Lady Rootes, Viscount and Viscountess Rothermere, Sir Arthur Sutherland, Sir Robert Webber, Viscount Weir, Lady Yule and the Attorney-General, Sir Hartley Shawcross.

There was one steward who had been aboard the old *Mauretania*. "The trouble is" he said, "this ship has been pushed around so much, what with trooping, royal visits, official tours and Press parties that she has become impersonal. It'll take the maiden voyage to shake her down and give her a soul of her own."

Naturally, the BBC made special preparations to cover the maiden voyage. Listeners were able to follow the course of the ship right across the Atlantic to the moment she entered New York harbour. BBC engineers had a special studio on board and, in conjunction with the ship's radio officers, sent out broadcasts to shore over the *Queen Elizabeth*'s own transmitters. Nine separate points – from the bridge to the children's playground – were wired for microphones. In addition a full set of recording gear was carried.

Every day, principally immediately after the news bulletins on the Home and Light Programmes, Stewart MacPherson and Wynford Vaughan Thomas sent reports of the liner's progress. There were special broadcasts too, in the popular Woman's Hour, on Thursday and Friday. But three programmes in particular were of longer duration. The first of these, at 1.10 pm on the Home Service, was of the departure from the Ocean Dock giving a first description of the scene, the last minute arrivals and the bustle of the

This post-War view of the First Class Restaurant makes on interesting comparison with the picture on page 46, when the room was filled with troops.

Customs Hall. Then, at 1.50 pm on the Light Programme, was broadcast the actual sailing with Stewart MacPherson, stationed on the bridge and relaying all the excitement to the listeners. At 3.30 pm that same afternoon was broadcast the first of the reports, over the ship's radio – prefaced by the magic words, 'At Sea.' By Friday the 18th October, with the *Queen Elizabeth* well out in mid-Atlantic, the broadcasters took the listeners on a tour of the ship. Commodore Bisset was interviewed on the bridge. Then, on the morning of Monday the 21st October came the big moment: the *Queen Elizabeth* steaming up the Hudson River to an ear-splitting chorus of welcome from the shipping in the harbour.

But well before her arrival in New York there was that buzz of excitement aboard – would the *Queen Elizabeth* make a record crossing? Richard Viner, the *Daily Graphic* special correspondent, telephoned his report from on board the ship as she gathered speed into the Atlantic. "As the mighty prow of the *Queen Elizabeth* cut through the first Atlantic waves, passengers danced in the Veranda Grill in celebration of a dream come true. They stepped from seven years of austerity to a hundred hours of luxury. And what luxury!

"Last night I heard that the liner had already been thrusting her way ahead at 30 knots for seven hours. Then she was in the St. Georges Channel, heading towards Ireland. Now, in the early morning she is well past the Bishop's Rock

and on the Blue Riband course. There are reasons for hoping there may be a record run after all."

Despite the boyish enthusiasm of the *Daily Graphic*'s correspondent for the *Queen Elizabeth* to make a grasp for the Blue Riband, when the Commodore was asked about it he responded: "Absolutely not. The *Queen Mary* has that. Why should we raise all hell to take it from her?"

Bishop's Rock was passed at midnight; the *Queen Elizabeth* was actually maintaining a steady 29½ knots and on her first full day at sea had covered 609 miles. However, the Commodore had said that if the weather held and with the prevailing following wind, he really only needed to maintain the ship at 27 knots in order to make the tide in New York. The sea was a little rough but she was proving herself to be a steady sea boat. The only people under the weather were those who found a dinner and breakfast with a choice of about fifty different dishes a little too much for the digestive system. It was all very tempting after the years of austerity.

Mr. Molotov and Mr. Vishinsky were out early on deck. Both hatless, they clambered about the Sports Deck examining everything like a couple of schoolboys. They were invited by the Commodore to the bridge and they remained there for twenty minutes. Mr. Molotov was plainly delighted when asked to take the wheel, steering the ship for five minutes, and putting her a couple of degrees off-course. Through his interpreter he asked the Commodore many questions and said that he was delighted with the ship and the comfort on board. He was in a very jovial mood and expressed a wish to return to the bridge the following day, so interested was he in the radar, the gyro compass and other navigational instruments.

While Mr. Molotov filled the rest of his day watching the games of deck tennis and shuffle board, promenading with his three companions and talking with passengers that he knew, there was a full programme of events for the passengers' entertainment. There was a cinema show, housey-housey, an auction pool and dancing in the ballroom and veranda grill. The orchestra leaders Geraldo, Jack Hylton and Bert Ambrose, who were travelling as passengers, were asked if they would be guest conductors to the orchestras on board.

There was but one blot to mar what was otherwise a seemingly flawless maiden voyage – New York. There was a strike of the tug boat men in the port and Commodore Bisset had said that he would take the *Queen Elizabeth* in without tugs if the strike situation made it necessary. The president of the International Longshoremen's Association, Joseph Ryan, announced that all work on towing foreign ships into New York harbour would stop and bring the whole of the New York docks to a standstill if there was any attempt to dock the liner without tugs. Members of the U.S. shipping unions representing masters, mates and pilots and marine engineers had been idle since the beginning of October through various wage disputes. The commodore was preparing for the eventuality of having to take the *Queen Elizabeth* into Halifax instead, as indeed was everyone at Cunard. It would not be known until the Saturday, when they knew the position at New York, whether they would be going there instead of New York. "I might have a stab at New York without tugs," Commodore Bisset said, "but everything depends on the weather and what labour there is ashore to take our lines and tie us up. Everything is going like clockwork and everyone seems happy. If we go to Halifax, arrangements have been laid on to get the passengers to New York in the quickest possible time."

On Friday the 18th October Commodore Bisset conducted a simple memorial tribute to Sir Percy Bates. One of the dance bands played the hymns and Sir James gave an address to 'shipmates and fellow travellers'. Of Sir Percy he said: "He was a man of great integrity, strong purpose and sympathetic understanding."

The weather had deteriorated that day: to quote the ship's official log 'a very rough sea with a moderate north-westerly swell'. It resulted in many empty spaces on the deck and in the public rooms. Mr. Molotov was seen walking briskly around the deck at 7 am but it was later reported that "He was not feeling too well." Nor was his bodyguard and as a result Inspector Wilkinson of Scotland Yard took over his duties, temporarily. The *Daily Mail* correspondent, Rhona Churchill, reported for her column: "We don't feel so

good today and Mr. John Shepherd, millionaire owner of an American radio network and a Boston department store, did not improve matters when he joined us in the Observation Bar before lunch for cocktails. He was dressed in a sea-sickly lemon jacket, sky-blue trousers, gold and royal blue socks and the Airborne beret he bought in Piccadilly because he liked the colour. It took courage for me to face that lemon jacket when more than half the passengers, including Mr. Molotov and his bodyguard, were prostrate in their cabins, calling for sedatives. We have been told that we shall be in calm waters before tonight's fun begins."

Jack Hylton threw a lunch-time champagne cocktail party in the Smoke Room to celebrate his winning £655 in the day's forecast on the ship's run. "Everything that man touches turns to gold," disgruntled losers were saying. The Commodore asked Jack Hylton to organise a concert, which included the film star Roland Young. Mr. P.J. Noel-Baker, a government minister, was to have met the Press that morning to chat about the forthcoming United Nations meeting but he could not risk leaving his cabin. Sir Hartley Shawcross, who agreed to substitute, announced that he was trying to organise a cocktail party so that the British, Russian and American delegates could meet informally.

Despite the weather, the *Queen Elizabeth* sped onwards, maintaining her high speed: 742 miles to noon on the 18th, at an average speed of 29.68 knots. The reportedly 40-mile-an-hour gale was sending spray across her bows. When the sun broke through the clouds it shone on some very pale and wan faces. Mr. Molotov was sufficiently recovered to attend Mr. Noel-Baker's cocktail party. Senator Connally, Sir Norman Birkett, Baroness Ravensdale, Sir Alexander Maxwell, Air Chief Marshal Sir Guy Garrod and a hundred other distinguished passengers were present. At 6 pm the *Queen Elizabeth* reported that she was on the west side of a depression. She recorded better weather but with winds approaching gale force. There were many familiar faces absent from the dining room that evening.

Under vastly improved weather conditions and with a rising barometer, the *Queen Elizabeth* raised her speed to 29.50 knots. As she steadied, many passengers who had been upset by the pitching found their sea legs once more. Though the sea remained rough, with a fresh westerly 22 m.p.h. breeze, the swell was moderate. She had, up to Friday covered 1,351 miles in 45 hours 36 minutes, at an average of 29.63 knots, well above the 27.50 knots required to bring her into New York on time.

"New York to welcome 'Queen E' today" proclaimed one newspaper report from New York. "Americans, with all the glitter, noise and pomp they can muster are preparing a riotous welcome for the *Queen Elizabeth* when she docks here at 12.30 G.M.T. tomorrow. With memories of her war-time visits still vivid, this great ship will be acclaimed almost as America's own. Ex-GIs who returned home in her will be in the forefront of the vast welcoming crowds.

Now, like so many of the veterans she brought home, the *Queen Elizabeth* is herself returning home on a demobilisation visit, and 12 tugs, two fire boats, naval blimps and scores of aircraft are ready to escort her up the Hudson to her berth opposite midtown New York. Reporters from the whole of this continent are covering the event and more than 250 will be on the quayside when she docks. Mr Vincent Impelliteri, New York's acting mayor, will lead officials in the city's formal welcome."

But, as New York prepared to welcome the glamorous new Cunarder and as the directors of the Cunard-White Star Line smiled in satisfaction that at last their new ship was in service and, before too long to be joined by her half-sister, all was not as it should be. Rhona Churchill filed another report back to the offices of the *Daily Mail*.

"We will be steaming into New York Harbour as you sit down to lunch tomorrow. They say that New Yorkers will be lining the Hudson's banks to welcome us, as we shall be lining the *Queen Elizabeth*'s decks to see their famous skyline.

"We have drunk 1,700 bottles of champagne, 2,500 bottles of French and German wine and 3,000 bottles of spirits. We have had eggs every day for breakfast and again at night as snacks in the ship's night club. We have consumed more meat per head in five days than a British housewife sees in five weeks.

"And yet, somehow, amid all this luxury, there has been an indefinable something wrong. The ship has never come to life. She has not found her soul. You hear the passengers discussing it as you walk the decks. You hear them say: 'What's wrong with this ship?' And if you ask the seasoned Atlantic crosser what he thinks of the new Queen, it is ten to one he'll tell you: 'Well, she's not the old *Berengaria*' or 'They loved the old *Mauretania*'.

"I went 'below stairs' last night in search of the answer, and drank beer with the crew in their 'Pig & Whistle'. The crew's pub is slap alongside the engines. The heat and the din are appalling. As the men drank iced lager from their pint mugs, so the sweat poured out of them. 'Comes out faster than what goes in', said a seaman. They were mostly

standing jammed together, wearing only their vests and trousers because of the stifling heat. There seems to be only one seat for 30 men – and hard backless benches at that. With them in all this heat and beer swilling were the ship's 13 pageboys, knocking back Pepsicola and looking as though they should be in the ship's nursery.

"The men were calling it 'The Glory Hole'.

"A dining room steward told me: "We work 14 hours solid a day, with short breaks for late meals, then knock off exhausted at night to come down to this". 'This' was an iron bunk in a tiny, six-bunk cabin on the ship's lowest deck, and immediately over the screws. They had one wash basin between them, and a locker each, and they told me that, apart from the din, they could not sleep at night for the heat. They have white cotton sheets on their bunks but no cloths on their meal tables. The able-seamen complain they have to scrub their dirty overalls clean in tiny hand-basins, 'which just isn't possible, Miss', and they have nowhere but their already steamy cabins to dry them. This grievance could be easily righted, but the biggest one is the long hours and unbelievably hard work involved in a ship like this new Queen.

"Many of the old Cunard stewards have been watching the new post-war recruits to Britain's merchant navy. They believe that the young men will not stand up to the strain, and will soon be leaving the sea for jobs ashore. The stewards are up at 6.30 cleaning the ship from end to end while we still sleep. Then they are running to-and-fro to our cabins with fruit juices and breakfast, valeting the men's clothes and polishing shoes. The dining room stewards, who also clean decks, carpets and cloak rooms, must wash and polish their own silver and glass.

"In their own words, they are 'on the go solid from 6.30 am to 10 at night, with only a two-hour break every other day'. I have talked to scores of the crew, and no one has a friendly word about this new Queen.

"Perhaps that is what is wrong with her.

"Perhaps a ship cannot find her soul until her crew first fall in love with her."

It was Trafalgar Day, Monday the 21st October, and the *Queen Elizabeth* was steaming slowly in order not to arrive in New York harbour too soon. It was still dark when she met the first stage of her welcome at Quarantine: here a reception committee of city officials boarded from a tender, along with 150 newspaper reporters. A coastguard cutter escorted the liner as she entered through the narrows, while aircraft and a helicopter circled above. She received a tumultuous welcome as she arrived in the harbour in the brilliant sunshine of an Indian summer, docking at Pier 90 at 7.39 am – an hour and a half early. The crowds had been waiting since dawn because of rumours that she would arrive early. The sirens and whistles of ships sounded in greeting; planes circled and dipped in salute and fire boats sprayed curtains of water. Hundreds of motorists stopped their cars and kept their fingers on the hooter buttons. People rushed from waterfront cafes with cups of coffee and spilled them

as they tried to climb onto railings and stone buttresses and pushed aside the hastily erected barriers, all trying to get a better view. The threat of action by the tug boat men was over as eight tugs took charge of her, guiding her alongside the pier. Four others stood close by in case they were needed. Even several hours later, and well after her passengers had disembarked, reserve police were still holding back the crowds that had gone to see the ship. Meanwhile, on board the *Queen Elizabeth* things were being made ready for the entertainments and celebrations that were expected to last almost until sailing time on Thursday.

The New York Sun recorded the great liner's arrival as being 'like a breath of happier times', while Commodore Bisset was reported as saying 'she performed beautifully, just like a sewing machine'. The crossing, from Bishop's Rock to the Ambrose Light, had been completed in four days, 16 hours, 18 minutes at an average speed of 27.99 knots. For the first

▽ The tight-lipped Soviet foreign minister, Vyacheslav Molotov, arrives in New York flanked by a military entourage. Behind are members of the New York press who have come on board to interview him.

three days the ship had averaged more than 29 knots but because of the bad weather her speed had to be reduced.

Expressing the feelings of great contingents of United States military and civilian passengers who had crossed the Atlantic in the *Queen Elizabeth* during the war, Robert E. Sherwood, the American playwright who helped the late President Roosevelt draft many of his speeches, sent the following message to *The Daily Telegraph*: "As one of the hundreds of thousands of Americans who travelled swiftly and safely on the Queens in war-time, I salute the arrival of the *Queen Elizabeth* on her first peace-time mission. I hope that she and her sister ship will have a long service carrying goodwill in both directions across the ocean and that these two proud and beautiful veterans will never again be forced to wear battle dress."

Many advertisers in the New York newspapers devoted their space, in some cases half a page or more, to bidding the *Queen Elizabeth* welcome. Expressing admiration for this 'graceful ocean queen' the *New York Sun* suggested that her 'deep-throated whistle may have reminded some of the more thoughtful that our own merchant ships have become pawns of labour strife, the results of which none can foresee'.

The criticism by some of the crew aboard the *Queen Elizabeth* regarding their accommodation had reached the ears of the new company chairman. He responded by saying that Cunard had always taken a pride in its men, both ashore and afloat, and that all that was wanted was a happy company of men who are as glad to be with the company as he was to serve them. An official statement was issued by the company: "The accommodation provided for the crew was carefully studied before and during the ship's reconversion and has been admitted to be of an unusually high standard."

Hoping that issue was behind them, the Cunard-White Star Line let it be known that they aimed to have five new ships on the Atlantic run by the middle of the following year but that they were not planning for any more liners of the size of the *Queen Elizabeth* or *Queen Mary*. Frederick Bates, the Cunard chairman was reported as saying: "They are not required. The two giant liners we have are sufficient to maintain a weekly service in each direction. Nor is the company searching for a further speed record." The report went on to indicate that one of the five new ships would be of a class similar to the *Mauretania*, two would be passenger-cargo ships and two cargo-only ships. Apart from the express service from Southampton to New York, Cunard were maintaining their Liverpool – New York service and their weekly services from both London and Liverpool to Canada.

Having completed her first commercial voyage, the *Queen Elizabeth* lies in New York. Next to her is the US battleship *Missouri* on which the Japanese surrender had been signed at the end of the War.

R.M.S. QUEEN ELIZABETH

Chapter 7

NORTH ATLANTIC ZENITH

The *Queen Elizabeth* sailed from New York at 6 pm on the 24th October 1946 with 2,246 passengers on board: they were being described in the British press as her first cargo of dollar-spending American tourists and Big Business executives. One newspaper report stated that the women of Britain would be in for a tremendous shock when they saw the American women who were travelling on the ship. "They are here with furs, diamonds, orchids and nylons, breath-taking hats, shoes, handbags and dress accessories. Every American woman on board seems to be dressed like a film star, and that is true of all three classes." The people of Britain, however, appeared to have another concern: Food. This led Cunard once again to emphasise that, apart from a few unimportant unrationed items such as potatoes, all the food for the *Queen Elizabeth* trips was imported with Government authority, the bulk being from the United States. The Cunard statement continued: "There is no question of it coming off rations – and it will not in future. Passengers are being carried in competition with foreign ship companies or air services, where there is no restriction on food supplies. To subject them to austerity meals would result only in seriously handicapping British business without increasing British rations. Dollar earnings of Cunard-White Star Line ships are considerably important, so is the money spent here by visitors."

Queen Elizabeth's return voyage generated almost as much press coverage as did the maiden voyage. In part this was because it was discovered that she had two stowaways on board, John Dick a 22 year old Canadian who wished to take up employment in Manchester and Kingsley Foster, 28, a lawyer who had been a captain in the United States Army Air Force. He was chafing at the delayed arrival in America of his wife and young child. There was a great deal of sympathy expressed by the passengers for the stowaways, who were allowed to move freely about the ship until 12 hours before she reached Southampton, when they were placed in detention to await the arrival of the police. The romantic story of the young GI separated from his wife for over a year was played out extensively in the newspapers. The fact that Charles Guttman, millionaire wine importer, who was also travelling aboard the ship, insisted on paying the young man's First Class fare – thereby preventing Cunard from prosecuting him - added more column inches. A British business man paid Dick's fare. Among the other passengers travelling in First Class were the film stars Ray Milland, Joan Bennett, Pat O'Brien and Dorothy Malone; Adolph Zukor, chairman of Paramount Pictures; Lord and Lady Vestey; Earl and Countess Poulett; and Sir William and Lady Stephenson. The dockside sheds at Southampton resembled a small scale Hollywood with cameras perched everywhere among the baggage, filming and photographing the screen stars as well as the other rich and famous passengers.

It had been an almost unnaturally calm crossing for the time of year and was made in 5 days, 3 hours at an average speed of 27.06 knots. The *Queen Elizabeth* slipped quietly into Southampton in the very early hours of the morning. The stewards had worked through the night to unload the estimated 500 tons of luggage before the passengers began disembarking at 8 am.

So while there were those who felt that the *Queen Elizabeth* was lacking in soul, she was nevertheless promoted in the press as 'a gold mine for Britain', with glamour as the keynote. There were 2,200 passengers booked on her next voyage back to New York. Among them, again, was Joan Bennett whose brief visit to England had been to attend the Royal Command film performance. However, the passengers who gleaned all the limelight on this particular crossing were the Duke and Duchess of Windsor. The Duke was invited up onto the bridge as the tugs manoeuvred into position to move the ship from her berth. He was quickly recognised by those on shore, including a gang of dockers, who gave him a cheer. The Duke smiled and waved in acknowledgement.

At the end of November 1946, Pan American World Airways announced that they would reduce by twenty percent the number of employees in their offices in London, New York and other centres because of the sea competition to transatlantic flying – offered largely by the *Queen Elizabeth*. It seemed as though other airlines might follow suit. Pan American officials said that the *Queen Elizabeth*, in one crossing, was carrying the equivalent of 56 flights by their planes which could accommodate 40 passengers at a time. A spokesman for the company said that they had reduced their number of transatlantic flights as a result. Although PanAm was facing competition from other airlines as well, it was admitted that the preference of the travelling public to cross on the *Queen Elizabeth* (soon to be joined by the *Queen Mary*) was the main factor.

◁   An impressive array of Alexandra Towing Co. steam tugs heaves the *Queen Elizabeth* away from her Southampton berth as she starts yet another transatlantic crossing.

POST CARD
This is a Real Photograph

THE WORLD'S LARGEST LINER
Gross Tonnage. ... .83,673
Length. ... 1,031 feet.
Breadth. ... 118 feet.

The Address only to be written here

Dear Joe,
I am having a smashing time on the Q.E. and I haven't been sea sick yet. the food is really marvellous and plenty of it. The ship is beautiful and there is plenty of entertainment going on. I will write soon and don't you forget to write.
Love. mom. xx

Miss J. Ford.

CUNARD WHITE STAR. R.M.S. "QUEEN ELIZABETH."

Meanwhile, those workers who had been brought south from the Clyde to help complete the transformation of the *Queen Elizabeth* from troop carrier to luxury liner had been transferred to the *Queen Mary*. She had arrived in Southampton on Friday the 27th September, her war service finally over. Some of the work planned would mean not just restoration to her peacetime finery but also modernisation which would bring her into line with the *Queen Elizabeth*. The work was expected to take six months to complete.

As 1946 slipped into 1947, the *Queen Elizabeth* settled into the routine of North Atlantic service but she was never far from the headlines, particularly during those first few years of her career. Commodore Bisset retired from Cunard in January and handed over command of the *Queen Elizabeth* to Captain Charles Ford. He had not been in command of the liner very long before she was to encounter one of the worst storms that she had so far had to face. For 11 hours she battled against winds of up to 65 m.p.h. which caused her to slow to barely 5 knots. On this particular voyage she was carrying the fabulously wealthy Maharajah Gaekwar of Baroda and his wife and child. The *Queen Elizabeth*'s arrival in New York was delayed 24 hours because of the storm and as a result she had to make a very quick turn-round of just 31½ hours in order to be ready to sail back to Southampton on schedule.

On the 25th February, 2,000 of her passengers found themselves involved in a strike by 230 stevedores at Southampton, who had been due to unload the luggage

from the ship. Instead, stewards staggered down the gangways, piling the baggage on the dock side. Eventually, the stevedores, who had objected to being transferred from piece-work, were persuaded to return pending negotiations. Meanwhile, the First Class passengers, including the Duchess of Leinster, hunted for their baggage amid the 'mountain' on the dockside. While the First and Cabin Class passengers eventually made it onto the London-bound trains – with the first boat train departing three hours late – Cunard offered the Tourist Class passengers their cabins back for the night, along with dinner and breakfast, at no extra charge.

On Friday the 7th March, as the *Queen Elizabeth* was being made ready to sail from New York with 2,288 passengers on board – including Noel Coward, Burgess Meredith and Paulette Goddard – fire broke out on the liner *John Ericsson*, which was moored at the adjacent berth. Like the Cunarder, the *John Ericsson* was just about ready to sail for Europe, with 400 passengers. While the *Queen Elizabeth* was in no danger, she was engulfed in the smoke as the fire swept through the main and promenade decks of the other liner. Hundreds of visitors to the *Queen Elizabeth* were urged to cut short their farewells and hurry ashore. Dr. Lawson, the surgeon on the *Queen Elizabeth*, treated members of the crew of the burning ship who were brought on board unconscious. The fire was brought under control within three hours and the *Queen Elizabeth* sailed for Southampton only one hour behind her scheduled time.

The following month, her schedule was to become totally disrupted. On the 14th April she made her way slowly towards Southampton, through thick fog off the Isle of Wight. With a pilot aboard who was inexperienced in handling either of the 'Queens', she ran aground on the Brambles Bank, just off Calshot. That was at 7.30 pm and there was just an hour available to refloat her, catch the high tide and enable her 2,446 passengers to disembark. Urgent calls were sent for tugs and seven were soon swaying around her. For two hours they pushed and pulled. As darkness came the *Queen Elizabeth* glowed with lights, her passengers silhouetted along her promenade watching the straining tugs. All efforts were in vain, however, and the liner refused to move. At 9.30 pm attempts to refloat her were abandoned until the following morning. She had run aground at a somewhat notorious spot: the *Majestic* had grounded there in 1934 and the *Aquitania* had done so the following year.

Next morning there were twelve tugs attached to the stranded 'Queen'. Water ballast had been pumped off in order to lighten her bow and 12,000 tons of oil was loaded into two barges. Her First Class passengers, including Lady Peel – better known as the actress Beatrice Lillie – were disembarked into tenders and their luggage was loaded into lighters that afternoon, all of this making the ship 15,000 tons lighter. The Cabin and Tourist Class passengers had to remain on board and when this was queried with Cunard the response was: "We always disembark First Class passengers first." That evening there were fifteen tugs attached to the liner. The plight of the *Queen Elizabeth* attracted crowds of sightseers, circling aircraft with press photographers and of course many column inches in the newspapers. By 7 pm there was but a thin hope of success: they knew that if she were not afloat that evening she would probably have to remain until the spring tide, which was not until Sunday, five days hence. To make matters worse another thick fog was rolling along the coast.

At 8 pm the *Queen Elizabeth* sounded three blasts on her siren. "I am going full speed astern." The tugs responded with their sirens, full speed ahead, and it seemed that the area for miles was blackened with smoke from this combined all-out effort. It failed. A few minutes later they tried again: the tugs at her stern pulling hard to port while those at her bows to starboard. After two minutes the stern of the *Queen Elizabeth* began to shift and from her decks her passengers sent up a cheer. Again the tugs pulled straight ahead while the liner struggled full speed astern. At 8.35 pm the cry went up 'She's moving!'. Slowly, she slid astern and then as she gathered some speed she sounded two blasts, the 'All clear',

▽ Fortunately, not for real. A Sunderland flying-boat of RAF Coastal Command uses the *Queen Elizabeth* as a target for mock bombing practice in June, 1948.

⚠ The Canterbury Pilgrims marquetry panel has pride of place in the First Class Lounge which was also notable for its veneered walls and indirect lighting.

on her sirens and disappeared from view into the fog. She did not berth that evening: instead she anchored in Cowes Roads and those passengers who had not been taken off remained for another night on board. While Beatrice Lillie had rejoiced at the delay, saying "Oh how wonderful it is to be back in England. I certainly didn't object to the delay. It was well worthwhile just for the sake of another of those simply lovely meals we got on board", her delight was not shared by everyone. Among her fellow passengers were some attending a conference on wool disposal, one of whom said that the delay had cost him a whole day out of the three days allotted for his visit. He was sailing back to the United States on board the liner *America* on the Friday morning.

A much pleasanter event happened off Cowes just three months later. The outward-bound *Queen Elizabeth* passed the newly refurbished *Queen Mary* on the evening of the 25th July. The *Queen Mary*, in-bound from a two-day trials trip in the English Channel, dropped anchor about a mile and a half off Cowes at 5 pm to await the sailing of the *Queen Elizabeth*, which steamed out of Southampton Water and into The Solent shortly before 7.30 pm. As the *Queen Elizabeth* passed

within half-a-mile of her running-mate, the two liners sounded first three short and then three longer blasts on their sirens. Then the *Queen Mary* turned towards Southampton to take the berth vacated by the *Queen Elizabeth*.

The Cunard Line was poised to fully establish its pre-eminent position on the North Atlantic: the somewhat smaller but equally grand fleetmate to the 'Queens', the 35,677 ton *Mauretania*, also recently refurbished after war service, had been re-introduced onto the Southampton to New York service in June. At the time it was expected that the 45,000 ton *Aquitania*, now a veteran of two world wars, would be given a new lease of life as a luxury liner. At that time, though, she was still wanted for service between Southampton and Halifax, operating under government control. Her crew were very loyal to her, referring to the 32-year-old liner as The Old Lady of the Atlantic, and assuring everyone that there was 'plenty of life in the old girl yet'.

Gradually, more liners were released from war service and the duties of repatriation of servicemen, war brides and refugees. Once overhauled, they were returned to commercial service. The United States Lines' *America*, like

△ Confident elegance. The spacious First Class foyer was a pleasant place for shopping and for meeting one's fellow passengers.

the *Queen Elizabeth*, had been due to enter service on the North Atlantic in 1940. Instead, her debut on the New York – Southampton route was delayed until November 1946. Holland America Line's *Veendam* was followed into Atlantic service by the line's flagship, *Nieuw Amsterdam*, in the late summer of 1947: her war-time career had been every bit as glorious as that of the two 'Queens'. The Polish liner *Batory* also returned to the North Atlantic run in 1947. Likewise, liner services were being re-established on other routes. The Union-Castle Line had restarted its mail service to South Africa in January with the return of its flagship, *Capetown Castle*. Even though she was soon followed into service by the *Warwick Castle* and the *Athlone Castle*, the company could hardly get its liners refurbished quickly enough, so rapidly did the list of people waiting for passage to South Africa grow. Although the liners of the P&O Lines and Royal Mail Lines were still on government service, the port of Southampton was beginning to resume its former peace-time bustle.

Originally, Her Majesty the Queen had requested that there should not be a portrait of her hung aboard the *Queen Elizabeth*. However, it seems as though her brother, the Hon.

David Bowes-Lyon, who was appointed to the board of Cunard-White Star after the war, persuaded her to change her mind. Thus, Sir Oswald Birley was commissioned to paint a portrait. It was, sadly, a rather pedestrian work: Her Majesty was shown in a sumptuous and elaborate crinoline gown and wearing the Order of the Garter. On the 28th July 1948, His Majesty the King, accompanied by the Queen and Princess Margaret, travelled to Southampton to unveil the portrait. It had been given pride of place in the First Class Lounge. This however, had required the removal of the very beautiful and much-acclaimed marquetry panel, The Canterbury Tales. This was re-positioned at the head of the Main Hall staircase. Also on that day, Her Majesty presented to the ship her personal standard, which was framed and hung in the Main Restaurant.

1948 had seen a record number of American tourists sailing across the Atlantic to Europe, even though it was still scarred from the years of war, and 1949 looked as if it would be an even more successful year. All, however, was not well on the other side of the Atlantic at this time. The New York City authorities, who owned most of the piers, announced their intention to increase their rental. As this would mean Cunard Line paying the US dollar equivalent of over £190,000 in 1948, and even more in 1949, the company began to consider looking for an alternative port. As both the *Queen Elizabeth* and *Queen Mary* had used Halifax, Nova Scotia during the war, very real consideration was given to this port instead of New York. A Cunard official said that the rental increase, virtually to double what the line were already paying, would greatly reduce the company's dollar earnings. Those earnings were already low during the winter months because fewer Americans travelled to Europe at that time. Although the ships were still sailing full, it was largely with returning Europeans who had paid their fares in Sterling. The leases of practically all the city-owned piers had expired during the war and the authorities refused to renew them. Cunard were anxious to get together with other shipping lines and plead with the city for reasonable rates but they did not expect to be listened to. The Dutch had already bought a terminal of their own at Hoboken, New Jersey and Cunard looked to the possibility of Nova Scotia. It was an accepted fact that influential and travel-wise passengers would be far from happy at this prospect and the resultant train journeys which would be involved. It was hoped that they might put pressure on their Congressional representatives to ensure some agreement with the city of New York.

Despite the worries over the rental of their New York piers, the future looked bright for the Cunard 'Queens' and all other transatlantic liners the late 1940s. There was a report that indicated that the United States Department of Commerce were looking at plans by Vladimir Yourkevitch – designer of the pre-war *Normandie* - for a 100,000 ton liner capable of a speed of 50 knots. The indications were that it was believed such a vessel would be commercially viable, particularly as shipping experts of the day were agreed that the two 'Queens' could earn over twice as much as three medium-sized ships. Before the war a return trip on the *Queen Mary* cost £126 10s. in First Class, £66 5s. in Tourist and £42 Third Class. The idea behind the Yourkevitch-designed giant liner was to have a one class fare of approximately £30 inclusive or £20 if meals were bought separately in the restaurant. It was envisaged that with a pay-load of 4,000 passengers her profits would be virtually double of those of either the *Queen Mary* or the *Queen Elizabeth*.

While the 'Queens' generally operated a flawless service back and forth across the Atlantic, there were those occasions when the sailing schedules were in total disarray. Such an occasion struck in November 1948. The *Queen Elizabeth* was held back from her scheduled departure from Southampton on the 17th because of a longshoremen's strike in the United States. All her passengers were contacted by telegram advising them of the delay. It was anticipated that, regardless of the strike, she would sail on Saturday the 20th, after a 76 hour delay, and that if it was still in force she would divert to Halifax, N.S. The dockers there, who had boycotted diverted ships in sympathy with the New York men, had resumed normal working. The *Aquitania* had

▽ It seems dramatic but the *Queen Elizabeth* is merely cleaning soot from her exhausts as she moves slowly forward while weighing her bow anchor.

After 1950, when they were in Southampton, the Cunarders generally berthed at the splendid new Art Deco Ocean Terminal – since, alas, demolished.

arrived in Halifax on the 17th after taking more than nine days for her crossing. She had delayed her arrival because the docks were overcrowded with ships. The New York dispute appeared to have been engineered by Communist members of the International Longshoremen's Association after the president of the organisation, Joseph Ryan, had tried to rid it of the extreme Left Wing members. The Communists aimed the strike partly at Mr. Ryan and partly at shipments to Europe under the aid programme. Not only was it affecting tons of aid shipments to Europe but it was expected that many thousands of Christmas mail packages would not be delivered on time. Cunard had, though, been able to arrange passage for a lucky few passengers aboard the Canadian Pacific liner *Empress of Canada* sailing from Liverpool.

With no let-up in the strike, Cunard announced that the *Queen Elizabeth* would sail for Halifax: the announcement was met by a threat from the New York longshoremen to 'bar' Cunard liners from the port once the strike was over unless the diversion of the ships ceased. Even Mr. Ryan, whom some of the strike action was aimed at, expressed his 'surprise' at the 'temerity' of Cunard in scheduling the *Queen Elizabeth* for Halifax. He also dropped the bombshell that the Halifax dockers were once again planning to reinstate their earlier boycott.

It was perhaps inevitable that some members of the *Queen Elizabeth*'s crew should also take strike action in sympathy with the US longshoremen. They demanded assurances that the liner would not sail for New York until the longshoremen's strike was settled. Other crew members, although still on board, had their bags packed and were ready to leave if no promise was forthcoming from Cunard that the 'Queens' would not be used as strike-breakers. At the time, the *Queen Mary* was in dry dock and it had been expected that once her overhaul work was finished she would take the berth vacated by the *Queen Elizabeth*. Now, she was stuck in the dry dock and 1,600 passengers were stuck aboard the *Queen Elizabeth* as yet another sailing was cancelled.

A notice was posted outside the Purser's Office. "The *Queen Elizabeth* cannot proceed to New York until it is reasonably certain that she can be properly received and handled there. Assurance on this point is not expected before tomorrow evening and the ship therefore cannot sail before Tuesday afternoon at the earliest. It is hoped that tomorrow's advices may be such as to enable the company to decide that a Tuesday sailing is possible. The company sincerely regret any inconvenience caused to passengers both on board the *Queen Elizabeth* and those waiting embarkation at Cherbourg."

Special trains returned more than 600 passengers from Cherbourg to Paris. The weary passengers, some of whom had waited four days, prepared for another night's emergency lodgings in hotel lounges, restaurants and municipal buildings. Meanwhile, for those passengers aboard the *Queen*

Elizabeth there was some semblance of normal onboard life – albeit with the ship very securely alongside her berth. There was Horse Racing in the Main Lounge and dancing in the ballroom but only to recorded music: while the musicians were on board they were unable to play because a Musician's Union ruling forbad them from performing while the ship was in port. All passengers leaving the ship were warned that, because of currency regulations, they were liable to Customs search when they returned. Church services were, however, held as normal. Passengers even lounged in deck chairs, wrapped in steamer rugs, reading their books and newspapers as though in mid-Atlantic. The cinema was open and every showing was packed for Somerset Maugham's new film *Quartet*. With many crew members on strike, everyone else had to lend a hand where possible. Stewardesses, bath attendants, beauty specialists all took it in turn to wait at tables and in Tourist Class women passengers helped clear the tables. By the 22nd, some passengers had had enough, among them Mrs. Douglas Fairbanks, Jnr., and decided to return to America by aeroplane. American Airlines even put on a special 'plane for the party.

This strike and the subsequent delay and disruption to the sailings of the Cunard liners had far greater implications than just the inconveniencing of several thousand travelers. It came at a time when Britain and Europe were still struggling from the effects of the war. The editorial in the *Daily Graphic* on the 22nd November was headed "Act now – the ships must sail." It read: "Cunard-White Star say *Queen Elizabeth* cannot sail before Tuesday. Sailing of *Queen Mary* due on Wednesday deferred." The text of the editorial read: "This is a blow struck at the very vitals of the whole European Recovery Programme. The present livelihood and the future prospects not merely of Britain but of the whole Western civilisation depend upon the swift passage of goods across the Atlantic. Indeed, time is the essence of the contract. Yet, in face of this most urgent need, men of the merchant marine in this country abet those who, for quite different reasons, are recklessly interrupting the flow of goods. The folly of their action and its danger to the well-being of themselves and their families, no less than to all the rest of us, must be swiftly brought home to them. If ever there was the most compelling reason for immediate intervention by the Government, it is here. The interruption of the sailing of these great ships across the Atlantic is a challenge – a challenge of symbolic significance – to every effort this country has made and is making to secure recovery at home and abroad."

The situation became even more ridiculous when on Wednesday the 24th 800 Cabin and Tourist Class passengers decided to stage a 'stay-aboard strike' in the face of Cunard's announcement that passengers would be disembarked on either Friday or Saturday. This decision was made following a new deadlock in New York regarding the strikers' demands. The decision came as a blow to many emigrant families who were without homes and with very little money,

certainly not enough to spend on hotel accommodation for an indeterminate length of time. Even so, they turned down an offer to be flown to New York, being determined to sail on the liner – although it meant missing plane connections to take them on to San Francisco and then to New Zealand and Australia.

Suddenly, on the following day, the news came – the dispute in the United States had been settled! The unloading of luggage from the *Queen Elizabeth* was halted. News that the strike was over had been picked up from an American broadcast. Most of the 1,500 passengers aboard were at breakfast but smiling waiters whispered it as they served. Excited passengers left their breakfasts and crowded around the notice-boards in the purser's square. There chalked up was: "The strike in New York is settled and it is expected that the ship will sail approximately at 8 am on Sunday."

The shouts of those who read the announcement brought others hurrying to the board. Passengers were given shore leave until 10 pm on Saturday and special boat trains were organised to bring other passengers from London during that afternoon and evening. A Cunard official announced: "We are all ready but Sunday morning has been fixed because it is the next high tide in daylight. We don't take out the big liners from Southampton at night because of the turn just outside Ocean Dock." (After leaving the Ocean Dock stern first, the *Queen Elizabeth* needed 2,000 feet from the dockhead while swinging round before proceeding down Southampton Water.) "She will sail with 2,200 passengers, her full complement. The vacancies through those who cancelled passages will be taken up from the *Queen Mary*'s passenger list. The *Queen Elizabeth* will definitely call at Cherbourg for the 600 passengers who should have come aboard there. Vacancies through cancellations will be filled up."

The Sunday sailing meant that the *Queen Elizabeth* would be departing eleven days late and the cost to Cunard was about £40,000. No new sailing date was fixed at that time for the *Queen Mary*. No sooner had preparations begun for the delayed departure than news came of fresh threats of renewed strike action, with two thousand New York dockers rejecting a new pay agreement. The dispute was eventually resolved but a thick fog enveloped Southampton at around midnight on Saturday. The *Queen Elizabeth* had been scheduled to depart at 8.15 am and there was even time up until 10 am for her to sail before the tide became unsuitable. The fog lifted just too late. The decision not to sail was telephoned to Paris in time to prevent the two special trains taking the passengers to Cherbourg. Those passengers aboard the *Queen Elizabeth* took the news philosophically. The Polish liner, *Batory*, however, was able to sail for New York only an hour behind schedule. Fortunately for her passengers, she had been in what was referred to as the New Docks, on the River Test and therefore had a straight run down Southampton Water. Tuesday 30th November saw

↑ In this dramatic picture of the ship at speed, one can appreciate her large expanses of open deck space.
↓ Just another day on Luxury Liner Row, Manhattan. From top to bottom: *America, United States, Ile de France, Georgic* and *Queen Elizabeth.*

another planned departure cancelled with the thick fog making the difficult manoeuvre out of the Ocean Dock impossible. The *Aquitania*, with passengers for Halifax, was also unable to sail. A further lightning strike by Southampton stevedores added to the misery. They were unhappy because they were expected to work with three men who had not joined the earlier strike. This meant that 1,200 passengers who had arrived on boat trains to board the *Queen Mary* had to handle their own luggage and this was made all the more difficult when a power failure plunged the departure hall into darkness. Those passengers who had abandoned the idea of sailing to New York and instead decided to fly found that London Airport was also fogbound. Some of them even returned to the liner.

On Wednesday the 1st December, the fog lifted and the *Queen Elizabeth* was at last under way – 14 days late. Her passengers lined her decks and cheered as the wintery sun was breaking through. The *Queen Mary* followed her

an hour later but then anchored in Cowes Roads for the night as the port of Cherbourg could not handle both the 'Queens' together. One hundred and thirty passengers who had been waiting at Cherbourg boarded the *Queen Elizabeth* and after them came a mountain of parcels and 2,000 postal bags. Later, two special boat trains brought a further 600 passengers from Paris. To enable the 'Queens' to get back onto their scheduled sailings it was necessary for them to be serviced and embark passengers in New York all within 24 hours and as the liners headed out into the Atlantic there was anxiety as to whether this logistical feat could be accomplished. The *Queen Elizabeth* was due to arrive in New York on Monday the 6th December and would leave the following day, when New York hoped to welcome the *Queen Mary* - but not until the *Queen Elizabeth* was heading back to Europe. On the 2nd December, the United States Lines announced the cancellation of the Christmas cruise which was to have been made by the *America*. Instead, she

▽ The imposing funnels of the steamship *Queen Elizabeth* make an interesting contrast with those of the motorliner *Britannic*, which continues to wear the livery of her former White Star Line owners.

would make two voyages between New York, Le Havre and Southampton and thus help to ease the congestion caused by the recent strike action.

The *Queen Elizabeth* reached Quarantine at the entrance to New York harbour shortly after 7 pm on the Monday evening, several hours later than planned. It had been a stormy crossing and the bad weather was also delaying the *Queen Mary*, which did not arrive until late Wednesday afternoon. It was not until 3 am that the *Queen Elizabeth* was eventually alongside her New York berth. "Hello there! Can you hear us, crew of *Queen Elizabeth*?", a voice boomed out by loudspeaker as the liner neared her berth. The loudspeaker was mounted on a jeep sent to the pier by the International Longshoremen's Association. The voice continued: "The men of the Longshoremen's Association extend heartfelt thanks for your demonstration of support and solidarity in our recent strike. Your action gained the admiration of union members throughout the world." Pickets from the Longshoremen's Association and the Seafarers Union paraded outside the pier with placards reading: "Boys of the Queen, if ever you need a hand, just tell us"; "Thanks a million, we doff our hats to you"; "Grateful thanks, Liz's crew" and "Three rousing cheers, hip hurrah for the British tar." The demonstration put on for the crew far outdid the welcome given by 3,000 people waiting to greet the passengers.

Many American passengers were highly disgruntled by the repeated delays, first by the strike and then by the fog and finally by the additional 12 hours because of the rough weather. However, British passengers, among whom were Lady Stanley, Sir Alexander Maxwell and the former Land Speed Record-holder Captain G.E.T. Eyston, did not join in with the complaints but many others confirmed that for some American passengers the voyage had been 'one long grumble fest'. British passengers agreed the delay had been irksome but added phlegmatically: "After all, what did it matter – the food was marvellous, and it never gave out. It wasn't necessary to ration anybody, or even to cut the size of the meals. We haven't eaten so well for years. Some people don't know when they are well off." Over 350 men were ready to work in shifts to refuel and victual the liner during her stay in port. She was due to leave at midnight on the Wednesday.

While the late 1940s and early 1950s did see more than their fair share of labour unrest, the events of November 1948, coupled with the bad weather, were not exactly common occurrences. The *Queen Elizabeth*, *Queen Mary* and *Mauretania* generally maintained a well regulated service across the Atlantic and gradually they were being joined by ships of other lines and from other countries. In July 1949, the much rebuilt French liner *Ile de France* made her first Le Havre to New York voyage after an absence of ten years. At 43,500 tons she was the fourth largest passenger liner in the world. At the same time the former Norddeutscher Lloyd liner *Europa* was undergoing extensive rebuilding that would transform her into the elegant *Liberté*, the French Line's replacement for the burned out *Normandie*.

At the time of the *Queen Elizabeth*'s first commercial sailing to New York the announcement from Cunard's new chairman was that the line had no plans for any further liners to match the 'Queens'. However, in late December 1949 tantalising newspaper reports appeared that gave the impression that Cunard were poised to order a new and superior 'Queen'. The *Daily Graphic* reported with

▽ A rare occasion. The outbound *Queen Elizabeth* encounters the incoming *Queen Mary*. Normally, they would have passed some distance apart in mid-ocean.

One of the many famous people who crossed on the *Queen Elizabeth* was the popular British singer and comedienne Gracie Fields.

considerable confidence: "Britain is to build a new Queen liner which will be the future mistress of the North Atlantic. She will cost at least £15,000,000." The report implied that Cunard were unwilling to rest on their laurels. With trade booming and several other countries announcing construction plans for new liners, and with Cunard's desire to remain pre-eminent on the North Atlantic, a ship would be needed that was more up-to-date than the *Queen Mary*, a more suitable running mate for the *Queen Elizabeth*.

The report continued: "With a tonnage expected to be near 90,000, she will be larger and faster than the *Queen Mary* and the *Queen Elizabeth*. Cunard-White Star are almost certain to place the order with the famous Clyde firm of John Brown and Co. Some 20,000 workers will have a share in the huge contract. Three other maritime nations are preparing challengers for the North Atlantic passenger traffic. An American 60,000 ton liner will be in service in 1952. France has in view another *Normandie* (83,000 tons) and the Dutch a liner at least as big as the *Nieuw Amsterdam* (36,667 tons).

"Britain cannot afford to lag in the historic race for the Atlantic Blue Riband and the new Cunarder will be her answer. She will take at least three years to build and will not be in service much before 1954. Since the *Queen Mary* was launched over 15 years ago there have been more revolutionary improvements in building, equipping, propelling and navigating ships than in all previous maritime history. Cunard-White Star tradition is to make each new vessel the last word in design. Demands for higher standards of accommodation for both passengers and crew, for more luxurious public rooms and for the thousand-and-one

amenities expected on board ship today have all grown. Constructional costs have passed their peak. Although they will never fall to their pre-war level, British yards can produce a super-ship more cheaply than any other nation."

Sadly, it was a report based upon no foundation at all. However, like the *Daily Graphic*'s report, various others had been of such a confident tone that Cunard felt impelled to deny them. Thus on the 29th December 1949 the following announcement appeared in *The Times*:

"No new Atlantic liner in view – Cunard Statement."

"Cunard-White Star officially stated yesterday that it was not contemplating placing any orders for new tonnage at present. The company described as 'misleading' reports, circulating yesterday, that it proposed to build a transatlantic liner larger and faster than the *Queen Elizabeth*. "In the ordinary state of affairs," it was stated, "the company, like other shipping companies, has continually under review the types of ships that may be required from time to time for its various trades, either to supplement or replace existing tonnage as and when circumstances warrant and conditions permit.

"Our shipping correspondent writes: The *Queen Mary* was completed in 1936 and the *Queen Elizabeth* in 1940. Both of these great ships should normally have many years of life before them. Nevertheless, it may be assumed that the Cunard management is looking ahead, considering future needs. It is certain that the company has much in mind current costs of construction."

Also in December 1949 it was reported that the 35-year-old liner *Aquitania* was to be withdrawn from service and broken up. It was estimated that she had sailed 3,000,000 miles and had carried approximately 1,000,200 passengers. During 1949 she had made 13 round voyages to Halifax carrying over 22,000 passengers. On the 19th February 1950 *Aquitania* sailed for the final time from Southampton, her departure delayed by four hours because of fog. Her destination was the Clyde, her birthplace, and it was there that she would be broken up.

In September 1951 the *Queen Elizabeth* made her 100th Atlantic crossing since entering commercial service in October 1946. Back at that time it was sometimes said that the most dangerous street in New York was the West Side Highway along the Hudson River when the *Queen Elizabeth* was berthed at Pier 90. Motorists would be so busy looking at the ship that they would forget the car in front or the pedestrian stepping off the sidewalk. While from the highway the liner would have seemed, to those passing motorists, quiet and serene she would in fact have been a hive of activity preparing her for the return voyage. While there were normally about 2,000 passengers carried on each voyage this would rise to around 2,300 during the 'tourist season'. Preparations would have to be made to receive them and the liner would also take on her main stores in New York. 1,700,000 gallons of fuel oil and almost the same amount of fresh water would be pumped aboard. Six miles of carpet was cleaned and 100,000 pieces of linen changed. The normal turn-round time was two and a half days.

Enough food had to be brought onto the ship in New York to serve 100,000 meals: 10,000 a day. Escalators took it up in a set order for storing in the refrigeration space: tinned foods first, then cereals, vegetables, meat, poultry, fish, eggs and milk. Among the items would be twenty tons of meat, 10,000 pounds of sugar, 1,000 lobsters and 10,000 pounds of ham and bacon. The kitchens were staffed by 126 cooks under four chefs and a head chef. In the Main Restaurant, where the chief steward and chef would hold their daily consultation, steak was still in the late 1940s and early 1950s the passengers' favourite, despite the choice of trout, salmon, lobster, lamb, ham and beef.

Strangely, the ship's butcher (there was also a ship's gardener on each of the 'Queens') was responsible for all the pets carried on board. The trans-Atlantic fare for a cat was £2.10s. On the *Queen Mary* a crate of 10,000 live turtles once broke open in heavy weather and the turtles crawled about the butcher's shop. It was rumoured that not all of them were ever found …!

There was usually a fine mixture of celebrities travelling in First Class. In those days of the early 1950s they would include the likes of Joe Louis, Christian Dior, Gracie Fields, Edith Sitwell and Mae West. And for those select passengers travelling in First Class there was no greater honour than to receive the printed card presenting the Commodore's compliments and requesting the pleasure of their company for cocktails in his quarters. Passengers – usually eight –

honoured with an invitation to sit at the captain's table in the Main Restaurant were selected from a short list. Normally, those VIPs were British and American (though on the maiden voyage the guests at Commodore Bisset's table were Molotov and Vishinsky, Spaak (the Belgian Prime Minister) and Jan Masaryk of Czechoslovakia.

The rich and famous did not, however, make up the majority of the passengers carried on the *Queen Elizabeth* - they were just the ones who made it into the newspapers, magazines and the news reels. Cabin and Tourist Class passengers outnumbered First Class by more than 600. In those classes travelled college professors, business men, students, migrants and a large proportion of tourists of average means. The Tourist Class fare for a single crossing was £41 for a berth in a four-berth cabin. The 'high spot' for a passenger travelling Tourist Class was the Winter Garden Lounge with its great seaward-facing sweep of windows. Here, there was a tea-time orchestra and there were evening dances, amid the flowers. There was, however, no regular dance band for Tourist Class but one of the ship's bands played there at stated times and dance music was relayed at other times by loudspeaker from First Class. In Tourist Class, dancing finished early whereas in First Class the fun and entertainment in the Veranda Grill, sustained with Champagne and bacon and eggs, went on until the small hours.

Transatlantic travel took on a whole new dimension on the 3rd July 1952 with the entry into service of the American super-liner *United States*. Dominated by two huge streamlined funnels she was the face of modernity: her interiors were

▽ The American liner *United States,* which entered service in 1952, wrested the Blue Riband from the *Queen Mary* and posed considerable competition to the Cunarders.

sleek and smart and more importantly, she was fast. When she docked at Southampton at 6.40 pm on the 8th July there were 4,000 people at the Ocean Terminal waiting to greet her for she had lowered the *Queen Mary's* fourteen-year-old record for the west–to–east, Ambrose Light to Bishop's Rock crossing by 10 hours and 2 minutes. Arriving back in New York on the 15th July, having made the east–to–west crossing in just 3 days 12 hours, 12 minutes at an average speed of 34.51 knots, the Blue Riband for the fastest Atlantic crossing was well and truly hers.

The Cunard Line had always assumed a rather curious attitude with regard to the Blue Riband. On the one hand, they refused to accept the Hales Trophy once the *Queen Mary* had established herself as the fastest Atlantic liner, stating that they were not looking to break records but purely to maintain a regular and reliable Atlantic service. On the other hand, they were not at all inhibited in promoting the *Queen Mary* and the *Queen Elizabeth* as being the fastest and largest liners on the Atlantic. Even so, it is not beyond the bounds of imagination to consider that Cunard would have been more than happy to regain the Blue Riband for reasons of both company and national prestige. The *United States* had proved herself to be a faster liner than the *Queen Mary* but the *Queen Elizabeth* had not been pushed to her limits. There were indications when planning her secret maiden voyage dash across the Atlantic that she might well be capable of speed in excess of 32 knots, and that was an assumption made of a then untested liner. After the war Cunard had stated that it would be foolish to have the *Queen Elizabeth* trying to better her near-sister's speed – but once the *Queen Mary's* record had been irrevocably broken, what then?

On one crossing, in August 1952, the *United States* sailed from Le Havre about thirty minutes after the *Queen Elizabeth* had left Cherbourg. At about 10 am that same morning, shortly after passing the Bishop's Rock light, the American flagship spotted the *Queen Elizabeth* up ahead, with 'a large bone in her teeth'. It was judged that she was making her normal cruising speed of 28 or 29 knots, about right for her first day out, but clearly she was not making her best possible speed. The *United States* was making 31 knots. The two ships were about a half-mile apart. Messages passed between the masters of the two liners. Commodore Cove on the *Queen Elizabeth* wished Commodore Manning on the *United States* "Pleasant Voyage". Manning replied "Thank you". Within four hours the *Queen Elizabeth* had disappeared to the stern of the *United States*. However, although the log of the *United States* showed that she covered 776 miles at an average of 31.04 knots on her first day out, and the *Queen Elizabeth* averaged 27.84 knots and covered 720 miles for the same period, the Cunarder still arrived in New York only nine hours behind the *United States*. Later, both Commodores made emphatic denials that they had been racing. But if they were not, then one is left to question why it was necessary for the Commodores to make the statement. It has been said

that many of the passengers and crew aboard both liners knew that the ships were racing. Perhaps it was after this that Cunard conceded defeat. After all, they still had the largest liner in the world.

In January 1953 the *Queen Elizabeth* entered the King George V dry dock at Southampton for her annual overhaul but additional work was planned as well. It was Coronation year and the North Atlantic route was expected to be particularly busy bringing Americans in their thousands to see the great days of pageantry in London. The *Queen Elizabeth* was overhauled in every department. This annual undertaking involved the employment of 2,000 men. The additional work involved increasing her oil storage capacity, so that more fuel could be bought on one side of the Atlantic than on the other, according to where it was cheaper. To provide the extra capacity, tanks which had been used to store boiler-feed water were converted to hold an additional 1,000 tons of fuel oil. Also, the air-conditioning plant, which had been limited to the First Class public rooms, was extended to Tourist Class cabins on one deck. Because of the Coronation it was expected that passengers would begin to cross the Atlantic earlier than usual: Cunard were already experiencing heavy bookings. The line stated confidently that competition from the express liner *United States* was not likely to be felt to any great degree. Unfortunately, the refitting work was marred by fires that broke out in some of the passenger cabins and it seemed very likely that these were the work of an arsonist, though this was never proved. It was only by good fortune that no serious damage was done.

Having sailed aboard the *Queen Elizabeth* on her second voyage to New York, in early November 1946, the Duke of Windsor, unaccompanied by the Duchess, made another crossing on the liner in April 1953. He was travelling light – with just 30 pieces of luggage. (On the voyage he had made with the Duchess aboard the *Queen Mary* the previous December, they had travelled with 101 – and two dogs.) The Duke and Duchess made several voyages aboard the 'Queens' before ultimately transferring their allegiance to the *United States*.

Her Majesty Queen Elizabeth, the Queen Mother held considerable affection for the *Queen Elizabeth* and had expressed a desire to sail on her. The opportunity came in October 1954 when she embarked on the liner at the beginning of an official tour of the United States and Canada. With regrettable timing, a strike was again affecting the Southampton docks but in anticipation of what might have been a highly embarrassing situation, with the Queen Mother on board and the liner dependent upon tugs to get away from the dock, the *Queen Elizabeth* had been berthed with her bows pointing outwards. This would enable an easier departure should the strikers attempt to disrupt the sailing. Perhaps it was that special magic that the Queen Mother seemed to exude but there was no problem with the tug men and the liner sailed on time. The Queen Mother

△ The *Queen Elizabeth* arrives in an icy New York after a winter crossing.   Already her hold has been opened and her cargo gear is poised to begin discharging.

occupied a three-roomed suite on Main Deck and although it was a very rough crossing she toured various parts of the ship, attended Divine Service on the Sunday and dined in the Main Restaurant and in the Veranda Grill. It is doubtful that the liner ever again carried such an illustrious passenger. Even the passengers in First Class must have found it an unusual experience, dining with royalty every night. There was great excitement when in mid-Atlantic the *Queen Elizabeth* passed the Southampton-bound *Queen Mary*. Passengers lined the decks of both ships but of course for those on board the *Queen Mary* there was the added excitement of knowing that the Queen Mother was aboard the *Queen Elizabeth*, although for them the only evidence of this was her personal standard flying from the masthead. The Queen Mother sent a message to the *Queen Mary*: "I send you my greetings and good wishes to all on board. I hope that you get better weather soon. Elizabeth R." The bad weather followed the

Queen Elizabeth all the way across the Atlantic and right into New York harbour, where she arrived on the 26th October. It was so bad, in fact, that disembarkation was delayed for twelve hours.

During her annual overhaul in January 1955 the *Queen Elizabeth* was fitted with Denny-Brown stabilisers. She was the largest ship to be fitted with these devices. Once the work installing the stabilisers was completed, along with the other usual refurbishments, she sailed from Southampton on the 27th March for a series of trials so that her crew could become familiar with how the ship responded to these additions. She was back in port on the 30th to be made ready for her first Atlantic crossing of the season.

At the very height of the summer season of 1955 the *United States*, perhaps the most significant competitor to the 'Queens,' carried more passengers than on any of her previous voyages. For all liners serving the United States and

Canada this proved to be a significant year, with 942,245 passengers making transatlantic crossings one way or the other. This represented an 18 percent increase eastbound and a 21 percent increase westbound. Involved were 1,239 crossings by 55 companies or services according to the Trans-Atlantic Passenger Conference. In July and August of that year the *United States* carried more passengers than the *Queen Mary* and slightly less than the *Queen Elizabeth*. (The *United States* carried 15,400 passengers, the *Queen Mary* 13,861 and the *Queen Elizabeth* 15,848.) The slightly greater operating speed of the American ship enabled her to gain three days on each of the 'Queens' during that 60-day period, thereby permitting her to fit in one extra crossing. While the two 'Queens' averaged considerably more passengers than did the *United States*, they made one fewer trip. Neither of the French Line vessels, *Ile de France* nor *Liberté*, approached the 'Queens' in regard to the size of their passenger lists – even though they were far more like the *Queen Elizabeth* and *Queen Mary* in style but with that added continental chic that even the mighty 'Queens' were unable to emulate. The *United States*, along with her similar but smaller fleet mate, *America*, the French *Ile de France* and *Liberté* and the two Cunard 'Queens' were at the time regarded as the 'Big Six', the most significant liners then employed on the North Atlantic run.

A record was set for the port of New York on the 25th September 1956, with five liners, the *Cristoforo Colombo*, *America*, *United States*, *Queen Elizabeth* and *Mauretania* bringing in more than 7,000 passengers.

In May 1957 Colonel Denis H. Bates, chairman of the Cunard Steam Ship Co. Ltd., made his statement to the company's 80th annual stockholders' meeting. He began by saying: "A year ago I warned that the costs of running ships are still rising and that it will be very difficult to increase revenue to cover additional expenditure. We were then faced with heavy increases, especially in bunkers and wages, and it appeared questionable if the balance surplus could be maintained. However, the 1956 surplus is actually £433,002 above 1955 despite the difficulties." He continued: "We have carried more passengers across the Atlantic, cruise business has been good, earnings of the cargo ships have increased. During operational difficulties our sole considerations have been the safety of our ships and the comfort of our passengers: to terminate voyages at intermediate ports is not the service Cunard aim at and I am grateful to the many passengers who have written not only to forgive us, but to add their thanks for our success in meeting those interjections." Further on in his statement he referred to competition from Atlantic air travel. "From time to time I have been asked what effect the air has had on our passenger business. In my view, sea and air passenger traffic have been complementary rather than competitive; so far Atlantic travel has largely promoted its own traffic and total numbers by sea and air have continued to increase. If economic law were allowed to prevail, that process would be maintained, but the airlines appear to be able to ignore such normal factors of transportation as cost and profit margins.

"Air fares are arranged through the International Air Transport Association. Its decisions require Government approval, but profit and loss do not seem to have been given much consideration, either by airlines or the Government. It is not surprising to read in the Press that the two State air corporations of Britain have had so far the benefit of capital expenditure of £126 million of public money, while their losses to date amount to nearly £40 million. We ourselves can fairly ask why people who want the speed of air travel should not pay the economic price for it and why they should expect to be subsidised by their fellow taxpayers. Further, is it wise policy for Britain to authorise its State air corporations to quote uneconomical fares in competition with British ships when in two world wars and more recently over Suez it has been proved how dependent this island is on its Merchant Service?"

Despite his unhappiness over the State-owned air corporations, the chairman advised the shareholders: "Last year a record number of passengers crossed the Atlantic by sea and we are convinced that for the foreseeable future the demand for Cunard travel will be well sustained." Nevertheless he bemoaned the fact while in pre-war years the cost of a passenger liner for the Canadian service would be in the region of £1 million, in 1957 it would be in excess of £5 million. "We are convinced that shipping will remain essential to Britain and the constitution of the group's fleets is continuously under review, but the steady drain of our available resources under the guise of taxation of so-called profits has forced us to delay unduly the provision of new tonnage and to retain passenger vessels built in the 1920s." However, he was able to remind the shareholders that during the summer the liner *Sylvania* would join her sister ships *Saxonia*, *Ivernia* and *Carinthia*, thus completing the company's present Canadian building programme. Colonel Bates was reluctant to attempt any forecasts "in a world frequently disturbed by industrial strife and incidents of international near-war." He also expressed concern for the company's cargo services which were having to be re-routed via the Cape rather than go through the Suez Canal. Dock and tug strikes in America and engineering strikes in Britain were another woe and while he never specifically mentioned the 'Queens' in his statement it was evident that they had been subjected to the industrial unrest in America. He nevertheless ended his statement on an optimistic note: "Against the background of difficulties ahead, a cheering feature is that the skill of our managements and the loyalty of our staffs surmounted these obstacles in 1956 and all are determined to repeat the effort in 1957, especially if we are allowed a clear run."

The 1950s were truly the 'golden era' for the Cunard Line: the *Queen Elizabeth* and the *Queen Mary* sailed to capacity on virtually all of their voyages, earning enormous profits for the company. It was not, however, just the 'Queens' that were successful: by 1958 the company had twelve passenger liners in service between Britain and the United States and Canada (if one includes the cruising liner *Caronia*). This was the very pinnacle of ocean liner transportation across the North Atlantic. In July the Trans-Atlantic Passenger Conference announced in New York that nearly 10 percent more people had gone by ship from New York to Europe during the first half of that year than in the same period in 1957. This accounted for 230,000 passengers – a new record for a six month period. The total number of passengers sailing across the Atlantic for the whole of 1958 was 1,036,000: an unprecedented figure. However, on the 4th October that same year also saw the introduction of the first commercial jet airliner across the Atlantic, from New York to Paris. The effect was almost instantaneous, for business travellers particularly. Several hours – even if they were not particularly comfortable – in an aircraft were preferable to the better part of two weeks travelling back and forth across the Atlantic in a liner. Time was money and the world had made its first tentative steps into the 'jet age'.

A 1958 advertisement for Boeing, promoting their 707 and 720 aircraft read: "Only seven hours to brush up on your French. The superb Boeing 707 jet airliner goes into service first across the Atlantic and within weeks across the United States. You'll be delighted with the feeling of solid security you get from flight aboard this swift new sky-liner. It begins the moment of take-off, as abundant, jet-smooth power lifts the 707 effortlessly to cruising altitude. You'll fly serenely through high, weatherless skies. In just 60 minutes, you're almost 600 miles out of New York. In scarcely six hours you'll be trotting out your best French for the douanier at Paris. The spacious cabin is peaceful and quiet and completely free from vibration. There is only luxurious comfort and a sense of exhilaration from the almost magical ease and smoothness of 707 flight."

Seductive words indeed and for many it was advertising copy that was far more tempting than Cunard's "Getting there is half the fun." It was, however, not just Cunard who felt the effect of the tiny silvery speck streaking across the skies high above the liners. Holland America, Norddeutscher Lloyd and French Line along with many others saw a falling off in their passenger numbers. After that immediate decline however, passenger numbers held steady for a few years and in fact the late 1950s and early 1960s saw a veritable renaissance in ocean liner building, not just for the North Atlantic but for liner services worldwide. In the late 1950s the age of the ocean liner was far from dead but change, radical change, was on the horizon.

At 3.30 pm on Wednesday 29th July 1959, when the *Queen Elizabeth* was outward bound from New York, she was in collision with the United States Lines cargo vessel *American Hunter*. Both ships had been in the Ambrose Channel when a thick fog had closed in. The *American Hunter* collided with the starboard bow of the liner. It was lucky that all her passengers were at lifeboat drill at the time. They were requested to remain at their lifeboat stations until the liner was towed back to her berth. The incident only delayed her departure by one day as the damage was confined to her starboard hawse pipe. A year later, on the 25th September 1960, as the *Queen Elizabeth* was in the Western Approaches, nearing the end of her voyage, an electrical fault caused a fire to break out damaging three cabins on A Deck. Fortunately, with the aid of the automatic sprinklers the crew were soon able to put out the blaze.

◁ The crumpled bow of the *American Hunter* after the collision in July, 1959.

▽ Welders at work on the *Queen Elizabeth's* damaged hawse pipe.

Chapter 8

CROSSINGS, CRUISES & CHANGES

Although by 1960 the competition from the airlines was being felt by all the passenger shipping companies, June of that year saw the entry into service on the Mediterranean to New York run of the Italian liner *Leonardo Da Vinci*. *The Maritime Reporter* hailed the event as being one in which the shipping industry could take much pride: "In building this lovely ship the Italian Line demonstrated a faith in the future of steamship travel …" Just nine months earlier Holland America had taken delivery of their new flagship *Rotterdam*, which was also employed on the North Atlantic service. Furthermore, the Canadian Pacific liner *Empress of Canada* was due to enter service in April 1961. She would normally be employed on the St. Lawrence run but was destined to use the port of New York as a terminal for her winter cruises.

A report in March 1960 had noted that concern had been expressed in Parliament over Cunard's acquisition of Eagle Airways. Fears were felt that shipbuilding would be sacrificed in favour of subsidised aircraft construction. British shipbuilders were reported to be worried that too much money was being spent on aircraft research at the expense of shipbuilding and ship operation. (It was at this time that designs for the aircraft which would become *Concorde* were being worked on.) At the heart of the issue was the fear that plans to replace the *Queen Mary* and the *Queen Elizabeth* with two new super liners might be abandoned.

Back in 1957, at the time of the construction of *Sylvania*, the last of their quartet of liners designed for the St. Lawrence service, Cunard had been looking towards the ultimate replacement of the *Queen Mary*. Also at that time, with the *Britannic*, the last remaining White Star liner, due for retirement in 1960 and with several other shipping companies taking delivery of new liners, Cunard had felt it prudent to reserve a berth at John Brown's shipyard. But not long afterwards the plan to replace *Britannic* was dropped and Cunard took no further action concerning new ships for their express service, other than to indicate that they were contemplating the construction of two large liners which would cost about £20 million each.

It has been suggested that with the remarkable success of the *Queen Elizabeth* and the *Queen Mary* (at one point Cunard ships carried 50 percent of the total North Atlantic traffic) Cunard became complacent and disregarded any threat of competition from the airlines. This, however, is far from the truth: what they seem not to have fully appreciated was the immense impact that aircraft would have on the way that people would travel the world over. Cunard were, in fact, under the impression that, while a certain proportion of people would consider travelling by air, there would always be a significant number who would continue to travel by sea. They certainly did not ignore the significance of air travel and indeed, they made very positive moves towards acquiring a significant slice of that market for themselves.

While on the one hand Cunard gave consideration to the plan for new ocean liners, on the other they had looked squarely at the new competition. The company had in fact amended its Articles back in 1935 to include the possibility of transporting passengers by air and as early as 1955 they had entered into exploratory talks with BOAC regarding some form of collaboration, but nothing came of this. One suggested objective had been to try to arrange for the discount on a return ticket (then about 10 percent) to apply to a journey which was one way by sea and one way by air. (Later it became possible to obtain this kind of discount, but outside the peak traffic season.) Then in May 1960 Cunard bought Harold Bamberg's Eagle Airways Ltd., which had traded as British Eagle over a network of European routes and holiday charters operated mainly by their subsidiary, the Lunn-Poly travel organisation. In September 1960 British Eagle was renamed Cunard-Eagle Airways. Apart from operating on several European routes, Eagle possessed one licence to fly the Atlantic, to the Bahamas and Bermuda. However, Cunard wished to operate a service from Britain to the United States. By an unexpectedly swift decision of the Air Transport Licensing Board in mid-June 1961, Cunard-Eagle Airways received approval for a daily transatlantic service to New York. Cunard-Eagle proposed to start operations from May 1962, using Boeing 707 aircraft which they had already ordered. The licence was granted for a fifteen year period from the 1st August 1961 to the 31st July 1976. The aircraft were to offer First Class and Economy Class seating and would carry about 140 passengers. While the company also had ambitions to provide service to both the Mid-West of America and to Canada, the licensing board did not give their approval for this. BOAC (British Overseas Airways Corporation) regarded Cunard-Eagle as a considerable threat and lodged an appeal. This was successful and Cunard's licence was revoked in November 1961, only a few months after being issued. The Cunard-Eagle venture was

---

◁   This mid-ocean view of the *Queen Elizabeth's* immaculate foredeck also shows how one row of forward-facing windows has been blanked out.

Fading glory maybe – but still looking fabulous. The *Queen Mary* photographed from the deck of another Cunarder, the Canadian route's *Saxonia.*

effectively grounded. The Cunard directors were frustrated by all of this: as a shipping line they were used to 'freedom of the seas' and they found it incomprehensible that there was not the equivalent 'freedom of the air'. While this was a setback which might have been only temporary, it was certainly embarrassing for the new company. In fact, had they overcome it, they still might have faced real difficulty in competing on the North Atlantic with so limited a fleet. Things were not helped by the fact that Cunard-Eagle's first year coincided with a downturn in trade, prompting Sir John Brocklebank to describe it as 'the worst financial year in the history of commercial aviation'.

However, BOAC and Cunard entered into secret negotiations, the result of which was the formation, in June 1962, of a new airline, BOAC-Cunard, to operate on trans-Atlantic routes with Cunard holding a 30 percent share of the operation. The services were initially operated by Boeing 707s but during 1965 Super VC10s also joined in, carrying the attractive dark blue and gold BOAC-Cunard

livery. Meanwhile, Harold Bamberg re-acquired 60 per cent of the Cunard-Eagle airline from Cunard in 1962 and the remaining 40 per cent at the end of December 1966. He renamed it British Eagle International but it never really recovered from the whole debacle and was eventually forced out of business. All initially went well with the BOAC-Cunard operation but in 1966 BOAC warned that more money was needed to enable them to order more and larger aircraft. The request could not have come at a worse time for Cunard: it seemed that every ship in the fleet was being operated at a loss and by then they had a new liner on the stocks as well. Thus, Cunard were unable to provide the capital required. It was therefore decided that the joint venture should cease and BOAC bought Cunard's share of the company for £11,500,000.

In April 1959, prior to its involvement in the airline industry, Cunard had entered into talks with John Brown's and with representatives from the Department of Transport regarding the potential replacement of the 'Queens'.

Cunard's initial intention – even with the very evident threat from the airlines - was to replace them with another pair of 80,000–ton liners. They were firm in their belief that there would always be a very large proportion of people who would prefer to make their journeys across the Atlantic by ship. However, such an ambitious plan could not be realised without the aid of some form of government subsidy. Cunard's main argument in favour of this was the national prestige that would be attached to such ships, as indeed it was to the *Queen Elizabeth* and *Queen Mary*. While this was, at the time, still a valid argument questions were nevertheless raised as to whether two 80,000-ton liners would be viable.

The government set up a committee chaired by Lord Chandos and he was given the task of reporting on the whole question of replacing the 'Queens'. The committee ultimately recommended that the government should provide a grant of £18 million towards the building of a single 75,000-ton vessel that would be a replacement for the by now rather dated *Queen Mary*. The total cost of the ship was set at £30 million and it was expected that she would be ready to enter service in 1966. Just one month after the official agreement to provide Cunard with a loan to build this replacement had been announced in the press, the *Queen Mary* arrived from New York with just 437 passengers on board. In March 1961 Cunard invited tenders for the new ship but meanwhile the North Atlantic Shipping Bill was debated in Parliament. The statistics cast a pall over any enthusiasm for a new transatlantic liner. In 1948 a mere 240,000 people had crossed the Atlantic by air. Then it was noisy and slow, the propeller-driven aircraft taking at the very least sixteen hours, and it usually involved stops at Shannon and Gander for refuelling. By 1958 the introduction of the jet aircraft had reduced the non-stop journey to seven hours and in that year alone 1,193,000 people had travelled across the Atlantic by air and each year the figure was increasing as the number travelling by sea was decreasing. Nevertheless, the 'Q3' project as it had become known gathered momentum and tenders for the liner's construction had been invited.

Not everyone, however, greeted the news of the proposed subsidy for the new Cunard liner with approval and there was much criticism of it both in Parliament and reported in the Press. The editorial of the highly respected journal *The Syren & Shipping* (on the 10th May 1961) was naturally in favour of the project and wrote about it at length:

▽ The difficulty of docking these huge liners between the finger piers in New York is summed up by this view of the *Queen Elizabeth* being edged into her berth opposite one of Cunard's intermediate steamers.

"It is difficult to understand the extravagant criticisms in Parliament last week and in the National Press on the proposed subsidy for the *Queen Mary* replacement ship. The nasty remark was made in the House of Commons that while the Russians were launching a man into space, we were launching a white elephant into the ocean. No one said this about the recently-completed *Oriana*, *Canberra* or *Empress of Canada* - so was it the subsidy that rankled? The amount which the taxpayer is expected to find amounts to the magnificent total of £3¼ million. If the unwarrantedly pessimistic view is taken that this is merely a prestige venture – then no one with a memory can fail to note that fifty times this sum has gone 'up the spout' in recent years for the good of causes far less worthy. Why should it be taken for granted in some circles, however, that the new 'Queen' would not and could not be a commercial proposition? The Cunard Company, who stand to lose far more heavily than the Treasury if this is so, should be given some credit for knowing what future prospects are for the North Atlantic seaborne passenger trade. They have been in business some time and have presumably gained unrivalled experience in the business. With a reputation as safe and solid as the Bank of England they are hardly likely to wish to commit commercial suicide."

The editorial went on to report that during the second reading of the North Atlantic Shipping Bill the Minister of Transport, Mr. Ernest Marples, had stated that the owners of transatlantic express liners in other countries obtained a much better deal from their governments than Cunard was supposed to be getting from the British taxpayers, with the U.S. government providing 58 per cent of the capital cost and France providing 20 per cent. He also pointed out that the U.S. government gave a 28 per cent subsidy on running costs while the French made good any loss sustained. The £3¼ million the British government was granting Cunard represented just 11 percent of the capital costs while the rest of the sum to be advanced would be lent at gilt-edged rates of interest. Mr. Marples went on to say: "By no stretch of the imagination can it be said we are subsidising Cunard excessively as compared with other countries abroad".

The Syren & Shipping reminded its readers that the Chandos Committee had recommended that invitations to tender for construction of the ship should go to any shipyard in the country. The contract was to be given to the firm which submitted the 'best' tender. That would not necessarily be the lowest but the best in terms of value for money.

During the second reading of the North Atlantic Shipping Bill the Chancellor of the Exchequer, Mr. Selwyn Lloyd, pointed out that three fundamental questions had been raised: Should the Government get themselves mixed up in the North Atlantic service? If so, was the 'Q3' the right sort of ship for them to have? And were the financial terms tolerable? In answering the first question Mr. Lloyd referred to the large subsidies given to other operators, and said that there was a long tradition of financial help for the route. He was of the view that without Government action the ship would not be built but he was unable to accept that the Government took on the entire risk of building the ship. He went on to say that in 1958 and 1959 the dollar earnings from the *Queen Elizabeth* and the *Queen Mary* amounted to about $25 million gross and about $20 million net. It was estimated that the new ship would earn about $15 million gross and $13 million net annually. He also felt that if Britain withdrew from the North Atlantic express service there would be a tendency for the country to be by-passed.

▲ Cunard's artwork tended to be predictable and lacking in excitement. This view of the two Queens passing each other was nevertheless a popular image.

In dealing with the second point, the Chancellor said that it had been suggested that to have more and smaller ships would be a better use of public money. "All that I can say about that is that Lord Chandos' Committee was set up to examine that very point." On this question, the committee was absolutely specific. Going on to the third question, Mr. Lloyd stated that the financial help was to be an open subsidy. He thought it was better to have an open cash grant instead of a concealed subsidy at an artificially low rate of interest. Mr. Lloyd pointed out that since the war Cunard had spent £30 million of their own money building 200,000 tons of shipping. He thought that it was a very remarkable indication of the company's confidence in the future of the 'Q3' project that they were prepared to back it with £12 million of their own money.

While it had been expected in many quarters that Cunard would in fact follow the precedent set with the two previous 'Queens' and place the order with John Brown & Co., the lowest, and presumably the best, tender of £28 million, was submitted by a consortium of shipbuilders: Vickers Armstrongs Ltd. and Swan, Hunter and Wigham Richardson. So instead of Clydeside, it seemed as though the new Cunard Queen would be built on Tyneside. It was envisaged that the new liner would be 990 feet in length and in all probability nearer to 80,000 tons than the 75,000 that had been proposed. Although with only eight boilers instead of twelve as in the *Queen Elizabeth*, she was expected to have a very similar machinery arrangement to the two 'Queens'. However, provision was to be made for eventual conversion to nuclear propulsion. It seemed as though everything was set for the order to be placed and for construction to begin,

when several things conspired to make Cunard think again. Poor trading results caused some disquiet amongst the shareholders and one in particular, a Mr. R Gregory, led some very fierce opposition to the whole 'Q3' scheme. Later, speaking out at a shareholders' meeting, he said: "If we can only prevent shareholders and the people of this country from being afflicted with a floating groundnut scheme for the next quarter of a century then I think we will have done some good".

Also, by now Cunard's directors had begun to feel less than confident about the design concept of the proposed new ship. Much of the initial thought process towards it had been guided by Colonel Denis Bates, the then chairman. However, he had died in September 1959 and had been succeeded by Sir John Brocklebank. Sir John was of the opinion that an 80,000 ton liner built purely for North Atlantic service was no longer a viable option and instead the company should consider building a smaller, dual-purpose liner that would be able to maintain North Atlantic sailings during the high-season summer months and yet have world-wide cruising capabilities. Thus, in October 1961 Cunard announced the indefinite postponement of the 'Q3' order and took a long hard look at the future of the company.

The reality was simple but ugly. The world had changed. Those people whose faces had filled the newspapers, the smart magazines and the gossip columns: the film stars, theatre impresarios, actors and actresses famous on Broadway and in London's West End, industrialists and bankers, minor royalty and the glamorous crowd, had largely gone – to the First Class departure lounge at Heathrow Airport! They had become 'the jet-set'.

	Queen Elizabeth			Queen Mary		
	Passengers Carried	Number of crossings	Average Passenger List	Passengers Carried	Number of crossings	Average Passenger List
1956	73,875	44	1,679	61,954	44	1,408
1957	68,719	44	1,562	58,193	42	1,386
1958	69,806	44	1,587	54,928	40	1,373
1959	65,722	47	1,398	52,293	43	1,216
1960	61,323	44	1,394	49,440	42	1,177
1961	56,048	44	1,274	47,032	44	1,069
1962	53,104	43	1,235	48,449	47	1,031
1963	54,887	40	1,372	52,543	43	1,222
1964	44,391	33	1,345	44,718	40	1,118
1965	52,177	41	1,273	43,458	40	1,086
1966	28,501	27	1,056	28,904	34	850
1967	36,858	34	1,084	28,774	30	959

△ A later view of the First Class Lounge. The Canterbury Tales panel had by now been replaced by Sir Oswald Birley's portrait of Queen Elizabeth, the Queen Mother.

The First Class Restaurant. The richness of the room's decoration seems curiously at odds with the Art Deco-inspired linoleum floor covering.

One decision, announced in May 1962 and no doubt inspired by Sir John Brocklebank's view that some element of the company's future lay in cruising, was that the *Queen Elizabeth* would for the first time ever undertake a programme of three cruises from New York to Nassau in the Bahamas. While the Cunard Line had considerable experience in operating cruises - *Mauretania* sailed regularly from New York to the Caribbean each winter and the *Caronia* was at the time one of the world's most highly regarded cruise ships - the idea of sending the *Queen Elizabeth* off on five-day jaunts to the Bahamas was regarded by many as a desperate measure and it was questioned whether, with her high operating costs, she could even be operated successfully as a cruise ship.

In June of that year Sir John Brocklebank had to face a very stormy meeting of shareholders. It was made all the more unpleasant since the company's losses had amounted to £1,700,000 in the previous financial year and no dividend was being paid. Now it seemed that there was no way that Cunard could afford to replace the 'Queens'. However, Sir

John's focus was on cruising. The *Saxonia* and *Ivernia*, two of the ships on the regular St Lawrence run, were to be refitted to make them suitable for cruising while the *Mauretania* was to be given the familiar Cunard green cruising livery and placed on a Mediterranean to New York service.

During her annual overhaul, which was undertaken between mid-December 1962 and January 1963, the *Queen Elizabeth* underwent changes and modernisation to some of her cabins and public rooms. Sir John Brocklebank, was much impressed by the work (the *Queen Mary* had also undergone some up-grading) and he described the ships as being 'the best hotels travelling between Southampton and New York'. Further modernisation of the 'Queens' was planned to enable them to retain their premier position on the Atlantic.

It is frequently said that during the 1960s both the *Queen Elizabeth* and the *Queen Mary* were crossing the Atlantic as virtual ghost ships with, on occasion, as few as 200 passengers on board. Whilst this may have sometimes been the case on

◁ The conservative and comfortable First Class Smoke Room compares interestingly with its more daring equivalent in Cabin Class (see
△ page 122). The superb First Class Observation Lounge would later be allotted to Tourist Class in the far-reaching 1962-63 refit.

winter crossings, for the *Queen Elizabeth* at least, between 1956 and 1967 her average passenger list was always in excess of 1,000 (and on one crossing in June 1963 she carried an almost full complement of passengers, in excess of 2,000). While these figures only show the total number of passengers and the average passenger lists for any given year, the averages do show that both the 'Queens' enjoyed great popularity even into the later 1960s, which one might regard as their twilight years. At the same time, these figures do help dispel the commonly held belief that the *Queen Mary* was the more popular ship of the two, as in every year during the period 1956 – 1967 the *Queen Elizabeth* had the higher average passenger lists.

The airlines continued to take a greater share of transatlantic passenger traffic, although Cunard's share was still quite a reasonable slice. In 1954 the ships operating across the Atlantic had carried nearly a million passengers and the airlines just under 600,000. By 1964 the airlines accounted for 3,500,000 passengers while the

ships' traffic had shrunk to just over 700,000. At this time Cunard were not alone in offering passenger liner service across the North Atlantic. From 1957 to 1962, the balance on Cunard's profit and loss account deteriorated year by year and heavy losses were incurred in 1961 and 1962. While the distribution on the ordinary capital naturally fell away from the 1956 peak of 11 percent, shareholders went without a dividend in only one year, 1961. In the following period payments were resumed, with 4 per cent and subsequently 5 per cent, paid out of reserves. After a long decline a turning point seemed to have come in 1963. A further improvement in 1964 which produced a pre-tax profit of £454,000, against losses of £3 million in 1962 and £4 million in 1961, inspired hopes of a return to sustained profitability for the company.

The basic reason for this disappointing record was the long depression in shipping generally, coupled with the group's emphasis on passenger traffic in the highly seasonal and competitive North Atlantic trade. The regular services of some other shipping lines were on what might be regarded as 'cruise routes' where seasonal fluctuations were less severe. Cunard did, however, have shipping and other interests outside the North Atlantic trade: the two main wholly-owned subsidiaries were Port Line, operating a fleet of some 300,000 gross tons of cargo liners (mainly refrigerated meat ships) from Britain and North America to Australia and New Zealand; and Brocklebank Line, with 160,000 gross tons of cargo ships plying between Britain and and the Middle East, India, Pakistan and Ceylon. In the three years to 1963 the gross operating profits of Port Line were around £2 million a year; and those of Brocklebank, after falling from around £1 million in 1958 to a low point of £130,000 in 1961, had recovered to over £500,000 in 1963. Operating losses elsewhere (including those of the abortive Cunard-Eagle venture) approached £2 million in 1962 and £1,500,000 in 1963. The group's total operating surplus rose to £3,900,000 in 1964, compared with £1,100,000 in 1963. It seemed that, if progress went according to plan, Cunard's finances were likely to look much healthier by about 1970. Sadly, things would not work out that way. Instead, they would get an awful lot worse before they began to match the Cunard accountants' hopes.

The *Queen Elizabeth* arrived in New York on 19th February 1963 after another Atlantic crossing. She sailed on the 21st but instead of heading due east towards Europe she went south, towards the sunny Bahamas on the first of her cruises. She was in fact lucky to get away as New York's tugboat men were on strike. The *Queen Elizabeth* was under the command of Commodore Watts and he successfully undocked her without the aid of tugs. For her cruises *Queen Elizabeth*'s passenger capacity was reduced to approximately 1,500 and the minimum fare was the equivalent of £66. An extensive programme of entertainment was provided: the Queen of the Atlantic was in festive mode. On each of the cruises she had a lengthy stay in Nassau so that her passengers could fully enjoy the varied nightlife that was available. It was during one of these cruises, when the liner was 90 miles off Cape Hatteras, that a light aircraft crashed into the sea only a few hundred yards from her stern. The pilot was killed and there was little that the Captain of the *Queen Elizabeth* could do other than notify the coastguard. The strike of tugboat men had continued and so the difficult manoeuvres had to be undertaken without the aid of tugs at the beginning and end of each of the cruises. On the 13th March the *Queen Elizabeth* resumed her normal Atlantic sailings.

Those first three cruises confounded the critics and met with some measure of success - so much so that Cunard announced that the *Queen Elizabeth* would undertake two further cruises to Nassau during November and four more in 1964, departing on February 5th, 12th, 19th and on March 26th. However, the most ambitious plan was to emulate the cruises of pre-war days, when it had not really been considered fashionable to go to the Mediterranean during the heat of the summer. The *Queen Elizabeth* was to depart New York on the 27th February for a 25-day cruise which would call at Las Palmas, Tangier, Piraeus, Naples, Cannes, Gibraltar and Lisbon before returning to New York.

John Shepherd joined the Pursers' Department aboard the *Queen Elizabeth* in 1963 and has stated that of the two 'Queens' the *Queen Elizabeth* was certainly the easier ship to work, at least from a purser's point of view. In many other ways he recalls the *Queen Elizabeth* as being 'streets ahead of the *Queen Mary*' and cannot understand why the *Queen Mary* has this supposed aura of greater popularity than the *Queen Elizabeth* (particularly when the passenger-carrying figures indicate otherwise). When he was eventually transferred to the *Queen Mary*, he said 'My heart sank'.

He recalled: "I received instructions to join the *Queen Elizabeth* at Southampton on the 18th March 1963 and travelled south the day before. The *Queen Elizabeth* was just back from a series of five-day cruises from New York to Nassau in an attempt to occupy her profitably during the slack off-season on the North Atlantic.

"The sheer size of the *Queen Elizabeth* was staggering. I was familiar with the *Caronia* and *Mauretania* from their visits to the Mersey but boarding the *Elizabeth* by the crew gangway and finishing up on the working alleyway was like entering a maze. I eventually found my way to the passenger accommodation and to the First Class Purser's Office where the relief staff were arriving for duty. I can't say that I was made particularly welcome – I would be an irritation in that I knew absolutely nothing about the Purser's Office routine and would have to be taught 'from scratch'.

"The *Queen Elizabeth* carried a purser's staff of about thirty split between four offices: First Class, Cabin Class, Tourist Class and the crew purser's office, which looked after the accounts of wages for the 1,000-plus crew. There was a chief purser who was a 'figurehead', two staff pursers – one to look after the ship's accounts and the other to supervise the passenger entertainments - and about twenty-five assistant pursers ranging from senior assistant pursers down to lowly purser's clerks. About ten of the purser's staff were female (known in Cunard as lady assistant pursers, not as purserettes as in the Union-Castle and P&O) and there was certainly a 'glass-ceiling' – the ladies never gained the dizzy heights of senior assistant purser. One exception was perhaps the social directress – one Elizabeth Sayers on the *Queen Elizabeth* – whose main function seemed to be arranging tables for bridge in the afternoons. Included in the purser's staff were three baggage masters – one for each class. They looked after the stowage and forwarding of passengers' baggage. An interpreter was carried, who worked in the Tourist Class purser's office. He had a reasonable working knowledge of most European languages, although the assistant pursers themselves were required to be fairly fluent in either French

△   A montage of First Class and Cabin Class public spaces.

or German. Coming under the control of the purser's department were the ship's printers, the orchestras and the entertainers.

"The accommodation for male assistant pursers was fairly good, given that the ship had been designed in the mid-1930s, and was vastly superior to that provided on the *Queen Mary*. It consisted of about twelve mainly two-berth cabins on the Boat Deck, on the starboard side forward: so at least we had fresh air and daylight. The ladies' cabins were scattered throughout the ship and the chief purser, the two staff pursers and the Cabin Class and Tourist Class pursers had cabins in the main passenger accommodation.

"From arrival at Southampton to the next sailing day was usually about 36 hours, but this was broken by the crew boat drill which took place during the morning of the one complete day in port. Unless you lived locally it was not possible to get home due to the compulsory attendance at this drill. It was stated company practice for all officers and crew to work five voyages on and then take one voyage off on leave. In reality, this rarely happened due to staff shortages, sickness etc. I worked for fourteen weeks (seven round voyages) before I got my first voyage off, which amounted to just ten days leave.

"The work in the port period was not particularly onerous and 'office hours' (9 am – 5pm, with two hours off for lunch) were worked. The paperwork for the forthcoming voyage was prepared as far as possible and passengers' mail was sorted and marked with cabin numbers for distribution on sailing day. The crew purser's staff were perhaps at their busiest when in port at Southampton, with maybe up to 250 crew to pay-off and replacements to be signed on. The *Queen Elizabeth*, and indeed all the Cunard liners, had ship's articles known as a 'running agreement' whereby the articles were open for a six-month period during which officers and crew were signed on and off as required. At the end of the six months the articles were 'closed,' necessitating a general pay-off and sign-on by all officers and crew, after which a new set of articles was opened for the next six months.

"The crew purser's office on the *Queen Elizabeth* was situated directly behind the First Class purser's office on A Deck, amidships, in the heart of the First Class passenger accommodation. A fireman or greaser with a query about his wages was not encouraged to come wandering along to see the crew purser! On the *Queen Mary* the situation was even more bizarre – the crew purser's staff had taken over the squash court viewing gallery, high up on the so-called Sun Deck, immediately aft of the forward funnel and adjacent to the dog kennels! At least there was plenty of fresh air and some natural light. The crew purser and his staff should have been down on the working alleyway, where all the crew could have had access. The crew purser's staff was strictly a male preserve – the ladies were never allowed anywhere near!

"During the time the ship was in port, meals were taken in the magnificent First Class dining room. A limited but totally adequate 'port menu' was available. When the *Queen*

Elizabeth was at sea the assistant pursers took their meals in the Cabin Class restaurant, whilst the senior staff remained in First Class. We were allowed to choose anything we wished from the extensive menu and the Cabin Class menu was the equivalent of the First Class menu on the *Carinthia* and *Sylvania*. We ate superb food but after a few weeks one just longed for fish and chips in Southampton or a hamburger from the Market Diner in New York!

"As mentioned, a full scale boat drill muster took place at Southampton. Each of the male assistant pursers was allocated a muster station on the Promenade Deck and it was his responsibility to arrange the passengers assigned to his particular boat station. The passengers were lined up in rows with the women and children to the front and everyone was required to don lifejackets, which had to be secured by means of a reef knot (or, as the American passengers preferred, a 'square knot'). After inspection by a senior officer, a taped announcement was made over the ship's tannoy system advising the passengers exactly what to do in the event of a genuine emergency.

"The departure of the *Queen Elizabeth* from Southampton was very much dependent on the time of high water and on my first voyage this necessitated what Cunard called an 'overnight embarkation' with the ship sailing at about 6.30 the following morning. Passenger embarkation commenced the previous evening at about 6 pm and three special trains were run from London's Waterloo Station right into the Ocean Terminal at Southampton. First to arrive was the train carrying the Tourist Class passengers, followed about an hour later by the Cabin Class train, and finally the First Class passengers arrived in their train made up of Pullman coaches. The purser's staff were on hand by the gangways to 'check-in' all the passengers and obtain passport details etc.

"In 1963 the shadow of McCarthyism still hung over the United States Immigration Service and a complete passenger manifest had to be prepared by the time the *Queen Elizabeth* reached Cherbourg. It was then air-mailed to New York so that passengers could be checked before our arrival. Computers were not even thought of in 1963 – everything was done on manual typewriters and with masses of carbon paper. We always seemed to cope and I cannot recall an instance when the manifest was not prepared by the time of our arrival at Cherbourg, even with 2,000 passengers on board. A similar rigmarole was required for the crew and manifests were prepared for a full-scale crew immigration muster on arrival in New York.

"The actual allocation of cabins and berths to passengers was done 'shore side' and representatives from the shore staff were on hand until sailing time in an attempt to sort out any problems. The Tourist accommodation on the *Queen Elizabeth* consisted mainly of four-berth (two upper and two lower) inside cabins and the usual complaints consisted of 80-year-old passengers allocated an upper berth, or the lack of any natural light. With a completely full ship (and in 1963

A Grey Wornum tour de force: the exclusive Verandah Grill was both restaurant and night club

Strangely, in this otherwise carefully composed publicity picture, champagne has been served in the wrong kind of glasses.

⚠ The First Class Ballroom, otherwise known as The Salon, was typically lofty in proportion and some of its walls were covered in quilted silk.

both 'Queens' were full to capacity on several peak-season crossings) there wasn't a lot that could be done.

"After the passengers had boarded on the overnight embarkation the purser's offices closed down about 11 pm and reopened at 9 am the following morning. When the *Queen Elizabeth* was at sea, the offices were open from 9 am to 12 noon and from 2 pm to 6 pm.

"The *Queen Elizabeth* left her berth at about 6.30 am and was off Cherbourg about noon. Depending upon the tide she went alongside or anchored in the harbour. Both the Cunard 'Queens' were too large to use Le Havre, which was a much more convenient port for passengers travelling to and from Paris, as it was about 120 miles nearer to the French

capital than Cherbourg. A boat train was run from Paris and after passengers, luggage and some express cargo had been loaded, the *Queen Elizabeth* sailed for New York. Immediately after departure from Cherbourg a boat drill was held for the newly embarked passengers and the ship settled down for the four-day passage across the Western Ocean.

"It was necessary to alter the clocks an hour each night to adjust the five hour time difference from UK time to Eastern States time. On the westbound passage this meant stopping the clocks for sixty minutes each night that the *Queen Elizabeth* was at sea. Generally, this was done at midnight but some masters preferred the option of stopping the clocks for three periods of twenty minutes each at 8 pm, 11 pm and 2 am the

For all the elegance of this First Class bedroom, the light fittings were curiously functional.

following morning. As can be imagined, this created huge confusion for the passengers – and with some of the crew.

"Each evening that the ship was at sea, the purser's staff were required to assist with the 'games'. These alternated between bingo and horse-racing. The bingo was quite straightforward. The horse-racing consisted of six wooden 'horses' placed on a canvas track across the dance floor. A passenger was invited to shake the dice which determined which horses moved and for how many places on the track. One of the deck sailors was on hand to move the horses as required. The staff purser in charge of entertainments called the bingo numbers and provided a commentary for the horse races while the assistant pursers sold the tickets between the games and races. To provide a musical interlude whilst the tickets were being sold, the *Queen Elizabeth*'s resident organist, Ray Baines, played selections of popular tunes. 'Games' usually started at about 9.30 pm and lasted for an hour.

"In an effort to win back passengers from the airlines, Cunard introduced professional entertainers on its vessels in the early 1960s. These were usually second-rate 'passed their-sell-by-date' cabaret artists. There was always a dance team (who were required to give passengers dancing lessons) and a vocalist. Names such as Flack and Lamar, Boyer and Ravel and Brett Stevens all come to mind. A regular cabaret artist was the magnificent Adelaide Hall, who seemed to enjoy criss-crossing the Atlantic entertaining Cunard's passengers. Rough weather always caused the dance teams problems but except on the stormiest nights, the show always went on.

"Following the cabaret there was dancing in the lounges until midnight to the music of the three orchestras on board. In First Class the junior assistant pursers were not required to dance with the passengers; in Cabin Class and Tourist Class they were and this was a job I hated above all others.

"The *Queen Elizabeth* settled down into sea routine very quickly. All the passengers had to be seen by both the

The Cabin Class Smoke Room. The rectangular decorative motif and the combination of brown and blue were recurring themes throughout the First and Cabin Class public rooms.

purser's staff (who issued landing cards for New York) and by the travel bureau staff (who dealt with their onward travel arrangements). A lot of time was spent selling duty-free alcohol to the passengers. Under U.S. Customs regulations each arriving passenger could bring in five U.S. quarts of liquor and Cunard had produced special 'five-bottle' packs, which were sold to the passengers during the voyage and then delivered to cabins just before arrival in New York.

"Both the 'Queens' carried branches of the Midland Bank for the purpose of changing passengers' currency. There were three branches, one for each class, and they saved the purser's staff one of the biggest jobs of the voyage. On all the other Cunard liners the purser's staff had to deal with cashing travellers' cheques and currency exchanges themselves.

"Whilst the purser's offices closed for general business at 6 pm each day, the First Class office remained open with a skeleton staff so that passengers might have access to the safe deposit until 8.30 pm. Many First Class passengers deposited valuable jewellery in one of the two hundred or so safe deposit boxes at the start of the voyage and several would require access to these boxes before dressing for dinner. One of the worst crimes the purser's staff could commit was to 'over-carry' the contents of a safe deposit box at the end of

the crossing: the boxes were all double and triple checked to ensure that they were empty on arrival in port.

"The schedule meant that every Sunday was spent at sea: the crew were delighted to see the Blue Ensign flying as it meant that they were entitled to a 'Sunday at Sea'. This ensured them an extra half-day's pay. For the passengers the Sabbath was marked by the ship's Divine Service, which was held in the First Class Main Lounge and passengers from all classes were invited to attend. The Staff Captain took the service, which was usually well attended. Ray Baines at the organ provided the accompaniment for the hymns. Unfortunately, he did not know many hymn tunes and the same old ones turned up with monotonous regularity every Sunday.

"Another significant event of every voyage was 'passing the *Queen Mary*'. The time the ships were expected to pass was made known to the passengers and the outside decks were always crowded long before she came into sight. Usually, the two 'Queens' passed each other at a distance of about five miles and it was all over in ten minutes, as they passed at a combined speed of almost 60 knots or 70 miles per hour.

"When the E.T.A. (Estimated Time of Arrival) at New York was confirmed the 'landing arrangements' cards were run-off by the ship's printers advising all passengers of the

procedures for U.S. immigration and customs. A cable was sent to the Port Health Authority requesting 'Free Pratique' and advising that there were no infectious diseases on board.

"The *Queen Elizabeth* took a pilot off the Ambrose Channel Light Vessel and proceeded under the newly completed Verrazano Narrows Bridge. Just beyond the bridge was the Quarantine Anchorage where the *Elizabeth* slowed down and the port, immigration and customs officials boarded by tender. The ship then proceeded slowly past the Statue of Liberty and across New York Bay to the North River where, under the care of about ten Moran tugs, she was manoeuvred, at high water slack, towards her berth alongside Cunard's time-honoured Pier 90 at the foot of West 50th Street in Manhattan.

"The passenger immigration checks were thorough and time consuming and it would be almost noon by the time the last of the Tourist Class passengers had been cleared and left the ship. All members of the crew also had to clear immigration and answer a series of questions, some of them of a highly impertinent nature. Only then were they allowed ashore.

"The *Queen Elizabeth* had a quick turn round in New York, being due to sail again at noon the following day. Embarkation

began at about 10 am and was complete by 11.30 am. There seemed to be an 'open ship' policy as regards visitors at New York, with the visitors almost outnumbering the passengers. About an hour before sailing time every effort was made to persuade the visitors to return ashore but inevitably one or two missed the last gangway and had to be transferred back to the pier by one of the harbour tugs. As the *Queen Elizabeth* sailed down the North River, passenger boat drill was carried out and was usually complete before passing under the Verrazano Narrows Bridge. The purser's staff were busy mustering all the passengers and obtaining details for the manifests for arrival at Cherbourg and Southampton. To expedite matters a British immigration officer sailed with the ship. Although he had absolutely nothing to do on the westbound voyage and was treated as a First Class passenger, he commenced interviewing the Southampton-bound passengers on the first day of the eastbound voyage. With perhaps 1,500 passengers bound for England on a busy crossing he had his work cut out to see everyone before arrival.

"The purser's office routine was very much the same as for the westbound crossing. General queries were dealt with, irate passengers soothed, onward travel arrangements confirmed and duty-free liquor sold. British Customs allowed

The Tourist Class Dining Room
The Tourist Class Garden Lounge.

Tourist Class public rooms were inevitably lower and less attractively decorated than those of the more expensive classes. The Tourist Class Smoke Room was cheerfully decorated.

each passenger to import just one litre and these 'one bottle' packs were distributed before arrival at Southampton.

"Arrival at Cherbourg was usually mid-morning and once again there was uncertainty whether the *Queen Elizabeth* would berth alongside or anchor in the harbour until the berthing instructions cable was received. All official radio messages to and from the *Queen Elizabeth*, and indeed all the Cunard liners, were sent and received in company code. This consisted of groups of five letters which were transmitted and received in Morse Code and the whole process was a nightmare for the radio officers. When a message was received one of the assistant pursers was required to decode it and then get the decode checked by one of his colleagues. The decode would then be typed onto the bottom of the original Marconigram and returned to the officer of the watch on the bridge. Similarly, all official traffic from the ship to the company's shore offices had to be coded, checked and then taken to the radio room for transmission. It was a long rigmarole, which of course could take place at any time of day or night.

"As the *Queen Elizabeth* crossed eastbound the ship's clocks had to be advanced one hour each day. Usually this was done at 1 am each morning but there were still some masters who preferred three blocks of twenty minutes each.

"On arrival at Cherbourg, French immigration and customs boarded and checked all the disembarking passengers. About 95 per cent of these were bound for Paris and special trains were waiting at the Gare Maritime. Depending on what time the *Queen Elizabeth* was required to dock at Southampton, there was occasionally 'shore leave' granted to passengers who then had the chance to wander to the town for two or three hours.

"Although it was not widely publicised, Cunard carried 'cross-Channel' passengers and about sixty or so were usually embarked for the passage to Southampton. The *Queen Elizabeth* crossed the Channel at a leisurely 18 knots and typically anchored at a point off Cowes, Isle of Wight to await the tide. She would eventually dock alongside the Ocean Terminal at about 11 pm and a handful of passengers would take advantage of the 'optional disembarkation' with the remainder sleeping on board before the general disembarkation at about 9 am the following morning. In actual fact, it took almost a full twenty-four hours from arrival off Cherbourg to disembarking the last passengers at Southampton, which somewhat negated the effect of the express ocean passage.

"The last night of the voyage was a busy time for the purser's staff and especially for the staff purser, with the ship's accounts having to be prepared and typed. All the takings from the ship's bars and shops had to be paid in to him and balanced, both in U.S. dollars and in pounds, shillings and pence. One of the lady assistant pursers typed the accounts and the whole process was usually completed by two or three in the morning.

"Looking back on the ten months I spent on the *Queen Elizabeth* in 1963, I recall them as a very happy, if extremely busy time. That year was probably the last when both 'Queens' were operating at full capacity during the summer season."

While Cunard had already planned further improvements and upgrading of *Queen Elizabeth*'s passenger accommodations in order to enable her to retain that competitive edge, the plan to use her as an occasional cruise ship had brought about some greater changes. She had arrived in Southampton on the 9th December, 1962 and during the following seven weeks she underwent not only her regular winter refit but some other alterations and reorganisation of her public rooms. The most significant, and perhaps most remarkable, was the down-grading of the impressive forward-facing Observation Lounge from First Class to Tourist Class. There was already a trend on the North Atlantic to favour Tourist Class over First Class, with several ships having mostly Tourist accommodation and just a token number in First. To compensate the First Class passengers for the loss of their spectacular Observation Lounge, the *Queen Elizabeth*'s ballroom was totally transformed: its quilted satin-covered walls, delicate furniture and gilded ceiling were dispensed with in favour of a mainly green, red and yellow scheme, with white shutters to give an illusion of windows. It was smart, modern and yet unremarkable - and totally at odds with the rest of the décor aboard the ship. It was a poor substitute for the 'lost' Observation Lounge.

Typical of the *Queen Elizabeth*'s five-day cruises from New York to Nassau was her 26th March 1964 sailing. Denny Bond Beattie Jr., ship enthusiast and inveterate cruise passenger was on board:

THE
QUEEN ELIZABETH
GOES TO
NASSAU

Take just the right touch of British formality, blend it with an equal amount of West Indian casualness—and the resulting delight will be the popular isle of Nassau. And you'll spend two sun filled days in this charming capital of the Bahamas when you take one of the three Queen Elizabeth five-day cruises to Nassau.

Bigger and busier and gayer than ever—Nassau has lost none of her quaint, pastel charm of the past. Narrow streets, made still narrower by the slanting walls of pink and blue and yellow houses... hibiscus-blooming gardens... powder pink beaches... vivid, clear waters sparkling with every shade of blue and green... and the delightful climate—always mild, always sunny.

You will want to shop along Nassau's popular and colorful Bay Street, where you'll find stores well stocked with rare and unusual imports—and a myriad of bargains that will please the pocket-book.

choose the cruise that suits you best

February 21st Cruise			February 28th Cruise			March 6th Cruise		
PORT	ARRIVE	DEPART	PORT	ARRIVE	DEPART	PORT	ARRIVE	DEPART
New York	(Embark 1:00 PM to 3:30 PM)	Thur. Feb. 21st	New York	(Embark 10:00 AM to 12:30 PM)	Thur. Feb. 28th	New York	(Embark 1:00 PM to 3:30 PM)	Wed. Mar. 6th
Nassau	Sat. Feb. 23rd AM	Sun. Feb. 24th PM	Nassau	Sat. Mar. 2nd AM	Sun. Mar. 3rd PM	Nassau	Fri. Mar. 8th AM	Sat. Mar. 9th PM
New York	Tues. Feb. 26th PM		New York	Tues. Mar. 5th AM		New York	Mon. Mar. 11th AM	

A new destination - Nassau was marketed as an attractive cruise port.
The *Queen Elizabeth* on one of her first visits to the Bahamas.

When the First Class Ballroom (see page 120) was converted into the Midships Bar, a false ceiling was installed to create a more intimate and more modern ambience – at odds with the rest of the First Class accommodation.

"We sailed with every cabin occupied and Cunard pulled out all the stops to see that everyone had a memorable 5 nights and 4 days. There was something for everyone in each day's programme. Activities included daily quizzes (delivered to your stateroom with the morning paper) with prizes; deck hikes; square-dancing by a professional group; table tennis tournaments; health and beauty culture classes; dancing classes; recorded and live classical music concerts during tea time; gymkhanas; a pre-teen costume parade; bingo; songfests; bridge and canasta tournaments; a concert of sacred music; party games; a get-together cocktail party for the unattached; a get-together party for the teenagers and people in their early twenties; horse-racing; and a pirate party for the pre-teen set. The cruise staff numbered 15 and included 3 social hostesses. Somehow, we managed to squeeze in two days and a night in Nassau.

"At cocktail time, the *Queen Elizabeth* was alive with music from stem to stern including piano music in the forward and aft Observation Lounges and Midships Bar. In the Caribbean Club the orchestra played for cocktail dancing. When not scurrying about with trays of drinks, the stewards plied us with platters of canapés.

"After dinner there were cabarets followed by dancing in the Main Lounge and Caribbean Club. The MCs introduced a dance team, soprano, baritone, marimba player and a comedian. The programme sequence was reversed in each room so that the entertainers could appear in both. All of the performers were good - no better and no worse than on other cruise liners. In the Midships Bar, an American trio with a female vocalist held forth for dancing from 10 pm until 2 am. This group was the best on board, both musically and from the viewpoint of being fun. The ship's orchestra in the Caribbean Lounge was adequate but nothing more - one beat, a brassy sax and a bored deadpan expression. Stamina they did have, for they would stay with it as long as there was a passenger capable of standing up on the floor.

"The new Midships Bar (First Class replacement for the forward Observation Lounge) is 'kissin kin' to the new public rooms aboard the *Franconia* and *Carmania* and just as un-Cunard. Predominant colours are dark green and claret red. Gold, grape and white are the accent colours, with the latter used in the dome over the dance floor and the shutters creating false windows on the forward partition and beyond the bar. The bar is shaped like a bow knot and

can comfortably accommodate fifty people. The furniture is contemporary in styling with clean lines and finished in very dark walnut. There are numerous sofas with low cocktail tables and end tables topped by good-looking brass lamps.

"Just forward of the entrance to the main foyer, the promenade deck is partitioned to provide additional enclosed deck space for Tourist Class passengers. These two verandas are furnished with tables and chairs taken from one of the other Tourist Class public rooms, creating a comfortable spot, popular with older passengers.

"For the pre-teen set and teenagers, several 'Clubs' had been created. One was on the enclosed promenade, Main Deck, aft. It was decorated with signal flags and animal decals. In addition to several Ping-Pong tables there was a juke-box that played continuously. Also, there was a Coke machine. The First Class squash court was for the teenagers and provided several Ping-Pong tables and a shuffleboard table. Again, signal flags were the main decorations. The Tourist cinema was allocated to the pre-teen group.

"My cabin was quite comfortable, even when the temperatures moved into the eighties and several hundred passengers took to the deck to sleep. (Those passengers had Cabin Class accommodations, aft on the lower decks.) The easy chair in my cabin did present something of a problem for it had to be moved each time I wanted to go into the bathroom or get to the dresser. The bed was soft and roomy and dresser space was fine, more than I needed. The closet was large with a light and a shoe rack. I would have liked a higher and moveable shower head and more luggage space. I could barely get my two-suiter under the bed. Although the cabin is equipped with an upper berth, I don't think two people would be too comfortable. One would have to either leave or stay in bed until the other had dressed. Most of the First Class cabins have been spruced up with new drapes (floor to ceiling, wall to wall) and bedspreads in good-looking contemporary print design.

"The crowd aboard was very nice. In age they ranged from a babe in arms to middle sixties. For once there was a large number of bachelors and very little surplus of unattached women. There were, as is to be expected at Easter, a large number of pre-teens and teenagers aboard. They were a nice group, attractive and well-behaved. I met a number of congenial and interesting people including the mayor of Baltimore, several titled Englishmen and members of the diplomatic set.

"The location of my table in the restaurant was excellent and the table steward was superb. The food was as good as I've had on any cruise ship but the First Class dining room is not one of the world's great restaurants. The menus were lengthy, offering a wide selection, including an international speciality each evening.

"In addition to luncheon in the restaurants there was a buffet on the First Class promenade, starboard side. Tables were set up on the Cabin promenade, aft of the Garden

Lounge. After you had made your selection, a steward carried your tray through to the tables. From 11 pm to 1 am there was an elaborate buffet to which I didn't go since I had just gotten up from the dinner table.

"A surprising number of passengers dressed for dinner, particularly on Friday evening. Many of the ladies wore full-length dinner gowns. Dress in the restaurants at luncheon is informal but many men adhere to the tradition of jacket and tie.

"My cabin steward was fine. The afternoon we sailed he came in to see if there was anything I needed or wanted. I mentioned that I preferred breakfast in my cabin instead of going to the restaurant. This, he said, was no problem and what time did I want it? Foolishly, I said at about 9.15. Every morning promptly at 9.15, a quick tap on the door then the light on over the basin and a rousingly cheery "Good morning" as he placed the tray in my lap. The only difficulty was that I hadn't been in bed for more than a few hours and was in no mood to wake up, much less eat.

"Service throughout the ship was excellent. The ratio of crew to passengers was 1-to-1. However, the crew is not as fond of the *Queen Elizabeth* as Cunard would like the public to believe. They much prefer the *Mary*. The *Queen Elizabeth*, they say, is cold and impersonal and a business proposition. I met several who were quite vocal on the subject. I had a ball talking with crew members who had served in the *Aquitania*, *Mauretania* and *Berengaria*. They seemed to appreciate talking about their experiences to someone in love with ships.

"The Cabin Class Lounge was dubbed 'The Caribbean Club'. The original writing areas have been converted into cocktail areas. A long bar is against the forward bulkhead between the entrances. This cocktail lounge is separated from the rest of the room by a curved red sofa. The room had been thoroughly 'hoked up' in trying to create a 'cruise' atmosphere. The cocktail corners were lined with corrugated cardboard printed with a cheap nautical design. This same decoration was applied to the windows. Fishnet was draped over the dance floor and strung with coloured seed lights. The bartenders were togged out in wild printed sports shirts.

"The Caribbean Night (Sunday Evening) was a howl! Not only the maddest hats but the craziest costumes. Parades through the restaurant, the lounges and the bars, with many prizes given out for various categories. Everyone entered into the fun with great spirit, except myself, who settled for navy blue and the usual head.

"Sailing time was loused up by a rousing rain storm. Friday, Saturday and Sunday were beautiful, with clear skies, bright sun and warm breezes. The Commodore had the throttles open Thursday night getting us away from New York and into the Gulf Stream. Monday was a beauty - a raging gale. It was impossible to go on deck. Safety lines were rigged in the foyers, lounges and bars for the benefit of older passengers. I felt like I was doing the limbo all day going from one side of the room to the other. The metal screens were put over the windows on the forward glass-enclosed promenade. Spray was pouring over the bow and sheeting over the open decks. The *Queen Elizabeth* rode it beautifully with little if any reduction in speed. About 4 pm the sea and wind abated and the lines came down for the evening. Vibration is quite noticeable in the aft Observation Lounge and in several other locations aft of the superstructure.

In the refit, formerly cosy cabins intended for Atlantic passengers were transformed in order to look cooler for cruising but some of them now had the air of hotel rooms.

"Nassau was jammed to the rafters. Every hotel and guest house was booked solid. In addition, there were six cruise ships in port: *Statendam, Anna C., Bahama Star, Florida* and *Evangeline* and, of course, the *Queen Elizabeth*. Cunard thoughtfully provided coffee for us while waiting for the tenders."

In fact, the *Queen Elizabeth* began to make for herself something of a reputation for her cruises and they became a regular part of her wintertime employment. In 1964 she made a five-day Christmas cruise to Nassau and this was followed by a similar cruise over New Year's Eve. Then, after a few more Atlantic crossings during January (when she might well have been better employed on further cruises), she made another five-day trip to the Bahamas. This was followed by another long cruise to the Mediterranean: it was largely the same itinerary as before, but this time also included a call at Madeira on her way back to New York.

As the *Queen Mary* was also losing money on her winter voyages across the Atlantic, Cunard decided that she should follow *Queen Elizabeth*'s lead and also make some cruises. Her first cruise was in December 1963, from Southampton to the Canary Islands. Although she would make several other cruises, the *Queen Mary* never enjoyed the same success as the *Queen Elizabeth* in this rôle. Indeed, it was remarkable that the *Queen Elizabeth* should ever have managed to be successful being operated in this way. After all, neither ship was built with even the remotest thought in mind of their sailing on anything other than the route, back and forth, between Southampton and New York.

Despite operating at a loss, Cunard decided to re-plan the whole 'new ship' venture. The 'Q3' concept was totally scrapped and they began again. This time the idea was for a ship of between 55,000 and 65,000 tons which, while well able to operate on the North Atlantic, could also pass through both the Panama and Suez Canals and would thus

be able to undertake a world-wide cruising programme. This project was to be known as 'Q4'. However, even with these more modern ideas in mind, the initial plan still called for the ship to be a three-class vessel. This aspect would be modified during the early days of her construction. Research undertaken by the Economist Intelligence Unit showed that, in view of changing lifestyles, the three-class plan was potentially less profitable. *The Daily Telegraph* reported that 'the day of the floating palace has been overtaken'. It quoted Sir Basil Smallpiece as saying: "In travel, separate class accommodation as a reflection of a hierarchical social structure is clearly out of date." What was remarkable was that it had taken Cunard so long to realise this. By 1965, they were even referring to the new liner as being 'a ship suited to the jet-age'.

This time it was the John Brown shipyard who submitted the best tender and the keel-laying ceremony took place at their yard on the 2nd July 1965. At the time, it was expected that the new ship would be delivered to Cunard in May 1968.

In January 1965 the *Queen Elizabeth* went aground at Cherbourg. Thankfully, it was not a repeat of the grounding off the Isle of Wight in 1947, when she was stuck for several days. In this instance she was free after just 40 minutes and there was no disruption to her sailing schedules. In March Cunard announced that she would be given a major overhaul that would cost £1,500,000. The aim of the extensive refitting was to ensure that she would be a worthy running mate to the as yet un-named 'Q4' and, again, to enhance her facilities to make her more suited to her increasingly dual rôles of cruise ship and Atlantic liner. The *Queen Elizabeth* was to be thoroughly redecorated and more of her cabins were to be fitted with private facilities, her Tourist Class cabins receiving new furnishings and brighter decor. A larger sea-water distillation plant was to be installed to enable her to undertake cruises of longer than just one week's duration. One of the most significant improvements was to be the installation of full air-conditioning in both passenger and crew accommodation, which would make her a far more comfortable ship when cruising in the Caribbean and other tropical regions. It would be particularly appreciated by many of her crew, who had often complained that much of their accommodation was very hot and therefore uncomfortable. (This was one of the most often quoted reasons why the *Queen Elizabeth* was said to be a less popular ship than the *Queen Mary*.) In addition, she was to be given a proper lido deck with an open-air swimming pool: along with the air-conditioning, these were the facilities that would make her more suited to her cruising rôle. The building of the lido was to be a major structural change involving much additional steel work and a change in her profile. To enhance the lido and protect the passengers using it from the breezes, glazed screens were to be constructed extending aft from her enclosed promenade deck to the docking bridge.

It was to the great disappointment of Southampton's shipyard unions that the contract was awarded to John Brown and Co. and the work would be carried out at their recently completed new graving dock on the Firth of Clyde. At that time John Brown's were building a new liner, the *Kungsholm*, for the Swedish American Line. John Rannie, managing director of John Brown's, said in regard to the contract from Cunard: "We are particularly pleased to receive this well balanced contract, providing work for all trades and ensuring continuity of employment for all our men when the Swedish American liner completes this year. The *Queen Elizabeth* will be in our hands from early next December to early March of next year, the three winter months, and will employ on board at the Firth of Clyde Dry Dock, Greenock, over 2,500 men. 2,000 will be from John Brown's of Clydebank, the remainder from the Dry Dock Company and the principal sub-contractors for the air-conditioning plant, J & E Hall and Thermotank Ltd.

"This contract will provide work under good conditions for large numbers of joiners, plumbers, electricians and painters at a time of the year when employment is scarce. We believe it was awarded to us partly because of a satisfactory job done on the *Sylvania* this winter and partly because the conversion is a large task to be completed in a short time and, having built the ship, we have the necessary data.

"Most of the steel work involved will be done by the Dry Dock Company and the engineering work by John Brown's

▽ Dressed overall, the expensively refitted *Queen Elizabeth* looks her best as she steams out of Southampton.

big top

The biggest shows on earth aren't on earth at all —
they're Cunard's Queen Elizabeth and Queen Mary plying the
sparkling Atlantic. (Pictured, the glorious new Lido Deck
of the completely air-conditioned Queen Elizabeth, that makes
a crossing more than ever a 5-day houseparty to Europe.)
The Queens reign as the biggest liners afloat by far, affording you
more room for more pleasure. And it's all in the fare.
Peerless international gourmet cuisine. Meticulous British service.
Sports and games. Dancing. Nightclubbing. Rejuvenating
and refreshing you as only the grand resort life at sea can do.
Begin your vacation with a vacation. Sail. Soon. Big.
Any Wednesday. **CUNARD QUEENS**

All Cunard liners are of British Registry...you'll appreciate the difference.
See your travel agent or Cunard: Main office in U.S., 25 Broadway, New York.

engineers. We employ close on 6,000 men but could employ another 350, a few vacancies existing in all trades."

Mr Rannie's fine words sounded very sour that November, when the *Kungsholm* was nowhere near ready to be handed over to her owners as planned. John Brown's had been bedevilled by labour problems and the ship was ultimately delivered to Swedish American Line four months late. John Brown's were reported to have lost £3 million on the contract. While Swedish American Line were undoubtedly disappointed not to get their new liner when they had expected it, they were very enthusiastic about the ship once they had got her. Nevertheless, the shipping press rather played down their enthusiasm and focused instead on her late delivery and the large sum of money John Brown's had lost on the contract. It was unfortunate publicity for the yard that was about to undertake such significant conversion work on one of the most famous liners in the world.

It was expected that the enhancements to the *Queen Elizabeth* would ensure her operational life up to about 1975. The *Queen Mary*, however, was expected to be retired from the fleet in 1969, Sir John Brocklebank having stated in January 1963 that he thought she still had six years of useful life left in her. Perhaps inspired by that statement, the British holiday camp entrepreneur, Sir Billy Butlin, offered Cunard £1 million for her. They refused. (With hindsight we can see that it was a foolish decision and one that would cost the company dear. Had they accepted the offer, Cunard might have been able to maintain the *Queen Elizabeth* in service at least until the completion of the 'Q4'.)

In 1957 they had spent £500,000 having the *Mauretania* fully air-conditioned in order to help give her a competitive edge in the New York to the Caribbean cruise market. Although this most elegant of Cunarders was to enjoy a few more years of success, by the early and mid-1960s she was being out-paced by much more up-to-date tonnage. These ships were modern internally (rather than looking like a set for a Ginger Rogers and Fred Astaire movie), were designed to operate as single-class ships when cruising, had attractive lido decks and cabins with smart and functional bathrooms and were more economical to operate. New York was at the time the 'cruise capital' of the world. When heading to the Caribbean the *Mauretania* was up against the likes of the Italian *Leonardo Da Vinci*, the German liners *Europa* and *Bremen*, Canadian Pacific's smart new *Empress of Canada*, the American *Independence, Constitution, Brasil, Argentina, Santa Rosa* and *Santa Paula*, Holland America's *Rotterdam* and *Statendam* and Norwegian America Line's *Bergensfjord*, while poised to enter service in 1965 were the *Sagafjord* and the *Oceanic* and 1966 would see the arrival of the magnificent Swedish American Line flagship *Kungsholm*. Although barely twenty-five years old, *Mauretania* represented another age. Cunard's attempt to operate her on a Mediterranean to New York service was a complete failure and with the introduction of the stunning pair of Italian liners *Michelangelo* and

Raffaello in 1965 she would certainly have been doomed. However, by 1964 *Mauretania* had been withdrawn from the Mediterranean service and was largely employed in cruising service from New York to the Caribbean. Unable to compete against the newer ships, she was withdrawn from service on the 10th November 1965 and barely two weeks later arrived at Ward's shipbreaking yard at Inverkeithing.

In July 1965 the Cunard Steam Ship Company celebrated 125 years of transatlantic service. On the 12th July *The Times* contained a twelve-page supplement with considerable information about the company, its background and more importantly, its future. Much was made of the design processes behind the 'Q4'. Also, there was an article 'Relaxing in the North Atlantic' that gave an appealing look at life aboard the *Queen Elizabeth*.

"From the Ocean Terminal building at Southampton a narrow passage leads to a spacious, well-polished hall with a reception desk, wide double staircase and an armchair or two in a distant corner. This might well be a set for the opening shot of a 1930s German film; only the potted palms are absent. It is in fact the heart of the world's largest liner, A Deck of the *Queen Elizabeth* with Purser's office. Except for a slight cant to the floor, rather felt than seen, it might be a building with a solid concrete foundation. There is no sense of having boarded a ship, or even of the butterfly-stomach urgency of departure which encompasses an airport lounge. The scene is chaotic, in a way that the preliminaries to a large conference might be.

"A Queen liner of over 80,000 tons is, they say, a magnificent sight: proud, majestic and awe-inspiring. For a passenger taking a journey in one there are few opportunities of getting the vessel into focus. It is simply too large. Smaller Cunarders, like the 22,600-ton *Carmania* and *Franconia*, are of the size to fit into the human eye. They can be usually seen from the dockside.

"Not that the Atlantic pays much respect to size. On its off days it can treat a Queen like a catamaran. On reasonable days relativity plays a part. There is a clear sensation on a liner the size of the *Franconia* that the vessel is moving through the water. Stand on the aft sports deck of the *Elizabeth* and the ship appears still while the sea rushes past at 35 m.p.h. A submarine ploughing its diminutive way through the Atlantic swell in the same direction appears, from the deck of a Queen, to be doing a steady 10 knots backwards.

"Unless the weather is rough, however, the sea plays little part in an Atlantic voyage. Most passengers go dutifully each morning for a few minutes to look at it and to smell it, but then for the next 24 hours the sea is ignored. The sun is what most passengers seek. For much of the year they are lucky if they can find it. The company's winter cruises are designed specifically to fulfil this desire.

"Life on board has a strange and unreal atmosphere. There are environmental differences in each class (three classes on the Queens, two on the other ships) but all passengers are soon aware of the luxurious protective cocoon in which they are ensconced; remote for five or seven days from the realities of life ashore. On the smaller ships, in First Class especially, the social atmosphere is more intimate because the number of passengers is considerably less. But common to each class and each ship is the sense of remoteness. Even the daily newspaper printed on board each Cunarder, *The Ocean Times*, does little to dispel the feeling of being cut off, for its news on the front and back pages is, except for the main story, a series of inconsequential snippets. Has the world, you begin to wonder, decided to relax also, at least for a few days?

"Dozing, eating and reading are the chief occupations of the daytime routine with deck games, except for a determined minority, an initial aberration. There are quizzes, the cinema, bridge, the shops and in the evening simple forms of gambling, cabaret, dancing and, of course, eating. Clearly the most important daily mental exercise is the choice of breakfast, luncheon and dinner from hypnotically large menus (nearly 50 items for breakfast alone); but most passengers get quickly into a routine which often means fillet or entrecote steak.

"The dining rooms and bars on ships which are British to the backbone in every other way are dominated by American culinary and drinking habits. Slices of toast, for example, are wrapped in paper, which might be good for hygiene but is bad for the toast. In the bar the assumption is that the basis of every drink is a scoopful of ice cubes. For one whose choice is a simple whisky and water without ice it means a process of re-education – either of the barman or the drinker.

"These sea crossings to and from North America are, of course, used more by Americans than anyone else. There are a fair number of Canadians, especially on the ships which sail between Montreal and Europe. In the Tourist Class the majority of passengers are going to, or returning from, holiday. Non-Americans generally combine a holiday with a visit to relatives in the United States or Canada, or are families moving because of a change of job. There is a sharp difference in age group between the classes. Tourist has always a large proportion of young people; in First (and in the Queens, Cabin Class) middle age predominates. These passengers are mostly holidaymakers, some of whom travel one way by air. Young students, eastbound for a few months in Europe, are almost exclusively confined to Tourist Class.

"Businessmen still tend to cross from one side of the Atlantic to the other by air. For these time is important, but increasingly the realisation is growing that time has also become obsessive. Transatlantic liners are today again carrying people on the kind of business trip that had for several years been lost to the airlines. Some firms have been told by their medical advisers that if the good health

of their senior men is to be maintained one transatlantic journey in about every five should be taken by ship. As one businessman said, in a Queen liner it is after all only a long weekend between London and New York. More men are now thinking that every so often they should take their wives on business journeys and one such person said he would only take the sea passage if accompanied by his wife because life on board ships was an experience essentially to be shared: 'for a man on his own it is no fun'.

"That is certainly one view. More generally these journeys look like an escapist's paradise. Some may be bored, especially on the seven-day Montreal route, although this is offset by two interesting days in the St. Lawrence River. Almost all people who cross, or who see themselves in future crossing, the Atlantic say they would go by sea if they had the time. Those who travel no other way argue vociferously that time is not important anyway. Perhaps they are right, for there are few experiences more idyllic than to progress from one point on the map to another in close proximity to a comfortable bed."

On the 6th November 1965 the *Queen Elizabeth* sailed from New York on a six-day cruise to Bermuda and Nassau. It was her first call at Bermuda. The day after the end of the cruise she sailed again for Southampton, arriving there on the 18th November. Then on the 4th December she sailed for Greenock where she would undergo the refitting work. The optimism that had been shown by John Brown's managing director, while undoubtedly sincerely meant, proved to be short-lived. To say that it was disastrous is perhaps over-stating it but it was a poor reflection on the shipyard that had once so proudly built the *Queen Elizabeth* and had worked at such a frantic pace to ensure her escape to the safety of New York back in 1940. Nevertheless, the shipyard gave priority to completing the *Kungsholm* – as indeed they should, given that she was already behind schedule as a result of their own labour problems. John Browns tried to cover by explaining that the yard had been hit by an epidemic of influenza. It was however, not just the late running of the work that was causing Cunard considerable concern: pilfering became a major worry. Seven hundred brass bolts (used for securing portholes) disappeared from the ship. These apparently had a 'marketable' value in the pubs in the area – one pint for one bolt. As would later be discovered, other non-ferrous items were stolen from the ship. Copper piping, to be used in the installation of the new shower units, was also easily saleable as scrap metal. Cut into short lengths, it was easily smuggled out of the shipyard. Even already installed piping was surreptitiously removed. So, with work on *Kungsholm* being given priority and with some workers more intent upon removing items from the *Queen Elizabeth* than actually installing them, it was inevitable that by the time the ship was due to leave the Clyde there was much left to be completed. Work on cabins on both A and C Decks had not even been started and Cunard realised that it would have to be completed in Southampton or perhaps even while the ship was at sea.

On the 7th March Cunard's newly appointed Commodore, Geoffrey Marr, journeyed up to Scotland to join the *Queen Elizabeth* and two days later she was eased from the dry dock. The typically March weather of blustery winds caused some concern during the manoeuvre but as even stronger winds were forecast for the following day it was decided to go ahead as planned. Nevertheless the windy weather caused it to be an anxious journey down to the Tail of the Bank. The *Queen Elizabeth* dropped anchor there and took on her newly reconditioned lifeboats as well as eight new motor launches that would be used as tenders when the liner was at anchor off various cruise ports. On the 12th March, when she departed from the Tail of the Bank, on board were many of John Brown's men continuing with the work that by this time they should have already finished. Several hundred more were to be sent by train to Southampton in order to complete the job while the *Queen Elizabeth* was alongside at her Southampton berth. It was a refit more extensive than any she had undergone in her almost twenty years of service. Several of the Tourist Class public rooms were renamed in an attempt to lessen the perception that the Tourist areas of the ship were less attractive to potential cruise passengers: a small and previously unnamed room that overlooked the Tourist Games Deck was reinvented as the Sun Room and on Main Deck the forward-facing Winter Garden became the Fastnet Room, while down on A Deck the Smoking Room was named the Ambrose Room and the small lounge on the starboard side of B Deck became the Eddystone Room.

On the 29th March the great ship sailed for Cherbourg and New York. Her passengers were the first to enjoy the rejuvenated 'Queen' but among them were thirty workmen. Their task was to attempt to complete the work on the C Deck cabins and at least to begin on the new cabins that were planned for D Deck. At this stage not even their basic structure had been started. Commenting on the refit, Sir Basil Smallpiece said, with typical British understatement: "It would be unrealistic to pretend that we are not disappointed …" It was with either remarkable irony or amazing cheek that soon after this John Brown's ran a full-page colour advertisement in shipping journals, showing an aerial view of both the *Queen Elizabeth* and *Kungsholm*, to promote their shipbuilding, ship repair and refitting skills.

The *Queen Elizabeth* arrived in New York on the 4th April and on the 7th her new out-door pool and lido deck were given the chance to be fully utilised as she departed on another five-day cruise to Bermuda. Water however, was for several passengers a particular feature of the cruise – at least at first. Cabins, particularly those on C Deck, were flooded with water several inches deep once passengers attempted to use the newly installed showers. It was then that the pillaging of the copper piping by the shipyard workers became apparent. With typical Cunard aplomb, the passengers were temporarily moved, the carpets and curtains replaced and the cabins dried out. The passengers were then reinstated and despite these problems the cruise was a great success.

In February 1962 the French Line had introduced the strikingly beautiful 66,348-ton liner *France* into service on the Le Havre - Southampton - New York route. At 1,035 feet she was the longest liner ever built. Her twin, winged funnels were stylish and distinctive and her interiors were up-to-the-minute modern. Prior to her maiden voyage she had been advertised as being "a new experience in ocean travel. She opens a new world of luxury for all. New grand luxe First Class. New concept of Tourist Class with hundreds of single and double cabins with bath." The *France*, although principally designed as an Atlantic liner, also undertook cruises from New York to the Caribbean. She was the new queen of the Atlantic and a tough act for the Cunard 'Queens' to compete with. Their virtue was that there were two of them and therefore they were able to maintain a frequent and regular service, whereas the *France* was a lone vessel.

While neither the 'Queens' nor the *France* were really suited to the role of cruise ships, both the *Queen Elizabeth* and the *France* had swimming pools. However, while the one aboard the *France* was easily accessible from the outdoor decks, it was nevertheless enclosed (and therefore suitable to be used in mid-Atlantic) while the one aboard the *Queen Elizabeth* was an open-air pool and thereby much more attractive for use during sunshine cruises. Cunard played up this fact. Glamorous advertisements appeared prominently featuring the expansive new lido deck. The wording of one such advertisement ran: "The biggest shows on earth aren't on earth at all – they're Cunard's *Queen Elizabeth* and *Queen Mary* plying the sparkling Atlantic. (Pictured, the glorious new Lido Deck of the completely air-conditioned *Queen Elizabeth*, that makes a crossing more than ever a 5-day house party to Europe.) The Queens reign as the biggest liners afloat by far, affording you more room for pleasure. And it's all in the fare. Peerless international gourmet cuisine. Meticulous British service. Sports and games. Dancing. Nightclubbing. Rejuvenating and refreshing you as only the grand resort life at sea can do. Begin your vacation with a vacation. Sail. Soon. Big."

The largest liners on the Atlantic, meticulous British service, a 5-day house party to Europe: all too soon this would turn very sour indeed.

After her cruise to Bermuda the *Queen Elizabeth* sailed again for Southampton and made two more voyages to New York. She was back in Southampton on the 16th May 1966 and there she was to remain until the 2nd July. On the 15th May the National Union of Seamen had called its members out on strike in a dispute over working conditions and demands for the reduction of their 56-hour working week to 40 hours. The strike brought all the ports around the country to a standstill. A week after the strike was called the Prime Minister, Harold Wilson, told the House of Commons that a state of emergency was being imposed. The new emergency powers would not be used until it was deemed absolutely necessary but they would allow the government to cap food prices; allow the Royal Navy to take control and clear ports; and lift restrictions on driving vehicles to allow for the free movement of goods.

The ports and docks around the country became increasingly congested as ships were brought to a standstill by the protesting members of the union. Most of the Cunard fleet was out of action and on the 23rd May 900 crew members of the *Queen Mary* stopped work when the ship arrived in Southampton from New York. On board were 850 passengers, including the evangelist Dr. Billy Graham who was about to begin a tour of Britain.

The Minister of Labour, Ray Gunter, negotiated with the NUS in an attempt to bring an end to the strike. He acknowledged that conditions and regulations governing the seamen needed to be modernised, but said that the pay demands could not be satisfied because the resulting amount of overtime pay would go counter to the prices and incomes policy that aimed to reduce inflation by limiting wage rises to 3.5%.

Shipowners at the time estimated that exports worth £40 million were delayed by the strike which saw 'dead' ships blocking berths in London, Liverpool, Southampton and other major ports. While the long weeks of the strike were to have far-reaching and serious repercussions for British merchant shipping, the port of Southampton presented an impressive and remarkable sight for those interested in ships. Passenger liners and cargo vessels filled every berth and in many cases were in fact berthed alongside each other. The *Queen Elizabeth* was at berth 106 and astern of her was the Union-Castle Line's flagship, *Windsor Castle*, while the Safmarine liner *S.A. Vaal* was in the berth ahead of her. All was not totally quiet aboard the *Queen Elizabeth* though. The work on the building of the D Deck cabins continued and was completed. Had the ship not been strikebound it could well have taken several more months.

It was not until the end of June that the strike eventually came to an end. While during the following weeks cargo was again being loaded and unloaded and passengers embarked or disembarked and the normal pattern of life seemed to have been resumed, British merchant shipping had for ever been changed by the many weeks of the strike. The effect on Cunard was devastating: as a result of the strike they had lost £4 million in revenue and the Cunard passenger operations had lost £14.1 million in five years. Added to the company's woes was the fact that its cargo operation, Port Line, had made a loss for the first time since it had come under Cunard's control, in 1916. It was far more than the already ailing company could bear and it was very obvious that drastic measures would have to be taken if it was to survive. It is a commonly held belief that it was the effects of this strike that hastened the withdrawal from service of the

Queen Mary. It would not stop, however, at just the withdrawal of this Atlantic dowager.

Meanwhile the 'Queens' picked up the threads of their Atlantic and cruising schedules. The *Queen Elizabeth* made seven further round trips to New York but one of these was again bedevilled by strike action, this time by the tugboat crews in Southampton. So, having departed from New York on the 14th October she made Cherbourg her European turnaround port instead. Arriving on the 19th, she remained there until the 21st, her passengers due to disembark in Southampton having been ferried across the Channel and likewise, those expecting to join the ship there were ferried across to the French port. Then, on the 28th October 1966 she sailed from New York on another long cruise, although this time it was not into the Mediterranean. Her first port of call was the ever popular Bermuda, then on to the Azores, Lisbon, Gibraltar, Madeira, Las Palmas, Dakar, Barbados, Caracas and St. Thomas before returning to New York on the 22nd November. This cruise was followed by another Atlantic crossing at the end of which the *Queen Elizabeth* was at Southampton for just over two weeks, during which time she underwent her winter overhaul. A further adjustment to her air-conditioning plant was made at this time, as her public rooms (the spaces that had originally been fitted with this facility) had proved to be uncomfortably hot during her recent long cruise - the air-conditioning for these rooms had been designed to cope with normal trans-Atlantic temperatures. Again refurbished, the *Queen Elizabeth* departed Southampton on the 16th December for New York and from there she went on to a cruise which enabled her passengers to enjoy Christmas Day in sunny Nassau. A further cruise saw her anchored off Nassau on the 30th and 31st December. She was back alongside Pier 90 on the 2nd January 1967. On the 4th January the *Queen Elizabeth* sailed from New York on an eleven-day Caribbean cruise: it was the first such cruise that she had operated, calling at St. Thomas, Caracas, La Guaira and Trinidad. This really was her most ambitious cruise programme as once back in New York after the Caribbean cruise she made two further Atlantic crossings and then sailed on another, even longer Caribbean cruise. Of fifteen days, this also included calls at Cristobal and Barbados.

Queen Elizabeth's early spring Mediterranean cruise was now something of a fixture and the 1967 one was the most spectacular yet – though not without its problems. She sailed from New York on the 21st February, non-stop for Las Palmas, then on up to Gibraltar. The next port was to have been Tangier but a heavy swell meant that this call had to be cancelled and instead a call at Palma was substituted. When the *Queen Elizabeth* sailed from Majorca shortly after midnight, there was a heavy gale blowing and a report came that a member of the crew had gone overboard. The weather conditions were such that only the most perfunctory of searches could be undertaken. It was later revealed that it had not been because of the weather conditions that he had fallen overboard but that he had deliberately jumped as a result of suffering severe depression. Unpleasant sea conditions again caused problems as the *Queen Elizabeth* approached Alexandria on the 4th March. As a result Commodore Marr had to seek permission from Cunard to rearrange the itinerary even further – and at considerable extra cost. Instead of calling at Alexandria, the *Queen Elizabeth* steamed for Piraeus (where she had been scheduled to call later in the cruise) arriving there on the 5th and remaining there until the 8th. She then returned to Alexandria for a stay of almost three days. The planned call at Rhodes was cancelled in order to make up time but from Beirut onward the *Queen Elizabeth* was back on schedule with calls at Haifa, Messina, Naples, Cannes, Barcelona, Lisbon and Madeira before arriving back in New York on the 31st March. Commodore Marr had apparently had misgivings regarding the company's wisdom in operating a Mediterranean cruise at that time of the year. The weather conditions certainly seemed to bear out his concerns. Then, soon after the ship had sailed from Madeira on her way back to New York, he slipped on some spilt detergent and cracked and broke bones.

On the 1st April and now under command of her Staff Captain, George Smith, due to Commodore Marr's incapacity, *Queen Elizabeth* once again resumed her more normal pattern of transatlantic sailings until October, when she again moved into cruising mode.

As Britain entered the era that was known as the 'Swinging 60s' (in reality only the final three years of the decade) the venerable institution that was known as the Cunard Line sank ever lower. The year 1967 was surely its lowest and bleakest point. The new chairman of Cunard, Sir Basil Smallpiece (ironically of BOAC background: he had been the chairman of the airline during the Cunard-Eagle Airways period) announced on the 8th May that the forthcoming summer would be the *Queen Mary*'s final season on the North Atlantic. She would be withdrawn from service that very autumn. There had after all been talk of her withdrawal before and the new ship then under construction was to be her replacement. So, while bringing her retirement forward was sad news, it was not as though her crew and the travelling public were wholly unprepared. What they were not prepared for was the announcement that the *Queen Elizabeth*, instead of remaining

▽   Although more modern entertainment was provided for cruise passengers, the traditional deck games still had a strong appeal.

The *Queen Elizabeth*, on a call at Naples during a Mediterranean cruise, is too large to tie up at the Maritime Station and so is moored in mid-harbour.

in service until the mid-1970s as had been planned, would follow the *Queen Mary* into retirement the following year – a good seven or so years earlier than had been expected. The facts seemed simple: each of the 'Queens' was apparently losing as much as £750,000 a year and Cunard decided that under those circumstances there was no possibility of being able to continue operating them. It appeared that, for all his apparent forward-thinking, Sir John Brocklebank's ideas for Cunard when he was Chairman were nevertheless still rooted in the earlier days of transatlantic liner travel (hence the initial concept that the 'Q4' would be a three-class liner). It seemed in those brash years of the late 1960s that the *Queen Elizabeth*, no matter how extensively refitted, could not make a suitable running mate to the very modern sleek new flagship – a vessel that was to become the very epitome of the image of Britain at that time. The idea of teaming the 'Q4' with the heavy late-deco-styled *Queen Elizabeth* was perhaps unrealistic. It was also highly doubtful that the two ships could have sailed together viably on transatlantic service into the mid-1970s, as Sir John had initially planned. However, whilst the *Queen Mary* was indeed losing money at this time, the *Queen Elizabeth* had in fact (probably in part due

to her extensive refitting) gradually begun to show a return to profitability. Although some of her Caribbean cruises had not attracted as many passengers as the company would have liked, in general she was becoming rather successful as a cruise ship.

Unfortunately, Cunard did not think that she was successful enough and Sir Basil Smallpiece said: "It had been hoped that the *Queen Elizabeth*'s cruise programme last winter would confirm the viability of the company's plan to keep her in service when the 'Q4' came along in 1969. In the event, the results had been far from satisfactory. The board's decision to withdraw her and the *Queen Mary* is part of the unrelenting process of facing realities in their determination to put the company on to a paying basis." Sir Basil went on to say: "There is no magic that will suddenly put us right - the road back to profitability will be a long hard slog."

Commodore Marr however, was of the opinion that had Cunard been willing to give her another year, alternating between cruises and Atlantic crossings, the *Queen Elizabeth* would once again have been fully profitable. He was strongly of the view that she should have remained in service much longer, stating: "It is my belief that we would not now be

Your Cunard ticket to Europe...
so much <u>more</u> than transportation

There's something about fancy headdress night aboard a Cunarder which *exactly* states the spirit and mood of this extra seagoing vacation to and from Europe. Everybody wins . . . those who participate and those who watch and applaud. Laughing, relaxed faces everywhere you look. Contagious fun. The varied invitations of the dance floor . . . a first-run film . . . cocktail fun, the exquisite pleasures of international cuisine served with British understanding. You find it hard to believe this complete resort vacation is included free in the cost of your Cunard crossing . . . and you're already planning to travel this way again!

Getting there is half the fun...Go CUNARD

Widest choice of ships, rates and sailings from New York and Canada to Europe. Consult your travel agent or Cunard Line. Main office in U. S.—25 Broadway, N.Y.

QUEEN ELIZABETH · QUEEN MARY · MAURETANIA · CARONIA · BRITANNIC · MEDIA · PARTHIA · CARINTHIA · IVERNIA · SAXONIA · SYLVANIA

sold if only we had promoted ourselves a little better with the cruise business. This ship should not die: she is young and she can go on for another thirty years at least." However, the decision had been made – both 'Queens' were to go. The company's future lay wholly with the new liner. Captain William Law was in command of the *Queen Elizabeth* at the time of the announcement and he was to later tell the press: "It will be awful to say good-bye to this magnificent ship. It has been an honour to command her."

There was, however, another aspect which Commodore Marr had perhaps not taken into account and which had rather forced Cunard's hand. The maritime safety organisation, IMCO (Intergovernmental Maritime Consultative Organisation) had recently introduced some new fire protection regulations. The American authorities therefore demanded that the *Queen Elizabeth* be fitted with additional sprinklers and have various structural changes made to staircases to prevent them acting as draught funnels in the event of a fire, thus bringing her up to the newly introduced standard of fire protection. Cunard estimated that while the work would cost approximately £750,000 it would ensure the liner's continued service on the Atlantic for several more years. It seemed that all would go ahead and Cunard requested that an inspector would be sent over from America to approve the work as it progressed. The request was declined. Instead, once the refitting work had been completed the U.S. authorities wanted the *Queen Elizabeth* to sail across to New York, empty of passengers, where she would then be inspected. If the work did not meet with their approval she would then have to be returned to Britain, still without passengers, for further work to be undertaken. Another voyage, yet again empty, would follow for further inspection and possible approval. The potential of several trips back and forth across the Atlantic, empty, just to attempt to please U.S. bureaucracy plus the loss of revenue while the work was being undertaken was just too daunting a concept for Cunard to accept; particularly at this time when the company was in such a difficult financial situation and after they had only recently spent so much money upgrading the ship anyway. This contributed greatly towards their decision to retire her much earlier than had been planned. So it was the United States maritime authorities who really dealt the final blow to the *Queen Elizabeth*.

Having announced the impending withdrawal of the 'Queens' from service, Cunard initiated formal talks with various shipbreaking companies, initially to see what the *Queen Mary* might realise in scrap value. According to Malcolm Finister, head of H.E. Moss & Co., Cunard's wholly-owned ship brokerage firm: "We had not the foggiest notion what these two ships might be worth. We first got scrap offers of up a million pounds sterling. We then sent word through normal commercial channels offering the *Queen Mary* for sale just as you would any piece

of real estate. We were astonished to find that she might be worth a good deal more than just her scrap price."

Among the people offering to buy the *Queen Mary* were Stanton and Robert Miller, along with their newly acquired partner in the Philadelphia landmark, the Drake Hotel, Charles Williard. However, they made it quite clear to Malcolm Finister that they were really more interested in acquiring the *Queen Elizabeth*. Nevertheless, they placed a bid of $3,360,000 for the *Queen Mary* and after it was announced

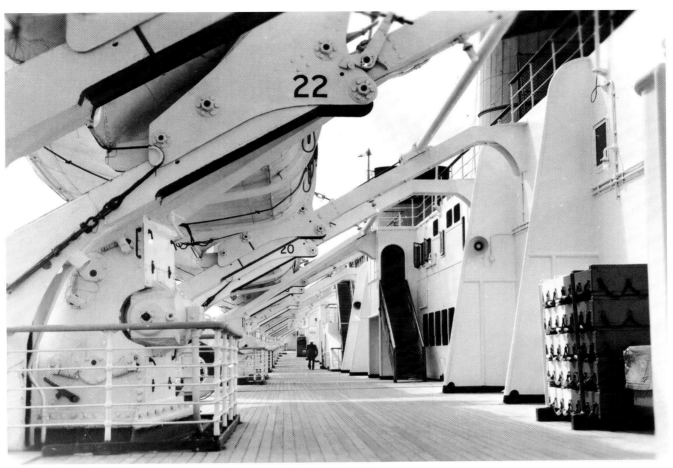

The sheer size of the *Queen Elizabeth* is well illustrated by these views of her Boat Deck and her enclosed Promenade stretching into the distance.

that Cunard had accepted the slightly higher bid from the city of Long Beach, California, the brothers Miller and Charles Williard again approached H.E.Moss and asked if a private deal on the *Queen Elizabeth* might be considered.

On the 20th October 1967 Sir Basil Smallpiece made another announcement that further shocked the shipping world. He told shareholders that the company had lost £2 million in the first six months of the year and that as a consequence three of the company's major liners would be withdrawn: *Caronia, Carinthia* and *Sylvania.* The *Caronia* was large and hugely expensive to operate. She was simply unable to compete against the likes of the new Norwegian and Swedish liners such as *Sagafjord* and *Kungsholm,* both of which were targeted at precisely the same market as *Caronia* and operated on similar cruises lasting many weeks and even months. These smaller, more efficient motor ships still offered cruises in a high degree of luxury and yet with fewer crew. *Caronia,* like many other ships of the Cunard fleet, was a representative of another time - one that was now past. Her décor was of a heavy and ponderous style and, although built in the late 1940s, internally *Caronia* was more akin to a liner of the 1930s while her competitors offered a lighter and fresher ambience. They were ships that looked and felt far more suited to worldwide cruising. Likewise, with the *Carinthia* and the *Sylvania* Cunard had followed public opinion when fitting them out: the travelling public of the 1950s had not warmed to Cunard's attempt at modernity aboard the earlier sisters, *Saxonia* and *Ivernia,* and the company had therefore returned to the more traditional look for the latter pair. They were in reality very large passenger/cargo liners and the time had really passed for ships of this type, for no matter whether they sailed with every berth full, if their cargo holds were not also full they would not make money. Thus, whichever way one looked at them, whether from a passenger's point of view or that of the company's accountants, they were unsatisfactory. Sir Basil told the shareholders that these ships would have to go and stated: "We do not intend to operate passenger ships just because they exist."

Although *Carinthia* and *Sylvania* had undertaken some cruises, neither of them had been designed with cruising in mind and, unlike their slightly older sisters *Carmania* and *Franconia* (the former *Saxonia* and *Ivernia*), they had not had the benefit of a radical refit to give them cruising capabilities. Thus they would have to be sold and, as Sir Basil said, their sale would be 'with no strings attached'. In other words, the company just wanted to be rid of them and they were little concerned as to who bought them or what they wanted to do with them. It was a cruel irony that they would, in fact, go on to be radically rebuilt and become two remarkably successful and long-lived cruise ships.

The *Carmania* and *Franconia* were to be retained but the real focus of the company was directed towards the 'Q4', which had, barely a month before, been launched by Her Majesty the Queen and given the name *Queen Elizabeth 2.*

The launching was the only bright spot for Cunard in that otherwise gloomy year.

The *Queen Mary* sailed from Southampton on her final transatlantic crossing to New York on the 16th September 1967. Six days later she made her final farewell to the city that had been her second home for the greater part of thirty-one years. The *Queen Elizabeth* had departed Southampton and Cherbourg on the 22nd and the two mightiest of Atlantic liners would meet mid-ocean for the very final time in the very earliest hours of the 25th. Notices of this last and brief encounter were broadcast and posted throughout the ship but at a little after midnight many passengers had retired for the night. Still, there were those who had waited, either out on deck or in the shelter of the enclosed promenade. Once the blaze of lights that could only be a large and speeding liner were spotted in the far distance, they grew quickly. The two liners veered closer to each other than they would have done previously. It was a spectacular sight, the lights on both the 'Queens' ablaze, their huge funnels floodlit, their sirens booming in one final salute to each other. In moments it was over - the *Queen Elizabeth* and the *Queen Mary* would never again pass on the Atlantic. An era had come to an end.

For the *Queen Elizabeth* it was business, more or less, as usual. Indeed, it was as though she were back to her very earliest days of Cunard service, sailing majestically alone. She arrived in New York on the 27th September, the day that the *Queen Mary* arrived to a great welcome in Southampton. The *Queen Elizabeth* made another Atlantic crossing to Southampton, arriving there on the 10th October. The following evening a young American, Theodore W. Scull, boarded the liner to return home. He was leaving England after having spent thirteen months of study at the University of London and was travelling Cabin Class. Along with friends who had gone to say farewell to him he toured the public rooms and, apart from occasional spaces, they thought the ship to be hideous in style and were disappointed by 'some strikingly misguided attempts at modernising, such as plastic palm leaves clinging to the columns in the Caribbean Room'. After his friends left to catch the train back to London, young Theodore wandered more around the ship. "I gazed out through the rain for a while and I could see the *Queen Mary* off in the distance with illuminated funnels, and just ahead, the *S.A. Oranje.*" The *Queen Elizabeth* sailed early the following morning with 1,702 passengers on board leaving the *Queen Mary* still floodlit at her distant berth. It was the final farewell: the two Cunard 'Queens' would never meet again.

Back in July Cunard had agreed to sell the *Queen Mary* to the Californian city of Long Beach for $3,444,000. She was to be used as a museum, hotel and convention centre but before she took up this static role she was to undertake one final and rather spectacular voyage. The 39-day trip from Southampton to Long Beach was to take her via Lisbon, Las Palmas, Rio de Janeiro, around Cape Horn, Valparaiso,

Callao, Balboa and Acapulco. Although Cunard agreed to provide the crew for the voyage, it was actually being marketed as a 'Final Fabulous Cruise' by the American travel company Fugazy. Passengers embarked the *Queen Mary* in the late afternoon and early evening of Monday the 30th October and the great liner departed Southampton for the very last time the following morning. Meanwhile, the *Queen Elizabeth* had returned to New York, undertaken another of her six-day cruises down to St. Thomas and Nassau and was now back again on the European side of the Atlantic. There was however, no further poetic encounter between the two ships for, as the *Queen Mary* was escorted down Southampton Water by a flotilla of assorted craft, the *Queen Elizabeth* was being manoeuvred alongside her berth at Cherbourg. She arrived several hours later at a now quiet Southampton, like a late guest arriving once the party has ended. The 'Queen' was now really alone.

Two more voyages to New York were undertaken and then she sailed on three cruises to Nassau, one over Christmas and then one over New Year. The *Queen Elizabeth* was anchored off Nassau on the 1st January 1968, the dawning of her final year of service. She made another cruise to Nassau before making a mid-January Atlantic crossing (a curious decision given that passenger numbers on the North Atlantic were at their lowest in mid-winter). By late January she was back again in New York and on the 26th she sailed on her final Caribbean cruise, twelve days to Cristobal, Caracas, Barbados, Fort de France and St. Thomas. Two further, shorter cruises to Nassau were interspersed between more Atlantic voyages - one in late February and her final one, an Easter cruise, departing New York on the 12th April.

There were 1,600 passengers aboard for this final fling down to the Bahamas. The ship arrived in Nassau on the 13th and remained there until shortly after 5pm the following day. As the *Queen Elizabeth* steamed away from the Bahamas towards New York for the final time evening fell and she glowed with that rich patina of an elegant Atlantic liner – rather than a cruise ship on a brief jaunt to the sun. During cocktail time a pianist played in the Observation Bar, there was dancing to the Dougie Ward Trio in The Midships Bar, the Neptune Trio played in the Club Room Cocktail Bar and there was dancing to Basil Stutely's Orchestra in the Caribbean Room. Much later in the evening there was an Easter Ball and Cabaret again in the Caribbean Room and at 11.15 pm there was an Easter Bonnet Parade. Meanwhile, there was Horse Racing in the Queen Elizabeth Lounge as well as dancing and other cabaret artists in The Midships Bar. From 10pm onwards in the Verandah Grill, once the very epitome of seagoing elegance, one could enjoy 'The With It sounds of The Applejacks', then a leading British pop group. There was also what was described as 'recorded entertainment from the Discotheque'. At least from 12.30am there was dancing to a live band, the Neptune Trio. The *Queen Elizabeth* steamed at a very sedate pace over the 961

The timetable for the *Queen Elizabeth's* final year of North Atlantic crossings. In the event, she was withdrawn from service before the year was out.

miles that separate Nassau and New York, not docking at her Manhattan berth until the 16th.

Commodore Marr considered that Cunard had announced the retirement of the *Queen Elizabeth* far too early and in his words she carried on sailing "like a cheap store

El barco de turistas más grande del Mundo en el Puerto de Cristobal. A Panamanian postcard records a visit of the World's biggest cruise ship to the port of Cristobal.

that has huge notices outside which say 'Final Closing Down Sale' more or less permanently displayed". Nevertheless, as if almost to spite the Cunard directors and regardless of Commodore Marr's view that the cruises had not been marketed as strongly as they should, her final cruises from New York were great successes attracting those who suddenly realised that it was 'now or never' to sail on this legendary liner. For over twenty years she had just been a regular part of the Manhattan waterfront and suddenly there was the realisation that in a few brief months she would no longer be there. Sadly, Cunard had also scheduled her to make some mid-winter Atlantic voyages but these only appealed to the most die-hard of travellers thus further enhancing the 'Ghost-Ship' stories that the press ran at the time, with pictures of virtually deserted lounges and empty windswept decks. But these voyages were few and her final summer season, like the winter cruises, attracted those passengers who realised now was their last chance to sail aboard the 'Queen'. It was either the voyage that they had always promised themselves or indeed one final nostalgic trip. There were of course also those regular trans-Atlantic travellers who had always been loyal to the *Queen Mary* and still regarded the *Queen Elizabeth* as too flashy and modern, the ship for 'new money' people. But with the *Queen Mary* gone, they were obliged to swallow their pride and travel with, if not exactly mingle with, what were

perceived to be 'not really our class of people'. As a result, on many of her voyages the *Queen Elizabeth* sailed virtually full and she was again making money for the company; and while they could not be dissuaded from their decision to retire her, the old liner was able to go with, metaphorically, her head held proudly high – even if she was looking somewhat shabby (due in part to the lack of a summer overhaul). For those for whom a transatlantic crossing or a cruise on the *Queen Elizabeth* was simply out of the question, there was still the chance to cross the English Channel to France on a ferry, just for the sheer pleasure of returning to Southampton aboard the 'Queen' and an increasing number of people took advantage of this excursion. Also, since the announcement of her sale the number of visitors to the ship when alongside at Southampton rose steadily. Everyone wanted just one more look at her.

There are conflicting reports of this period, with some indicating that by this time the *Queen Elizabeth* was presenting a rather sorry impression to those passengers who were, perhaps, looking upon this as their one last opportunity to sail on this legendary liner: that she was shabby and rust-streaked, that her carpets and furnishings were stained and worn and there was an air of something more than just genteel decay about her. However, one former passenger, John Dockray, sailed aboard the *Queen Elizabeth* in 1967 (and again in

Another scene at Cristobal, this time with the *Queen Elizabeth* sharing the limelight with her great American rival, the *United States*.

September 1968 just before her last voyage). He recalls the ship as being in fine condition. While admitting that she was by this time a far from new vessel, he maintains that there were in fact no faded carpets or signs of rust anywhere. His abiding memory is of polished wood, flowers everywhere and the lingering smell of furniture polish. She was pristine! "She looked great - still by far the most beautiful of all the liners. The broadside view was so perfectly balanced, with her two tangerine and black funnels sitting there, a joy to the eye."

Somewhat late in the day, a change was made to the sailing schedules and as from the 6th May the *Queen Elizabeth* began making occasional calls at Cobh. On the 23rd October she sailed from Southampton on her final voyage to New York. It was a quiet departure with none of the excitement of that October day in 1946. Indeed, it was a day marred by industrial dispute – the tug men, again. Nevertheless, she got away without any difficulties and arrived in New York on the 28th. The *Queen Elizabeth* was again in the spotlight (had she really ever been out of it?). During the following two days countless farewell tributes were paid to her and several functions, both private and official, were held on board. The English Speaking Union hosted a dinner at which guests paid $100 per head to attend: as they arrived at the ship they were piped aboard by the Glen Eagle Highlanders pipe band.

On the 30th, sailing day, New York's mayor, John Lindsay, went on board to bid an official farewell. He presented the ship with a plaque from the U.S. Department of Defence to commemorate the liner's war service, saying: "Today we can say 'The *Queen* is dead, long live the *Queen*' because in three months' time the Cunard Steam Ship Company will bring into New York the splendid new flagship, the *Queen Elizabeth 2*." (As things turned out, it was nearer seven months before New York saw the new liner arrive.) The *Queen Elizabeth* was thronged with visitors prior to her departure, each one of them wanting the moments to last just that little bit longer. The calls were made, several times, for all visitors to go ashore and as they reluctantly did so the band played 'Auld Lang Syne' and, for the final time, she backed out of her Manhattan berth into the Hudson River, with three resounding blasts on her siren. Small boats, yachts and excursion steamers accompanied her as she made her way past the famous skyline – and then, as she headed towards the Verrazano Narrows, they fell behind her and she headed into the Atlantic once more.

Voyage 495 was, by all accounts, a particularly happy one, perhaps inspired by the fact that it had been promoted as a gala trip – the final voyage. The much-loved comedian Frankie Howerd entertained passengers and crew during the voyage. Among the passengers were Lord and Lady

Four views of the *Queen Elizabeth* arriving at Southampton during the summer of 1968, with the now redundant *Caronia* in the background. The *Queen Elizabeth* was not only the World's largest liner but also arguably one of the most beautiful.

Montagu of Beaulieu. On the 3rd November Commodore Marr hosted a Farewell Dinner and on the 4th, the final night of the crossing, passengers and crew poured onto the dance floor at the end of the evening's entertainment for an emotional and very loud rendition of 'Auld Lang Syne'.

The *Queen Elizabeth* was back in Southampton on the 5th November but there was no particular welcome. She was a little delayed due to bad weather in the Atlantic but otherwise it was an arrival no different from any other. She docked at Berth 107 in the New Docks and remained there for two days. It had earlier been announced that as a tribute to the ship which she had launched, Her Majesty the Queen Mother would pay a visit to the liner on the 6th. So, once her final passengers from the Atlantic voyage had been disembarked, the ship was cleaned and polished throughout and other preparations made to welcome the Royal guest. Her Majesty arrived shortly before noon and was met by Commodore Marr and Staff Captain Law. She spoke to several members of the crew before being taken along to The Midships Bar to meet the senior officers as well as senior representatives from Cunard. Luncheon followed and then Commodore Marr conducted the Queen Mother on a tour of the ship. She had made a particular request to meet as many 'old Cunard hands' as possible. The tour included some of the open areas of the ship as well as the bridge, where Her Majesty reflected upon the time that she had taken brief control of the ship's wheel during the trials voyage off the Scottish coast twenty-two years earlier. She also took a last nostalgic look at the stateroom M64 which she had occupied on the one occasion when she had crossed the Atlantic on the liner.

The following evening, the crew held their own farewell celebration: a dance at a Southampton ballroom. Commodore and Mrs. Marr were invited as guests of honour and the Commodore was presented with a solid silver rose bowl bearing the inscription: 'RMS *Queen Elizabeth*, 2nd November 1968. Presented by the Ship's Company on the last voyage to Commodore Geoffrey Marr DSC, RD, RNR. In appreciation of his unfailing thoughtfulness and his many timely arrivals'.

On the 8th the *Queen Elizabeth* embarked her final passengers. They came on board for what was her only cruise from Britain: a seven-day trip to Las Palmas and Gibraltar. 'Auld Lang Syne' had become something of her theme song and once again its strains, played this time by Southampton's Salvation Army Band, drifted across the water as the *Queen Elizabeth* slipped away from her berth. On the 13th November, as the

Queen Elizabeth steamed away from Gibraltar, that bastion of the British Empire, she was escorted by various small craft and a flotilla of Royal Navy ships. Jet fighters roared overhead as the naval vessels prepared to turn back to Gibraltar. It was the final farewell to the great liner.

High winds slowed her progress towards Southampton, so the *Queen Elizabeth* was an hour late docking, again at Southampton's Berth 107 on the 15th November. That evening her crew were paid off. Some of them would be joining the new ship, *Queen Elizabeth 2*, while just 193 would sail again with the *Queen Elizabeth*, taking her to her new home. The last function to be held on board was a dance for nine hundred serving and ex-officers and for senior local dignitaries. The event was oversubscribed and, because the crew had been paid off, a local catering firm were brought in to provide refreshments.

Her career as a Cunard liner, as the flagship of the British merchant fleet, was at an end. Only ignominy would follow. What seemed like the final insult was the supposedly witty but distinctly tasteless advertising campaign to promote the entry into service of her successor, the *Queen Elizabeth 2*: 'Ships have been boring long enough …!'

It was hardly an appropriate way to acknowledge the very liners that had made your company a household name on both sides of the Atlantic, at their peak earning unrivalled profits. Boring? The *Queen Elizabeth* and the *Queen Mary* were undoubtedly the two most profitable Atlantic liners ever built and their stories, along with those of most of the other liners that had flown the Cunard house-flag, were far from boring. It was an advertising campaign that showed just how low Cunard had fallen and how desperate they were to prove that they might be down but were not yet out.

The *Queen Elizabeth* had crossed the Atlantic 896 times, had carried 2,300,000 passengers (excluding those carried during the war), had made 30 cruises and had steamed 3,472,672 miles.

big name

Q for Queen Elizabeth. Q...

Biggest names afloat. ...
room to give you more l...

Begin your vacation ...
resort life to Europe. It'...
you can eat, all the fun ...
Go nightclubbing. Dar...
So much so you'll wish...

Any Wednesday. Q...

See your travel agent or Cu...

Your last chances to sail on the Queen Elizabeth

This November, the greatest ship in the world goes into retirement. With her vanishes a whole era of sea travel. But it's still not too late to sample it. If you hurry, you're still in time to book yourself on one of Queen Elizabeth's final 4 voyages.

Sailing date	Arrival New Yo...
September 24	September 3...
October 9	October 1...
October 23	October 2...

Farewell cruise to Las Palmas and Gibraltar leaves on November 8.
7 days — fares from £100*

*Subject to availability

CUNARD

Telephone 01-930 7890 or contact your travel agent now.

Chapter 9

FOR SALE

Almost as soon as Cunard had announced her impending retirement speculation had begun regarding the future for the *Queen Elizabeth*. There were many who favoured the idea of her being used in a similar role to that of the *Queen Mary* in Long Beach, but in Southampton instead. At the time of the *Queen Mary*'s impending disposal there had been many people in Britain horrified that she would fall into foreign hands and there had even been the suggestion that a national fund be set up to buy her from Cunard so that she could be towed out to sea and sunk! Similar views, many of them barely more than whimsical, were held by some regarding the *Queen Elizabeth*. For one of the Cunard 'Queens' to be sold to foreigners was bad enough but the very idea that both of them should be was seen by some as akin to selling off the family silver. Others viewed it as an inevitability – particularly after London Bridge had been sold to be re-erected in the Arizona Desert.

Between September 1967 and March 1968 Cunard received many serious offers to buy the ship. They had sold the *Queen Mary* for £1,500,000 and they hoped they would be able to sell the *Queen Elizabeth* for rather more. Stanton and Robert Miller and Charles Williard (who liked to refer to themselves as C-B-S, Charlie, Bob and Stan) were naturally there, having made it clear in 1967, when bidding for the *Queen Mary*, that it was the *Queen Elizabeth* they were really after. Malcolm Finister at Cunard's ship brokerage firm H.E. Moss had become more than a little impressed by C-B-S and is quoted as having said: "It was important for us not only to get the best price for the ship but also to know that she would have a good home. Finally, we decided we could hold off no further." Although he favoured C-B-S and their plans, the decision could not rest with Finister alone so other bids had to be given consideration.

There was an offer from Japan to use her as a marine science museum: they wanted her in time for the Tokyo World Fair in 1970. Brazilian operators wanted to use her as a floating casino and Mexico wanted her as an attraction in Acapulco bay. The evangelist Dr. Billy Graham offered Cunard over £2 million for her with a plan to use her as a Bible school. The United States Institute of Technology suggested using her as a floating university. Meanwhile, there was an offer from Honolulu, as well as a suggestion that she be used for British holidaymakers. There was also an offer from an Australian syndicate headed by Sir Howard Hickman, a 49-year old director of Tinsley Robor, a London-based printing firm, along with Dr. Malcolm Mackay, a member of the Australian House of Representatives. In March 1968 they bid £3 million for the *Queen Elizabeth* with the aim of using her on an emigrant service between Britain and Australia and as an Australian-based cruise ship. There were also offers from interested parties in South Africa and Atlanta, Georgia. Cunard were particularly interested in the offer from the group of Japanese businessmen, while the Brazilian group was offering a tantalising $7.5 million. So Finister advised C-B-S that they were out of the running: it seemed that they had lost the ship of their dreams. Despite the Brazilian bid being the highest, the directors of Cunard decided that they did not want to see the *Queen Elizabeth* being reduced to the role of a gambling ship. As a result the Philadelphia group were invited to bid again.

Out of over one hundred enquiries, there were just six real offers. On the 5th April, in the Savoy Hotel, Cunard announced that they had accepted an offer of £3.23 million from the Miller brothers and Charles Williard and the deal was signed. It had been planned that Philadelphia's Mayor Tate and Council President Paul D'Ortona were to be present to lend the city's prestige to the ceremonies but they had decided to remain in the United States. Mayor Tate then announced the deal five hours before it was signed, much to Cunard's irritation. Back in 1967 C-B-S had had joined forces with a property developer, Philip Klein, and sometime after their successful bid was announced Klein is reported to have said: "They wanted us to have her all along. Where do you think the final bid was typed? In the Moss office. Who do you think dictated the terms? Finister. They wanted us to bring her to Philadelphia."

The brothers Miller, Charles Williard and Philip Klein had an ambitious plan to create a new 150-acre tourist complex on the Delaware River, adjacent to Philadelphia's Hog Island, a plan that would fully equal, indeed would surely surpass, the development around the *Queen Mary* in Long Beach. For the previous ten years Klein had been sitting on thirty acres of undeveloped marshland between the Philadelphia International Airport and the Delaware River. This unprepossessing piece of real estate was controlled by Klein's non-profit making Philadelphia Marina Corporation and was leased from the City of Philadelphia which, in turn leased it from Tinicum Township. The Millers had

---

◁ Even by 1968, the bridge of the *Queen Elizabeth* was looking curiously antique in comparison with those of some of the newer liners.

New owners take the helm with ambitious plans for the *Queen Elizabeth* to start a fresh career as a static attraction in Philadelphia.

initially approached Klein with the idea of creating a $25 million 'boatel' (a motel for boat owners) on the site and a corporation, Airport-Boatel, was formed. However, once the *Queen Elizabeth* became available the 'boatel' concept was scrapped in favour of using the space for the liner and entirely new plans were drawn up.

These were for a Disneyland-type development which would consist of a marina, museum, shops, hotels and convention and recreation facilities. The park would have as its theme the Modern Wonders of the World and it would include recreations of the seven original wonders, while the *Queen Elizabeth* would be presented as the eighth (modern) wonder. Stanton Miller, flushed with pride and confidence, said shortly after the winning bid had been announced: "We Americans have turned to your great nation so often for inspiration and instruction. We now come to obtain one of your prized possessions. Be sure the *Queen Elizabeth* will be welcomed and cared for in the fashion her long and illustrious career in war and peace warrants."

The London newspaper *Evening Standard*, reporting the deal, referred to the Millers and Williard as 'Three U.S.

Millionaires' in its headlines. *The Daily Mirror* reported: "They are tanned, bouncy guys who intend squeezing a bundle of fun out of the old Lizzie ... Now they're taking over the captain's stateroom on the Elizabeth for their own personal high jinks. There's a panache, a heedless zest about the three which makes success boringly inevitable…"

In order to create the planned theme-park, Airport-Boatel Inc. hired what Stanton Miller described as 'a top design firm', Athena Designs Inc. Curiously, Athena Designs Inc. was based at the Drake Hotel in Philadelphia, owned by the Millers and Williard, and was apparently a two-man operation, one a former used-car salesman and the other a rug salesman.

While Philadelphia's Mayor Tate was quick enough, indeed premature, in jumping onto the C-B-S bandwagon and announcing the success of their bid, there were allegations that no City Hall enquiries had been made regarding the plans for the ship or how the city would benefit from her, despite the fact that it had been well known for over a year that the trio were trying to buy her. Sources have claimed that it was only a month after the deal had been signed that Mayor Tate and President D'Ortona came to the realisation that the *Queen Elizabeth* was actually going to be located in the Tinicum township rather than in the city of Philadelphia. It was reported that they were very angry and that there was a loud confrontation with the Miller brothers.

Just five days after the purchase agreement was signed, Stanton Miller approached the magazine *Philadelphia* suggesting that they were the only publication in town which could clearly define the advantages of having the *Queen Elizabeth* as part of the Philadelphia scene after she finished her transatlantic service in November. He assured *Philadelphia* that plans were being completed to berth her permanently at a site near the International Airport and that they were the only publication who could help get City co-operation in awarding more land for a parking lot. He pointed to plans to make the ship an enormous tourist attraction which would excite even the most jaded conventioneer. There would be enough beautiful staterooms to accommodate 2,300 guests plus restaurants, swimming pools, nightclubs and bars located only a few minutes from downtown Philadelphia. Miller even indicated that the airport had asked if they could use the ship as a source for standby electrical power. Any problems of bringing such a huge ship up to Philadelphia had been ironed out, he said, as Army Engineers had agreed to dredge a channel from mid-river to shore to allow the *Queen Elizabeth* to dock. His own firm was already planning a $250,000 sewage disposal plant and one of his associate's engineers had made a feasibility study regarding noise. "No problem", Miller apparently said, "it is a quiet spot out of the airport's flying pattern" and he was adamant when questioned about the proximity to oil refineries: "It's one of the cleanest parts of the city". However, he did admit that the problem of getting a road down to the ship had yet to be dealt with. *Philadelphia* agreed that having the *Queen Elizabeth* could be of enormous benefit to the city and they went ahead and began to research the article.

What transpired, however, was quite the opposite of Stanton Miller's aim. The editorial of the magazine's June edition reported that, when they assigned one of their writers to do a piece on the ship, "The story he brought back was not the story he went after … (it) raises more questions than it answers". The editorial revealed that the Miller brothers and Charles Williard were well-known to the magazine from previous investigations. The Millers had, it alleged, been involved in a number of unsuccessful enterprises and several big money deals, some of which had ended in acrimony and legal proceedings.

Then, by 1964 they had become part-owners of the Drake Hotel. In the past the Drake had been something of a landmark institution in Philadelphia but by the early 1960s it was run down and seedy. The Millers had the building restored, with some of the work being done by a company owned by Charles Williard. While on the surface it appeared that all was now going well, the *Philadelphia* editorial suggested that it was odd that the Millers should go into the hotel business and remarkable that they would have the financial backing to do so after enduring so many difficulties in the business world. The magazine went on to reveal that the $2.5 million purchase price had actually been supplied by the Teamsters' Pension Fund and that the Millers were close friends with Jimmy Hoffa, the Teamsters' Union chief who, until he was imprisoned for jury tampering, was a regular guest at the Drake Hotel. According to the magazine, the Millers had emerged from the deal as owners of 45 per cent of the holding company. In 1965 Charles Williard became the owner of a one-third stake.

Under the circumstances it seemed curious that Stanton Miller had approached the magazine in the first place when the previous year it had attacked his business partner Williard for 'playing funny games with a free-wheeling labour boss'. Even though the *Philadelphia* report hardly showed the Miller brothers and Charles Williard in a flattering light, it did state that the *Queen Elizabeth* was an unparalleled opportunity for the city, one which it believed should not be lost.

C-B-S went ahead and requested 90 acres of public land near the airport so that they could create a larger parking lot. "If we get no co-operation," Stanton Miller said, "we'll have no other recourse but to sell her. We've already got a $14.3 million offer and the Brazilian group still wants it for a gambling ship." The city of Philadelphia had to co-operate in the venture and the State also had to help by developing a six-lane highway out to the ship. "If we can't get that we'll be out of business."

Controversy was already swirling around the scheme. Had any approach actually been made to the State Highways Department? And it was alleged that there had been no contact with the Federal Aviation Authority about any possible hazard to aviation. Furthermore, nobody seemed able to remember who had made the all-important decibel tests to see whether jets taking off from the airport every four minutes would create an unbearable level of noise on board the ship. And it was alleged that it was only on the 25th April, nearly three weeks after the contract to buy the *Queen Elizabeth* had been signed, that an approach was made to the Army Corps of Engineers about the possibility of a river survey. There were also concerns that the proposed location for the *Queen Elizabeth*, at the old Gulf Oil Hog Island dock, while not perhaps the ugliest section of the Delaware Valley, came very close with its flat and marshy land and with the river smells combining with those of the nearby refineries and docks for oil tankers. Was this unattractive piece of real estate a suitable location for the planned Modern Wonders of the World complex?

By June, just two months after having signed the contract to purchase the liner, the Miller-Williard group were discussing with the Philadelphia City Representative's Office the possibility of mooring the *Queen Elizabeth* at the proposed Penn's Landing site, near Independence Hall.

▽ The front cover of the investigative Philadelphia magazine succinctly sums up the troubled situation surrounding the once-prestigious liner.

This, however, was turned down on the grounds that such an enormous ship would ruin all the plans for the development of the old Philadelphia area and that as she would have to be moored so far out in the river she would become a hazard to navigation. Later, it was proposed to revert to the original plan to berth her by the airport but that a deal should be struck to give the city part of the enormous tax revenue that Tinicum township had been planning on receiving.

Meanwhile, as the *Queen Elizabeth* sailed back and forth across the Atlantic on her final voyages, it was unclear who exactly was buying her. C-B-S said that they were, as individuals. Philip Klein, on the other hand, claimed that the liner was being bought by Airport-Boatel Inc. There were even disagreements over who had raised the bank loan which had been used for the initial down payment of $600,000 made at the time of the signing of the contract. In addition, Klein claimed to be under the impression that Cunard would put up $1.9 million of the money he proposed to raise to complete the deal and develop the project. Cunard made no official comment on this but privately denied it. Stanton Miller, on the other hand, said that the rest of the money would come from a stock offering to the public.

The soon-to-be owners of the *Queen Elizabeth* were not happy and seemed resentful at having probing questions asked about just where they were going to get the money to complete the purchase of the world's largest liner and at being on the receiving end of a rather different kind of publicity from that which they had sought. Focusing on the problem regarding the highway, they let it be known that in their opinion the city was not geared up to their ambitious project and they were looking elsewhere for a permanent home for the ship.

They turned their attention to Florida and made suitable overtures to the officials at Port Everglades. They had, in fact, looked several months earlier at the possibility of locating the *Queen Elizabeth* in Florida instead of the Delaware River. At the time, city officials in both Fort Lauderdale and Hollywood, in Broward County, had been very receptive to the idea. Mayor-Commissioner Edmund Burry had envisaged the liner retaining her aura of a great Cunarder and had been keen that her very British atmosphere should remain intact and not be degraded in any manner. Although Florida Governor, Claude Kirk, was also in favour of having the ship as a permanent attraction in the state, the idea was not met with total approval and as a result it generated some degree of controversy. As with the proposed site at Philadelphia, the arguments centred upon who was to pay for the essential shore-side services which the ship would need: road access, water supply, sewage disposal, police and fire services.

Even so, the idea that the *Queen Elizabeth* might be able to do for Port Everglades what the *Queen Mary* had done for Long Beach was too great an opportunity to let slip through their fingers and the two cities remained enthusiastic. Long Beach had, after all, paid Cunard $3,444,000 for the *Queen Mary* and

had got off to a good start in recouping their investment even before they had begun to remodel her to incorporate tourist-oriented attractions. Nevertheless, the controversy continued to such a degree that C-B-S went as far as to threaten, yet again, to take 'their ship' elsewhere if the agreements could not be finalised at Port Everglades. Cunard were unhappy at the messy way in which things were developing and matters reached such a pitch that they announced that instead of going ahead with the sale to Messrs. Miller and Williard they would sell the *Queen Elizabeth* for scrap if things could not be satisfactorily finalised regarding her future in Florida.

On the 16th August 1968 the Miller brothers and Williard and the Port Everglades management signed an agreement regarding the positioning of the *Queen Elizabeth* in the port as a static attraction. Larry Corcoran, the Chairman of the port authority, was very optimistic about the project and stated: "I think this is a historic event for Port Everglades and the benefit to Broward County will be stupendous". But, in fact, it seemed to be a repeat of the Delaware River project, with too much attention being paid to the idea of having the largest ship in the world in the port and not enough to the realities surrounding it. This was reflected in the statement by the Vice-President of the Greater Fort Lauderdale Chamber of Commerce, Sydney Banks, when in support of Corcoran's statement he said: "It's good for the community - I'm happy it's going to be down here rather than somewhere else".

It was against this backdrop of uncertainty regarding her future that the *Queen Elizabeth* operated her final cruises and Atlantic sailings – thus it was little wonder that Commodore Marr was unconvinced about her future success.

As the summer waned it became clear that the Miller brothers and Williard were unable to raise the balance of the agreed purchase price of the liner. Remarkably, they turned to Cunard for help. What was even more remarkable was the fact that Cunard were willing to oblige, rather than wind up as the creditor of this rather large debt. The fact was simple, they wished to dispose of the *Queen Elizabeth* with as much good grace as was possible and they wanted to see her employed in a (static) role that would reflect well upon them as well as upon the old liner herself. On the 23rd October, the day that the *Queen Elizabeth* departed Southampton on her final voyage to New York, they announced their intention to step in and rescue the situation by more or less taking over the new venture themselves. It was either that or being stuck with the ship and having to set about eliciting bids for her all over again. Sir Basil Smallpiece had agreed that the Cunard Steam Ship Company would put $1 million into a new company called The Elizabeth (Cunard) Corporation, and this would give them an 85 percent share, with the Millers and Williard holding the remaining 15 percent. As it appeared that Long Beach were going to make the *Queen Mary* into a huge and successful attraction, Cunard hoped that their continuing involvement with the *Queen Elizabeth* would likewise bring them substantial dividends in the years to come. The arrangement was that the Millers and Williard would lease the ship for $2 million a year and that they would have the option of taking her over completely after ten years.

Sir Basil Smallpiece told the press that the new agreement would benefit Cunard considerably once the project was underway. He was confident that it would be capable of generating its own finance and he added that the new contract would enable Cunard to retain control of the policy and development of the Elizabeth Corporation for as long as they wished.

It was also announced that the terms of the sale called for the ship to be referred to and advertised as *The Elizabeth*. Sir Basil explained that a formal renaming would not be required but that in deference to the Queen Mother, and to avoid confusion with the new liner *Queen Elizabeth 2*, it was best for all parties involved if the name of the liner was shortened in this way. Meanwhile, when in mid-Atlantic Commodore Marr told a gathering of four hundred crew members that the company would be retaining an active interest in the *Queen Elizabeth*'s future after she was withdrawn from service. The announcement was met with considerable enthusiasm. However, while it seemed that at last the *Queen Elizabeth*'s future had been secured in a safe haven, all the uncertainties that had lead up to the new arrangement contributed to a somewhat unsettling and distinctly shabby atmosphere.

While the departure of the *Queen Elizabeth* from Southampton, on the 29th November 1968, brought to a close a significant chapter in ocean liner history, it was a closure that happened quietly and without the pomp and circumstance that perhaps the *Queen Elizabeth* deserved after such an illustrious career. In effect her transatlantic career ended in much in the same way as it had begun, very quietly and witnessed by relatively few. At the end of her cruise to the Canary Islands and Gibraltar she had been berthed at Berth 107 in the New Docks and facing upstream. In the pre-dawn darkness of that cold November morning she was made ready for the voyage across the Atlantic to Florida. No flags dressed her, though there was the Southampton Albion Band on the dockside playing appropriate laments. A crowd of about 500 people had gathered to see her off. Six tugs, *Ventnor, Romsey, Chale, North Isle, Calshot* and *Thorness* had been detailed to attend to the *Queen Elizabeth* for that final time. However, the *Thorness* was delayed by the late arrival of another ship so it was only the five that responded to the pilot's radio instructions to 'Take her off'. They did so but it required considerable effort. "She's reluctant to come off" said the pilot watching from the bridge wing at the straining tugs. Echoing the pilot, one of the tug skippers was heard to say "She doesn't want to go".

Given that she was making the voyage with a reduced number of seamen on board the mooring lines had been slipped a little sooner than had been planned. As a result, Commodore Marr's wife and daughter, along with several officials, had to be landed by one of the tugs. Because she had been berthed facing 'the wrong way' the tugs had not only to move her away from the dockside but also to turn her 180 degrees so that she was facing down Southampton Water. Even though the *Queen Elizabeth* was not dressed with all her flags, each one of the five tugs and all the other ships in Southampton were. It was a dull grey morning with daylight seemingly reluctant to appear and in the gloom it was just discernable that the jibs of the dockside cranes were being dipped in salute as the liner slowly made her way out of the harbour. The other ships in the port sounded their sirens as she passed and the tugs as they began to leave her all gave three long blasts on their whistles. As the *Queen Elizabeth* was about to answer them with her booming siren an electrical fault developed with her whistle control gear and she left Southampton in silence. A little group of small boats accompanied her as she disappeared, ghost-like, into the November mist.

Commodore Marr was unhappy about the almost furtive way in which the *Queen Elizabeth* made her final departure from Southampton, comparing it to the more effusive farewells that she had been given in New York and in Gibraltar. He described it as being "… a British understatement with a vengeance, as though the British world of ships and shiplovers looked the other way until she had gone." Mrs. Marr shared his disappointment, referring to the quiet departure as 'a disgrace'. They were opinions that were also shared by many who recalled the almost carnival-like atmosphere when the *Queen Mary* departed the port on her voyage to Long Beach.

However, it has to be remembered that the *Queen Mary* was full of happy passengers off on what really was a voyage of a life time! Likewise, when the *Queen Elizabeth* had sailed for the final time from New York, she was full of passengers and the dock had its usual crowd of well-wishers. Also, when she sailed from Gibraltar it was the middle of a sunny day and again her decks were lined with happy, albeit nostalgic, cruise passengers. Her final departure (without passengers) from Southampton was on a cold late November in the gloom of pre-dawn. Why Cunard planned it so we cannot say but that 500 hardy souls braved the cold and the gloom was in itself remarkable. Perhaps Cunard had wanted to draw people's attention away from the past and look to the future. As the now redundant *Queen Elizabeth* steamed away from Southampton her successor, the sleekly-styled *Queen Elizabeth 2*, was undergoing the first of her trials voyages off the Isle of Arran. As the *Queen Elizabeth* made her way down The Solent and past Spithead she was cheered by the ship's company of HMS *Hampshire* and later that evening as she steamed down the English Channel she passed the inward bound *Carmania* and messages of farewell were passed between the former fleet mates.

As darkness fell and the *Queen Elizabeth* headed out into the Atlantic she was once again on her own – only this time she was on her own as never before.

Chapter 10

DOOMED BUT DIGNIFIED

It was a largely uneventful voyage, except for the fact that the ship's stores ran out of beer. Somehow, this rather set the tone for what was to come.

On Saturday the 7th December 1968, the *Queen Elizabeth* arrived off Boca Raton and was soon surrounded by hundreds of pleasure craft, with four helicopters hovering above. A USAF fighter plane roared overhead, tipping its wings in salute, and a pair of more graceful bi-planes made their sedate way towing banners proclaiming 'Welcome'. While Fort Lauderdale was more than pleased that the *Queen Elizabeth* would find her final home in its Port Everglades dock area, it was not ready for her. The dredging of the port had not been completed. As a result, Commodore Marr was requested to cruise the ship slowly along the Florida coast in a 'flag-waving' exercise. The stately progression, a little over a mile offshore, down as far as Key Biscayne, attracted thousands of sightseers. That night, floodlit from stem to stern, the *Queen Elizabeth* looked every bit the ocean liner of everyone's dreams. Early the following morning, assisted by six tugs, she steamed slowly into Port Everglades harbour. It was a tricky operation turning and manoeuvring her but by 11.15 am she was alongside a somewhat barren berth and Commodore Marr rang 'Finished with Engines' on the bridge telegraph to the Engine Room for what he thought was the final time.

It took almost ten weeks to turn the *Queen Elizabeth*, the former pride of the North Atlantic, into *The Elizabeth*, billed as being 'Queen of the Seas - one of America's foremost visitor attractions'. She was alongside berths 24 and 25 and the plan was for her to remain there for six months during which time a deeper channel would be dredged in the Intracoastal Waterway that would then allow *The Elizabeth* to be towed, stern first, one mile south to her permanent location. It seemed that there was always someone anxious to make 'a fast buck' where *The Elizabeth* was concerned. Just a month before she was due to be opened to the public, the General Manager of the Port Authority of Port Everglades was indicted by a Grand Jury for soliciting bribes in connection with The Elizabeth Project and for involvement in a cleverly-crafted and somewhat convoluted 50-year parking lot contract for the ship. This would have given him full control over this lucrative concession. He quickly resigned from his position at the Port and not long afterwards was murdered under rather curious circumstances. The case was never solved but there was more than just a hint of Mafia involvement.

The Elizabeth was opened to the public on the 14th February 1969. The visitors entered the ship on Restaurant Deck and the prescribed tour took them first up to Sun Deck, just aft of the forward funnel, from where a short walk took them into the Bridge. They then went down on the starboard side, to Boat Deck and then to Promenade Deck and the Observation Bar. They went down again to the former Tourist Class Winter Garden and then out onto the fore deck for a view of the impressive Bridge front and the towering funnels. Returning inside, the visitors were guided to the former First Class Main Lounge, the Midships Bar and the First Class Smoking Room. In the cinema a film about the *Queen Elizabeth*'s career was shown before visitors continued out onto the Lido Deck and then down to the Caribbean Room (formerly the Cabin Class Smoking Room). This was followed by the opportunity to see several former First Class suites and then they went down to the First Class restaurant, through the vast galley and into the Cabin Class restaurant, which had been turned into a shopping area selling a whole variety of *Queen Elizabeth*-oriented souvenirs. At various points throughout the tour there were recordings telling one about the room or area that one was looking at and there were photo murals of aspects of the ship's career both in peace and during the war.

A leaflet issued to guide the visitors around the ship summarised her career with two brief paragraphs: '*The Elizabeth* in War' and '*The Elizabeth* in Peace'. A third paragraph, '*The Elizabeth* in Retirement' stated: "Now *The Elizabeth* lies moored in the beauty of Florida's tropical sunshine in Port Everglades, Florida. Here she awaits the thousands of visitors who will once again bring her decks alive. Some will come and stand here in favorite haunts of happy voyages once made, others will lean against her rails and see the icy flume of the North Atlantic and search again for the enemy. Then there are those who only knew her by reputation and pictures and they will stand in wonderment at her majestic size and power. Here *The Elizabeth* will be accorded the loving care of skilled custodians who will preserve and protect the 'Queen of the Seas' for generations yet unborn to know."

When the exciting plans for what was to become *The Elizabeth*'s new home were revealed to the public, they

◁   As always, the *Queen Elizabeth* attracts attention. She is approaching Port Everglades with an accompanying flotilla of small craft.

The huge liner being carefully manoeuvred into the cut leading into Port Everglades harbour.   Hopes for her success are high.

proved to bear a strong resemblance to the development that was being planned near to the *Queen Mary* over in Long Beach, California. *The Elizabeth* would be moored alongside a 209-acre site just south of Port Everglades. The area would include what was referred to as an 'international village', a beach club, tennis courts, a golf course and six terminal buildings. Connecting all of these facilities would be a monorail. Meanwhile, plans for *The Elizabeth* herself revealed that she would have 700 'hotel rooms', two theatres, seven restaurants and bars and a 5,000-person convention facility. It was estimated that *The Elizabeth* would attract in excess of 3,000,000 visitors a year and generate $50,000,000 in annual revenue.

For the time being, however, she was operated in a much more modest way and, indeed, attracted large numbers of visitors, all anxious to see the most famous ocean liner in the world. She was in fact clearly visible to the passengers aboard other liners and cruise ships which regularly called at Port Everglades. On more than one occasion she was in the company of her former fleetmates *Carmania* and *Franconia* when they called there during Caribbean cruises. However, the public would ultimately demand more than just the chance to tour a retired liner, no matter how famous. Words of warning were given to the Elizabeth Corporation by the former United States Navy Admiral John J. Fee, a

director of the *Queen Mary* Project. "You people in Florida will need a lot of planning. It isn't enough just to buy a big ship and put a snack bar and calypso band on board. You have to think in terms of a whole cultural and recreational complex. You are almost creating an entire city when you get involved in something like this." In fact, the whole *Queen Mary* project would spiral grossly over budget and lag way behind schedule, ultimately coming under the scrutiny of a California State Congressional investigation.

Luckily for the Elizabeth Project, the Port Everglades Authority expressed their gratitude at having *The Elizabeth* in their port by not charging any docking fees – berths 24 and 25 were a gift. Given that the liner was burning up to 40 tons of bunker-C every day just to remain self sufficient, not having also to pay docking fees was most welcome. The simple fact was that despite a regular flow of visitors to the liner the Elizabeth Corporation was facing a financial crisis. Commodore Marr and 118 Cunard crewmen had been retained on board in order to supply power and ensure the safety of the ship. Their wages, coupled with *The Elizabeth*'s thirst for bunker-C, far outweighed the revenue that was earned from the visitors and the on board concessions. A report from a New York firm of management consultants showed Cunard that the Elizabeth Corporation project was not likely to be as attractive as they had first thought. It was costing approximately £1,250.00 ($3,000) per day just to keep *The Elizabeth* at Port Everglades. A conservative estimate put the total loss suffered since the ship arrived in Florida in December at $500,000. The visitors to her had initially been spending about $35,000 to see her but those earnings were beginning to fall. To make matters worse for Cunard, their new Atlantic liner *Queen Elizabeth 2* had encountered various mechanical and technical problems during her sea trials and these were of such a serious nature that her first six voyages had to be cancelled. This left the company desperately short of working capital, let alone enough to provide the additional funds to keep the Elizabeth Corporation functioning. Yet again disaster loomed over the former *Queen Elizabeth* and seemed to be threatening to engulf Cunard as well if they did not get rid of their former flagship - and very quickly.

For what had seemed like all the right reasons, Sir Basil Smallpiece had allowed the company to take on the Elizabeth Project. At the time to ensure a dignified retirement for the *Queen Elizabeth* seemed appropriate: it showed that Cunard felt they had a certain responsibility. While retiring the liner, they were not going to allow her to be downgraded to some tawdry floating sideshow. She would, after all, be forever associated with Cunard and therefore any less-than-dignified use of the ship would have reflected upon them. However, this was business and the harsh reality was that the Elizabeth Corporation and the former *Queen Elizabeth* herself were luxuries that Cunard quite clearly could not afford. There was no choice: the company had to be rid of the *Queen Elizabeth* once and for all.

Barely three months after she had been opened to the public, Cunard let it be known that the liner was once again available for sale - and that meant available to be broken up if no firm offers were received by the 11th June. Once again, the Anglo-Australian group headed by Sir Howard Hickman, which had expressed interest before, attempted to bid for the liner, hoping to revive their plan to operate her both on the emigrant service between Britain and Australia and on Australian-based cruises in direct competition to P&O. Cunard rejected their request to make a survey on the ship before putting in a firm bid. While a survey was normal commercial practice when buying second-hand ships, Cunard rejected the request on the grounds that similar options would have to be granted to at least a dozen other interested parties who, they stated, had expressed interest in buying the ship. The Hickman group had indicated a willingness to invest £5 million to convert her. Their plan was to register her in Liverpool and to provide jobs for a crew of 1,100 British officers and men with the full co-operation of many of Cunard's own technical staff. The group claimed that, although the initial cost of bringing the ship up to the new international safety standards would be high, she could make a direct £4 million a year contribution to Britain's balance of payments.

COME ABOARD

the

ELIZABETH

QUEEN OF THE SEAS

The largest ocean liner the world has ever seen

The **ELIZABETH** *Port Everglades, Flori...*
TOUR TICKE
admit one adult — est. price 2.40 state tax .10 **$2.5(**
055960

ELIZABETH - *Queen of the Seas*

△ A postcard published while the ship lay in Port Everglades illustrates confusion over her exact name and also shows the windows over the Observation Lounge being rid of the paint which had covered them for some years.

While British passenger ship operators were traditionally unwilling to sell to others who might provide direct competition using Greek or other relatively low-cost crews, this was not an accusation that could be levelled against the Hickman group. It was suggested that by selling *The Elizabeth* for scrap instead of letting her go to Hickman, Cunard could be shutting out a newcomer who could give Britain a larger stake in the mass Australian cruise market which, despite P&O's efforts, was being increasingly eaten into by foreign shipowners. This was seen as being potentially embarrassing not only to Cunard but also to other British passenger lines at a time when the shipping industry was being examined by a Government Committee of Inquiry, which was due to report by the end of the year. The shipping industry was supposedly trying to show that it was changing, with efficient management and new attitudes. However, it seemed that the old restrictive practices of keeping out potential competition still prevailed.

Cunard refused an option to the Hickman group. Cunard was associated with P&O and other operators in the container consortium which was then carrying cargo between Britain and Australia and it was likely that Sir Howard Hickman and his associates were shut out from bidding for fear of pressure from Cunard's cargo business colleagues. There

was, though, speculation at the time that the proposal by Sir Howard's group was simply not viable. With such a large British crew and under British registry, the *Queen Elizabeth* would never be able to operate at a profit.

There were, however, three people who were convinced that they could make her a profitable proposition once again – and they were none other than Robert and Stanton Miller and Charles Williard. They had acquired new financial backing from the Utilities Leasing Corporation of Haverford, Pennsylvania. Now under the name The Queen Limited, they offered $8,640,000 for the ship and they were ready with an initial payment of $2,000,000. With the benefit of hindsight one can see that such was Cunard's desire to be rid of what they now regarded as being nothing more than an albatross around their necks, they signed the instruments of sale, apparently without hesitation, to the Millers and Williard on 19th July 1969. At last, the ship was finally theirs and all connections between Cunard and their former flagship were severed.

With Cunard no longer having any interest or involvement in *The Elizabeth*, Commodore Marr and the crewmen who had been under his command while the liner was in Port Everglades returned to Britain on the 4th August on a specially chartered plane. In place of the Cunard crew there was now a small team of American steam engineering staff. They were there to maintain the machinery and to ensure that sufficient power was generated to keep *The Elizabeth* fully illuminated.

The Queen Limited began to re-work the original plans of the now defunct Elizabeth Corporation. The ship would still be berthed at the location that had been designated for her, but now she would provide 1,000 hotel rooms, seven restaurants, eleven bars, an outdoor concert arena, a dinner theatre, maritime museum, international bazaar, cinema, shops and - in what had been her two forward cargo holds – a discotheque. The design of her berth was also changed: she would be land-locked on her portside as well as around her bow and stern. The Millers and Williard had revived their old idea of a yacht marina and *The Elizabeth* was to be the centre of it, with a nearby yacht club, condominium complex and a 500-berth marina all situated in a cruise ship turning basin that was to be built just south of berths 24 and 25 where the liner was currently docked. Ever optimistic, the Millers and Williard expected *The Elizabeth* to be alongside her new berth in June 1970.

In August 1969, just weeks after The Queen Limited had taken ownership, several problems arose. Four fires were discovered aboard the ship. It turned out that each been set intentionally by a security guard who wanted the attention and credit for having found them. While the fires were minor, they heightened concerns over whether or not this huge liner had a properly trained crew in attendance. Parallels were drawn between *The Elizabeth* and the *Normandie* which had burned in New York harbour in 1942. Some time later, the *Queen Elizabeth* was the subject of a bomb threat by Cuban exiles. While there was, in fact, no bomb, this again heightened the awareness of *The Elizabeth*'s vulnerability. Then there were rumours about the Millers and Williard and the questionable company they were alleged to keep. Again their connections with Jimmy Hoffa and the Teamsters' Union were being openly talked about and fears were expressed in some quarters that before too long *The Elizabeth* would become a casino run under the watchful eyes of Mafia and Teamster bosses.

On the 31st October, yet another fire broke out but it was extinguished without the need to call in the local fire brigade. Several days later, the Port Everglades Fire Chief, John Gerkin, went on board the ship. There were 1,800 visitors also on board at the time. Gerkin asked a security guard about the emergency procedures and evacuation routes. The guard apparently had no idea at all what he was supposed to do in an emergency or where he was supposed to direct visitors. As a result, Fire Chief Gerkin served papers to The Queen Limited, closing *The Elizabeth* to the public as an extreme fire hazard. She was not to be opened again until stricter safety standards had been met. Even then, visitors could only be allowed on board in controlled numbers for guided tours rather than being left

to wander at will. Although the Project Superintendent of The Queen Limited was convinced that *The Elizabeth* fully complied with all the latest fire and safety regulations for Broward County, he had no choice but to do as the Fire Chief demanded. (For whatever reason, Fire Chief Gerkin lost his job shortly after this.) The temporary closure cost The Queen Limited $10,000 in lost visitor revenues and a huge Thanksgiving Day gala party had to be cancelled at short notice, along with several other events. With the new safety standards in place *The Elizabeth* reopened.

It had been planned that in January 1970 The Queen Limited would become a public corporation by offering $13,750,000 of stock. The timing was completely wrong: the national economy was weak and, to make things worse, the New York Stock Exchange Commission were planning a full investigation into The Queen Limited. The sale of stock was cancelled and the company never went public.

In May 1970 there were rumours circulating that *The Elizabeth* would be the location of a high-profile boxing match between Muhammad Ali and Joe Frazier. But as this rumour circulated The Queen Limited filed for Chapter XI bankruptcy in the Philadelphia Federal District Court. The assets of the company were listed as $11,400,000 and debts were shown to be over $12,000,000. The ship, however, remained open for business and was still bringing in an estimated $25,000 each month. It just seemed that she could not makes ends meet – the sudden closure and cancellation of several highly lucrative events had not helped matters either. Edward Moldt, Project Superintendent of The Queen Limited was quoted as saying: "When the stock market went to hell so did our plans for the *Queen Elizabeth*".

Then a 70-mph hurricane hit Florida on the 25th May. *The Elizabeth* snapped her mooring lines, dock pilings bent and her gangways dropped as she broke free. It was as if the old liner had had enough of all these indignities and was making a bid for freedom! As it was, she just drifted one hundred feet out into the Intracoastal Waterway. The crews of nearby naval vessels were able to get lines aboard her and, once she was back alongside, her empty fuel tanks and forward cargo hold were flooded to keep her evenly on the harbour bottom and ensure that she was unable move. It really was the worst of times for the once regal *Queen Elizabeth*.

On the 9th September she was yet again made available for sale. The notice of her sale proclaimed that the liner would be offered 'free and clear of liens and encumbrances' and the sale catalogue listed forty lots that would come under auctioneer's hammer. The lots included furniture from passenger and crew areas, paintings, a tapestry, some navigational equipment as well as various other fittings. She was, however, also offered 'as is' – always assuming that there was still anyone willing to bid for the entire liner. The sale was to be held at the Galt Ocean Mile Hotel at Fort

Two further postcards from Port Everglades. The lower one shows the *Queen Elizabeth* in the company of the still-active *Santa Maria*, *Carmania*, *Federico C.*, *Ariadne*, *Franconia* and *Europa*.

Lauderdale during the 9th and 10th September. There were 204 creditors holding liens against The Queen Limited, with the Cunard Line being at the top of the list. For twenty-one months, apart from her momentary bid for freedom, *The Elizabeth* had been inactive in the Florida sunshine. She had endured fires, albeit small ones and a level of maintenance that was not as Cunard had once lavished upon her; and now she sat at her berth, partially scuttled. It was therefore hardly surprising when a Genoa-based shipbreaker made an offer of $2,400,000 for her.

This was topped by one from Isidore Ostroff who placed a bid for $3,200,000. He was acting as agent for an undisclosed shipping firm. There were no other bids and it was finally announced that Mr. Ostroff had been acting for the Island Navigation Corporation Ltd., part of the vast shipping empire of the Hong Kong-based magnate C. Y. Tung whose ships sailed under the name Orient Overseas Line. Mr. Tung's companies operated about 4 million tons of cargo and passenger ships trading all over the world and owned a repair and maintenance yard at Lai Chi Kok.

▽ A carefully posed picture, copies of which could be bought on board the *Queen Elizabeth* during her time at Port Everglades.

164

R.M.S. QUEEN ELIZABETH

Chapter 11

RE-BIRTH & DEATH

The Elizabeth was closed to the public on the 17th September. Commodore William Hsuan, along with 200 Chinese seamen, had been flown from Hong Kong to make her ready for the long voyage to her new home. It was an enormous task, rather more than the 200 men could cope with. Poor management coupled with almost two years of inactivity had rapidly taken their toll on the old liner, so that in December a further 100 men had to be flown to Florida to help make her ready to take to the sea once again. Commodore Hsuan summed the situation up stating: "This ship's been laid up for two years, neglected and rotting". It was perhaps rather an understatement and he may have wondered whether the initial plan to tow the *Queen Elizabeth* from Florida to Singapore might not have been simpler. The idea had been to dry dock her there before she steamed under her own power up to Hong Kong.

C. Y. Tung was a shipowner who loved ships and his Orient Overseas Line included tankers, bulk carriers and an interesting assortment of cargo/passenger liners. In 1965 he had acquired the American Export Line's 9,600 gt. passenger/cargo liners *Excalibur* and *Exeter*, which he had renamed *Oriental Jade* and *Oriental Pearl*. With their public rooms enhanced by the addition of oriental-themed decorative objects, these two liners became quite successful in the trans-Pacific trade. In 1968 he had acquired the Holland America Line cargo/passenger liner, *Diemerdyk* and in 1970 he bought her sister vessel, *Dinteldyk*. At just under 12,000 gt., these elegantly styled vessels had accommodation for 60 passengers in accommodation equivalent to First Class. Holland America had employed them on the Hamburg to Vancouver service. Also in 1968, Mr. Tung had bought the somewhat larger former New Zealand Line *Rangitane*. She had briefly been sailing for the Federal Steam Navigation Company but in May 1968 they had sold her to Greek operators who had renamed her *Jan*. Under their flag, she had made just one voyage, to Taiwan. On arrival there she was sold to be broken up. However, C. Y. Tung stepped in and acquired her for his fleet. Then in August 1969 *Rangitane's* sister vessel, the 21,809 gt. *Rangitoto* was bought by the Oriental South American Lines Inc., also part of the Tung empire. The *Rangitoto* was renamed *Oriental Carnaval* (note: not *Carnival*) and the *Rangitane* became *Oriental Esmeralda*. They were both now employed on a Round-the-World service, whereas, sailing from San Diego, the former

Holland America sisters were used in Pacific services. While the operation of cargo/passenger liners such as these was regarded by many shipping companies as uneconomic, particularly as the age of containerisation was beginning, C. Y. Tung was sure that he could continue to use these comparatively young vessels viably (*Dinteldyk* having only entered service in 1957) to ports that were not yet moving towards containerised cargoes. Tung would, in fact, go on to add other seemingly redundant liners to his fleet in the 1970s. However, the former *Queen Elizabeth* was to be the veritable Queen of the whole Orient Overseas Line fleet.

Inevitably, for a liner the size of the *Queen Elizabeth*, his plans were ambitious and he embarked upon them on the grandest possible scale. It was announced that, once arrived in Hong Kong, she would be given a $5 million refit that would transform the former Atlantic liner into a cruise ship with the capabilities to sail around the world. This, however, was to be only part of her rôle, for while her First Class accommodation was to be refurbished and brought up-to-date for 1,428 cruise passengers (this was to be reduced to about 800 when operating in the dual rôle of passenger liner and shipboard university), her Cabin Class and Tourist Class accommodation would be rebuilt to suit the needs of 1,800 college students and 80 faculty members. C. Y. Tung had announced that the actual registered owners of ship would be the Seawise Foundation Ltd., a Bahamas registered company. This Foundation was initially to finance the 'floating university' aspect of the ship but Tung hoped to persuade the United Nations to eventually take over permanent sponsorship. The idea of a floating university had first been suggested in a speech by the Secretary-General of the United Nations, the underlying purpose being to provide an environment in which students of many races could mingle in conditions which, it was hoped, would be especially conducive to the promotion of mutual dependence and co-operation. Tung approached Seton Hall's Institute for Eastern Studies in New Jersey to discuss a possible affiliation with the floating university. He also held talks with other schools and ultimately it was agreed that the educational operation of the ship would be run by Chapman World Campus Afloat. Chapman College, dating back to 1861, is one of California's oldest institutions of higher learning. Since 1965 the college had conducted two shipboard study semesters a year, each with

◁ Now called *Seawise University* following her purchase by one of C. Y. Tung's companies, the great ship lies at Port Everglades being prepared for the long voyage to Hong Kong.

up to 500 pupils studying aboard a chartered ship and in the various ports included in its itinerary. World Campus Afloat was therefore a unique aspect of the college's International Studies Program.

At last, it seemed as though there was a sound economic and realistic plan for the future use of the *Queen Elizabeth*. Orient Overseas Line was a large and successful shipping company, while the Chapman College was well respected and experienced in operating their semesters at sea programme. Once it had become known that the *Queen Elizabeth* would sail on cruises with nearly 2,000 students on board she was generally referred to within the Tung empire as "C. Y's University" and it appears that this was how her new name *Seawise University* evolved.

On the 4th August 1969 Commodore Geoffrey Marr and the 118 other Cunard employees had left the former *Queen Elizabeth* for what they had imagined was the final time. However, in November 1970 Chief Engineer Edward Philip and sixteen former Cunard crew members arrived back in Florida and Commodore Marr joined them on the 18th November. Orient Overseas Line had enticed Commodore Marr and Chief Engineer Philip out of retirement and hired them as advisors for the liner's return to sea. While the former Cunard hands had been more than willing to rejoin their old command in order to prepare her for sea once again, they were appalled by the mess that they found on board. One of several difficult problems was the disposal of 4,000 tons of oil-contaminated water.

It took five months and over $800,000 of engine parts manufactured in Britain, to get the *Seawise University* to a condition where it was felt that she was ready once again to put to sea and to make the voyage to Hong Kong. The inactivity and neglect of what was now 26 months had taken a severe toll and deterioration had quickly set into the mechanical parts of the ship that had not being regularly used. A great number of her fragile boiler tubes had corroded and only by replacing 600 of them was it possible to get six of her twelve boilers operational. The general feeling among the engineers was that it would still be better to tow the liner rather than attempt the voyage under her own, rather compromised power. Quite apart from her boilers, there was a great deal more that needed either to be repaired, tested or replaced. The radio, radar and other navigational aids had to be overhauled and the classification societies had to undertake the necessary tests before the ship would be considered in a condition to be allowed to go to sea. Classification and Safety Certificates were issued to enable her to undertake the single voyage to Hong Kong as a cargo ship. Berthed for over two years in still near-tropical waters there was a considerable accumulation of marine growth on her hull, which had to be cleaned off.

With so much work to be done, especially re-tubing the boilers, it was inevitable that the originally scheduled departure from Port Everglades in early December 1970 would not be met. It was not in fact until the 31st December that the first two repaired boilers were fired up and it was not until the 3rd February 1971 that engine trials were carried out. The old ship was once again trembling with life and now Commodores Hsuan and Marr and their Chief Engineers Cheng and Philip could decide on a date for sailing. There had been several days of gales and it was not until Wednesday the 10th February that a lull in the stormy weather coincided with the appropriate tides. Looking back to the time when he had brought the *Queen Elizabeth* into Port Everglades harbor, Commodore Marr expressed his concerns to the press over taking her out to sea now, as *Seawise University*, under-powered and with an inexperienced crew of just 300 Chinese (plus the 16 Britons). His comments caused worry to her insurers and as a result an increase in her insurance premiums. Neither Commodore Marr's comments nor the increased premiums pleased C. Y. Tung. As if to reinforce Commodore Marr's disquiet, shortly before the final mooring ropes were let go, a message was received on the bridge informing the officers that one of the six operational boilers had developed leaks in its tubes during the night and as a result could not be used.

Seawise University, poised to become the pride of the Hong Kong merchant fleet but flying the flag of the Bahamas, eased her way slowly away from her berth, out of Port Everglades harbour and once again towards the Atlantic Ocean - and blew out another boiler in the process! Now with just four boilers operational, she did not have sufficient power for her to manoeuvre but fortunately by this time she was facing the harbour entrance and she had momentum and the aid of tugs to get her clear. She was at last at sea once more, but only just, and was trailing a considerable pall of black smoke behind her.

Intended to run at up to 32 knots on her twelve boilers, she was barely able to make headway at 8½ knots with the steam produced by her few operational boilers. Even so, it seemed as though the *Seawise University* was once again alive and, albeit slowly, was heading towards a new career. Commodore Marr commented that: "There's a feeling one gets when one walks this ship these days, that she's trying to get born again."

It was, however, a painful re-birth. On the day following her departure from Port Everglades *Seawise University* suffered a massive loss of feed water in number 4 boiler room. While this was corrected just two days later, again in number 4 boiler room a fire broke out at 9 am. It took an hour before it could be brought under control and then once it had been, it was discovered that one of the boilers was seriously damaged along with the electrical cables in that area. *Seawise University* was now without power and drifting. A call was put out for a towing tug to come to her aid and meanwhile lights were rigged so that, come the night, other nearby vessels would be aware that she was helpless. At midnight on Sunday the cruise ship *Starward* swept a searchlight across the drifting liner, giving her passengers a remarkable show, and then offered assistance. Commodore Hsuan declined and waited for the tug.

It was not until Tuesday the 17th that the tug, *Rescue*, arrived. At first the intention had been to tow the *Seawise University* to Kingston, Jamaica but the winds and tides made this impracticable and they also ruled out the alternative of towing her to Curacao. The third choice was luckier, the island of Aruba. Although only a small island it has extensive oil industry installations and facilities for handling tankers and was therefore able to deal with the huge liner. However, the *Seawise University* was more than just the tug *Rescue* could cope with on its own so another tug had to be called. Fortunately, the salvage tug *Jacob Van Heemskerck* could be diverted from her voyage to the United States in order to assist. Even with the aid of this powerful salvage tug it was still a slow and tedious tow, making little more than three or four knots. It was not until the 24th February that they arrived off Aruba. Even then the problems for *Seawise University* were far from over. After the towing tugs had left, a wind blew up and *Seawise University* dragged her anchor and drifted out into deep water again with her trailing anchor embedded into a sandbank. It seemed as though help was at hand with the arrival of another tug, the Aruba-based *Schelde*. Having pulled the helpless liner so that her anchor was free of the sandbank the tug master then announced that his vessel had engine problems and left the *Seawise University*, once again adrift. However, all was not quite as it seemed for there was in fact no problem with *Schelde*'s engines. Her master's actions were a ruse to enable him to return to the liner and lay claim to salvage. After some enquiries were made by Tung's representatives, the *Schelde* and another tug, *Los Cocos*, towed *Seawise University* to another safe haven, six miles from Oranjestad and it was here that the liner was at last securely anchored.

A survey revealed that strong leaks had developed in four of the five operative boilers. The one remaining boiler was used solely for driving auxiliary machinery and was not capable of supplying the main engines. The repairs would include plugging damaged boiler screen tubes and renewing some sixty tubes in two boilers. Additional defective screen tubes were also discovered in two more boilers. In the end, the total number of tubes to be replaced had risen to 294. More men, more tubes and other essential equipment for the repairs were flown out to Aruba to be taken aboard the ship. It was going to be a lengthy stay with completion of the repairs expected by mid-April: so Commodore Marr and Chief Engineer Philip took advantage of this and returned to England for a well-earned break. During their absence C. Y. Tung arrived in Aruba to inspect his troublesome acquisition. One of his instructions was that the boiler and engine rooms were to be thoroughly cleaned and painted. So, by the time that Marr and Philip returned they found that she was beginning to look more like the ship they remembered.

▽ Because of uncertainty over the state of her boilers and engines, the *Seawise University* took a port-hopping route to Hong Kong. She is here seen approaching Rio de Janeiro.

While the cleaning and painting might well have helped raise the morale of the crew, there were further problems to contend with. A cracked steam drum delayed the hydraulic tests of the boilers until the end of April and it was not until the 8th May that *Seawise University* was again ready to take to sea. Even then it was agreed to steam her at a reduced working pressure of 360 pounds in order to lessen the load on her boilers. It had taken seventy-four days to repair her but they were indeed seventy-four days well spent as the general feeling was that at last her boilers were functioning and she was fully under her own power. She steamed the short distance to Curacao where she took on some fresh water and fuel oil and a similar stop was made at Port of Spain, Trinidad. At last, *Seawise University* was ready for the long voyage diagonally across the South Atlantic.

Her former Cunard crewmen had every confidence in her and were keen, after all the indignities she had suffered, that she would now show what she could really do. They wanted the old former Cunarder to speed across the open ocean with a bone in her teeth just as she had done when she was the pride of the North Atlantic. Commodore Hsuan was rather more cautious and continued to treat her boilers with great care. Instead of steaming directly for Cape Town he instructed a course along the coast of South America towards Rio de Janeiro and she arrived there, unannounced, as dawn was breaking on the 30th May. It was two weeks later that *Seawise University* made her stately arrival at Cape Town and received a very warm welcome. She then encountered heavy swells as she steamed at a very sedate pace across the Indian Ocean, her Master still unwilling to push the liner much beyond 11 knots. So it was not until the 7th July that she arrived in Singapore to a welcome by RAF aircraft flying above her in salute; but Hong Kong was to be her final destination and it was here that she was to receive the big welcome. On the 14th July, twenty-two weeks after having left Port Everglades, *Seawise University* arrived off Hong Kong and then, after all that time, she was too early and had to steam slowly around for almost a day, waiting for the right moment. Early the following morning, shabby and rust-streaked yet proud and decked with flags, *Seawise University* steamed into Hong Kong harbour accompanied by dozens of small craft, fire boats and helicopters hovering above. The Queen had arrived.

C. Y. Tung hosted a celebratory banquet on board the ship. Although the food, the waiters and even the table cloths were supplied by Hong Kong's Miramar Hotel, it was a brief moment of glory – a memory of days past and it was a flicker of hope for the days to come. This was, however, the only celebration - there was a great deal of work to be done and it began on the very next day.

Because of her arrival during the typhoon season, she was at first anchored to the north of Kau Yi Chau Island but later she was moved to the south-west corner of the western quarantine anchorage in Hong Kong harbour. It

was here that the former Cunarder was to undergo most of her transformation into C. Y. Tung's dream ship, *Seawise University*. Every day, over a thousand men were shipped out to her to play their part in her reconditioning. It was a project that has been likened to her transformation from troopship to passenger liner at the end of the war. The work entailed was three-fold with the majority of the $5 million earmarked for the conversion being devoted to the updating of her safety standards and making all the necessary repairs to the structure, the fittings, the machinery and electrical and other equipment that would restore the ship to Lloyd's highest class, +100 A1, and would entitle her to a Class 1 Passenger Certificate. Engineers installed more than 100,000 square feet of fire protection insulation for main vertical zone bulkheads and step-up deck ceilings. Four hundred automatic and manual 'fail-safe' dampers were fitted and 250 fire-screen doors were added to give increased protection to bulkheads and fire escape stairway enclosures. A new emergency electrical supply system was installed along with 150,000 metres of armoured cable. 1,500 tons of solid ballast was added to increase stability.

The second phase of the work was to make whatever alterations and additions were necessary to bring the ship into compliance with SOLAS 1948 (as modified by IMCO 1966).

▽ Having finally arrived in Hong Kong after a trouble-plagued voyage of no less than five months, the *Seawise University* almost immediately became the scene of intense activity.

Announcing

the Maiden Voyage of SEAWISE (formerly the R.M.S. Queen Elizabeth) 75-day Circle Pacific Cruise.

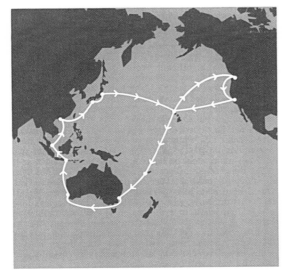

Sailing from Los Angeles on April 24, 1972. Rates from $30 a day first class.

Sailing from Vancouver, B.C. on April 18, 1972

	ARRIVAL DATE	DEPARTURE DATE
Los Angeles		April 24 PM
Honolulu	April 29 AM	May 3 AM
Suva	May 10 AM	May 12 PM
Sydney	May 16 AM	May 18 PM
Fremantle	May 23 AM	May 25 AM
Bali	May 28 noon	May 31 AM
Singapore	June 2 AM	June 5 AM
Hong Kong	June 8 AM	June 11 AM
Kobe	June 14 noon	June 16 PM
Yokohama	June 17 AM	June 20 AM
Honolulu	June 26 noon	June 29 AM
Vancouver	July 4 noon	July 6 PM
Los Angeles	July 9 AM	

Ports of call and dates subject to change without notice.

Still looking every inch a Cunarder, the *Seawise University* lies at anchor while work proceeds on her conversion into a university cruise ship.

This was a major aspect of the refitting work as the United States Coast Guard had been so insistent that she, as *Queen Elizabeth*, should comply with this. (It will be remembered that Cunard had been unhappy about the bureaucratic way in which the USCG had demanded that the work be done.) The third stage was to renovate and restore the passenger and crew accommodation and the public rooms to the standard required for the planned service. The total number of people to be carried was 2,700 in all: 900 students, 900 passengers and 900 crew. This was considerably less than the 3,653 that the ship had been able to carry when in Cunard service.

C. Y. Tung had initially thought of having the ship painted with a light grey hull and white upper works and with the funnels painted Orient Overseas Line's distinctive yellow with the red flower device. An early brochure for *Seawise University* promoting her 'maiden voyage' showed her in this livery. Indeed, although clearly shown with the name *Seawise University* on her bows, the brochure was headed 'Announcing the Maiden Voyage of *Seawise* (formerly the R.M.S. *Queen Elizabeth*) 75-day Circle Pacific Cruise'. Although she would initially be making a voyage across the Pacific from Hong Kong, the maiden voyage was being marketed as beginning from Los Angeles on the 24th April 1972, although a small note mentioned that she would in fact sail from Vancouver

on the 18th April. In reality, her maiden voyage would begin with her departure from Japan on the 28th March.

The voyage from Los Angeles would recall some of her wartime trooping voyages with calls at Honolulu, Suva and Sydney. She would then sail round to Fremantle and up to Bali, Hong Kong, Kobe, Yokohama then back to Honolulu, Vancouver and Los Angeles. Lengthy stays were planned in most of the ports: almost four days at Honolulu, two days at Suva and at Sydney, Fremantle and Bali. Three days were to be spent at Singapore, Hong Kong and Yokohama. This was to be no ordinary cruise.

The brochure stated: "For many people there was only one 'Queen.' And that was the R.M.S. *Queen Elizabeth* – the world's largest passenger liner. And what a ship to behold. 1031 feet long. 234 feet high. 82,997 gross tons. She has 700 electric clocks. 680 telephones. 30,000 lamps. And 4,000 miles of wiring. The statistics go on: 3 swimming pools. Squash courts. Three libraries. A 338-seat cinema. 11 passenger decks. There was never a ship to match her. And this is one reason why so many of you will welcome the opportunity to sail with the Queen as she sets out on a brand new career."

The brochure went on to mention the fact that it was intended that *Seawise* would become a seagoing university with part of her accommodation being set aside for this purpose – but that was to be in the future. For this maiden voyage, as the brochure so perfectly stated it – "she is a glorious passenger liner".

The problems encountered in getting the *Seawise* from Florida to Hong Kong had upset Tung's original plan of having her enter service on the 3rd September 1971. With that date in mind, the Chapman College had issued their own brochure with Fall 1971 and Spring 1972 semester cruises. The Fall cruise was to have seen *Seawise* sailing virtually all the way around the world, from Los Angeles to New York. There would have been calls at Honolulu and Pago Pago then on to New Zealand, Tasmania and Fremantle, up to Bali, Singapore and over to Ceylon, Bombay and across the Indian Ocean to Mombasa. Onward then to Cape Town and Rio, Trinidad, Caracas and finally New York. What a welcome she would have received back again at a Hudson River berth. The return voyage was to have been across to Africa, with calls at Casablanca and then Dakar, Freetown, Abijan and Cape Town. Up to Dar Es Salaam, Madras then Singapore, Manila, Hong Kong and on to Japan where she would call at Yokohama and Kobe. Then back across the Pacific to Honolulu and Los Angeles. It was an exciting concept and one that would probably have suited the large liner very well. But it did not, of course, happen. Instead, a programme of similarly ambitious World Campus Afloat cruises was now rescheduled to follow the maiden April 1972 Circle Pacific Cruise.

Orient Overseas Line were at pains to assure everyone that even though the liner was undergoing extensive refurbishing 'much of the classical décor - the best of a fabulous era' would be retained. It was a pity, really, that while they were anxious to acknowledge her glamorous past life, aboard *Seawise* things were to be totally informal with an emphasis on easygoing, casual shipboard life. No more dressing for dinner every night, no more black tie and elaborate evening gown events. To help make this casual shipboard life a reality, the Miramar Hotel was busy recruiting and training 1,200 men and women to work on board.

The *Daily Mirror* newspaper in London ran a story about the refitting of the ship under the headline: "Mr. Tung's Chinese Queen. He's treating her like a lady." The report read: "The thirty-three-year-old liner *Queen Elizabeth*, once the pride of Britain's passenger fleet, is rapidly being restored to her former grandeur – a few miles from Red China.

"The 83,000-ton vessel, which failed to make the grade as a tourist attraction at Port Everglades, Florida is now owned by Mr. C. Y. Tung. He is preparing to send her to sea again next year, renamed the *Seawise* after his initials, as a cruise liner and floating university.

"The £4,000,000 task of restoration will be completed in three months and after dry-docking in Japan, the old Queen will make her shake-down cruise.

"Then will come a cruise designed to publicise an anti-smoking campaign, followed by a 96-day Pacific run ending in Los Angeles.

▽ Another day's work done, crowds of men leave the ship which has already been partially repainted in her new livery, more suited to hot weather cruising.

Work in progress on the conversion and refurbishing. Compare the view of the Boat Deck with that to be seen on page 141.

This picture of the *Seawise University*, looking as imposing as ever while the work proceeds, recalls previous scenes of her earlier conversion from troopship to ocean liner.

"The liner will then begin her worldwide cruising role, carrying about 800 passengers First Class and 700 students in the Tourist section.

"Fourteen American universities and five Asian countries are supporting the *Seawise's* educational cruises.

"Mr. Tung already has one educational ship at sea.

"The *Queen Elizabeth* at present lies alone, aloof from the bustling traffic of Hong Kong harbour. Bare light bulbs and bobbing torches illuminate her. But the noise is deafening as nearly 1,500 workers carry out her transformation.

"Mr. Tung is retaining her 1930s style décor, which he thinks will have big appeal to present-day passengers.

"Work on some of the staterooms has already been completed. Richard Burton will be happy to know that the stateroom he booked permanently for Elizabeth Taylor's transatlantic crossings is being kept as it was – in ghastly pink. Much of the original wood panelling, fittings and leather-work are in good condition – a tribute to the British builders – and are being retained.

"Mr. Tung, sixty-year-old Chinese millionaire, is little known in Europe but he owns Asia's largest private fleet – more than 110 ships.

"'They say Onassis has the First Lady, but CY has the Queen' said an enthusiastic underling."

The article went on to question whether Mr. Tung's plans for the former *Queen Elizabeth* would actually work and answered its own question with – probably. It pointed out that Mr. Tung had started out as a shipping clerk and seemed to have the knack for buying ships that other people could not manage, turning them into going concerns.

During the five months that followed her arrival in Hong Kong harbour *Seawise University* was a hive of activity as the conversion went on to turn her from Atlantic liner to world cruise ship. It had been decided that instead of having a grey hull, *Seawise* would be all-white and as 1971 came to a close so the liner was utterly transformed. In the early January sunshine, with the external painting virtually finished she gleamed in her new livery, with the words Orient Overseas

As the transformation neared completion, tour groups were welcomed on board to inspect the ship which had been partially refurnished in a more eastern style.

Line in orange lettering on her hull below the bridge at Main Deck level. Along with the refurbishment of her public rooms and cabins, a great deal of work had been done to recondition her boilers and overhaul her engines. Mechanically she was fully restored to her prime as a Cunard liner as the remaining six inactive boilers, which had been stripped during the ship's stay at Port Everglades, were reactivated along with two additional turbine units. Although she looked magnificent in her fresh Orient Overseas Line livery, there remained a great deal still to be done and still well over one thousand men were being ferried out to her daily to complete the tasks. It had now been several years since the ship had been dry docked and this was to be done in Japan once the major internal work was completed.

While the world looked on in awe as the old *Queen Elizabeth* was gradually reborn as *Seawise University*, there were those who were less than happy with what was happening in Hong Kong harbour. Late in December it was seen that someone had painted on the funnels, in Chinese characters, 'C.Y. Tung go home – you are not wanted here'. This graffito was duly painted out and the funnels returned to their pristine splendour. The following day the graffito was there again, this time painted in another colour. Once again it was removed but for several more days the same message re-appeared - presumably having been painted in the quiet of the night.

On Sunday the 9th January 1972, a bright, sunny but cool day, the *Seawise* was being made ready to undertake her first sea trials the following week and then sail for Japan, even though there was still much internal work yet to be completed. Part of the problem lay with her fire doors. New fire doors were to be installed throughout the ship and these had been ordered from an Italian manufacturer. Whilst they had been delivered in sufficient time, the problem was that their frames were not of the correct dimensions. Therefore several of the fire doors that had been installed had subsequently been removed in order that they could be adapted to fit and thereby function correctly.

Although the *Seawise University* had assumed a new identity, she had not entirely lost her former queenly majesty.

Although there was work still being undertaken on board the ship, C. Y. Tung's son had planned that a celebratory cocktail party and a large formal lunch were to be held in the Peacock Lounge (the former First Class Lounge) that afternoon. As a result, there was considerable activity on board the ship in preparation, with the upper decks and main accommodation spaces being made clean and tidy. Decks were being swept and scrubbed while in the Peacock Lounge the Head Waiter, with a number of his staff, was organising the decoration of the tables. Also, the wives, children and other family members of the men working on the ship were going to be allowed on board for a sightseeing visit that day and, in fact, visitors had begun to arrive as early as 8 am and by lunchtime there were already 60 visitors on the ship. As it was a Sunday, there were just 294 workmen on board along with 250 crew members.

At about 11.30 am three cabin boys smelt, and then saw, smoke in a port side alleyway on A Deck, not far from the Main Square. Investigating further, they saw flames coming from a pile of rubbish near an open shell door. They ran to the Main Staircase raising the alarm by calling 'Fire!' As they did so, the special lunch-time fire patrol came along and they ran to the site of the fire with extinguishers. As this was happening, the master of *Seawise*, Commodore Chen, received on the bridge reports of other fires: one on B Deck and another on Sun Deck; and a short while later other fires were reported by one of the port side lifts on R Deck, in a central stairway aft on D Deck, in a smaller stairway aft on B Deck, on the B Deck central stairway and also in a central stairway forward between R and B Decks. It was also believed that there must have been a fire in the officers' accommodation immediately adjacent and below the wheelhouse as this very quickly became filled with dense smoke. Located mostly on stairways and in corridors and aided by the draft from many open shell doors and the fact that very few (if any) fire doors were closed, these separate sites of fire rapidly combined into one conflagration that covered the ship from stem to stern. Initially, Commodore Chen sent his Chief Officer to seek out the seat of the fire on B Deck and the Staff Captain was sent to the Sun Deck fire and attempts were made to fight these and the other fires that were later reported.

A call was sent, by V.H.F. radio from a Police launch, to the Hong Kong Fire Services Department just a few minutes after the cabin boys had discovered the fire on A Deck. However, it was not until 12.30 pm that the fire boats were on the scene and had begun to fight the fire, playing their hoses along the port side superstructure of the *Seawise*. While this was happening, fire service personnel went aboard the burning ship both to help fight the fires from inside and to search for survivors. By the time the fire boats had arrived, eighty per cent of the superstructure was already ablaze. A diesel-oil tank on board exploded, further feeding the raging inferno. The tongues of flame flickered over the exquisite and freshly restored veneers: lustrous panelling that had come from every corner of the British Empire cracked, bubbled and was consumed. The incomparable marquetry panel depicting the Canterbury Pilgrims and the beautiful tapestries in the First Class restaurant were destroyed within moments and were but a memory. As the clouds of smoke enveloped the upper superstructure and funnels of the *Seawise*, the visitors and crew members hastened to flee the ship, some of them sliding down ropes in order to escape the flames. Two hundred workmen had to be rescued and fourteen of them were injured. By 3.30 pm everyone had been evacuated from the ship.

Further firefighting equipment was brought out to the blazing liner on a ferry but it was far too late. The flames, unchecked by fire doors or sprinkler systems, continued to engulf the liner. Quite apart from the decorative woods on board even the main structural bulkheads were lined with two thicknesses of at least three-quarters of an inch plywood on each side and this, of course, provided a huge source of combustibility. In fact the heat became so fierce that it caused several decks to melt and, as a result of this intense heat, at approximately 3.30 pm the firefighting efforts had to be temporarily abandoned. By this time such an enormous quantity of water had been pumped aboard that the ship had now taken on a list of between 12 and 15 degrees to starboard. Two hours or so later the list appeared to have decreased slightly and the playing of the water from the fire boats was resumed and it continued until eight that evening

Throughout the night what had only a few hours before been a beacon of rebirth glowing in her fresh paintwork was now a beacon of disaster and the glow was now the slowly dying fire that had consumed her. The light of dawn revealed a pall of smoke, intermittent outbreaks of flame by the bows and the fact that what had once been a magnificent liner was now a distorted wreck. Her aft decks had all collapsed and her forward superstructure appeared to have fallen in on itself: much of the ship was distorted quite beyond recognition. By noon the once great ship died, capsizing due to a complete loss of stability as a result of the inflow of water through her open shell doors. The wreck sat with 80-degree list.

At the time of the fire C. Y. Tung was in London. Visibly shocked, he left for Hong Kong on the Monday morning taking with him the faint hope that she might be salvaged. "I feel so bad" he said "It is the only historical ship left. We restored it to her former glory. It makes me cry but I must be strong in my nerve." It was, however, not just C. Y. Tung who was shocked; the shipping world, too, was shocked, along with the thousands of people who had known and loved the *Queen Elizabeth*. It was an almost incomprehensible thought, that the great ship which had been the *Queen Elizabeth*, the largest liner in the world, was now nothing but a burned out wreck. But there it was, on the front of the morning newspapers across the world, photographs of *Seawise University* engulfed in clouds of billowing smoke.

The Times reported: "The hulk of the former luxury liner *Queen Elizabeth* started falling apart today as flames raked it from stem to stern outside Hong Kong harbor… Officials said the mainmast had collapsed and the aft promenade deck caved in during the night. The upper decks were collapsing too."

The *Daily Mirror*'s headline was 'A Queen Dies' and a huge picture of the burning liner covered most of the front and back pages. The newspaper quoted Commodore Marr who said: "It's terribly sad. It is a tragic end to a very beautiful ship – especially as we all thought that she had just received a new lease of life." Commodore Marr went on to say: "I do not believe that this fire started accidentally. The flames spread too quickly for that. It must be sabotage."

The Daily Express had the headline, "We'll never see the like of her again." *The Daily Telegraph* reported how, as the ship burned, executives of Mr. Tung's Island Navigation Company wept as they watched the fire tugs deluging her burning decks with hoses. "It's not the money – it's the tremendous efforts we have made to give her back the pride of the past that hurts so much", one said.

The London *Evening News* quoted the Hong Kong fire chief, Herbert Hutchins, the last man to leave the former *Queen Elizabeth*, "It nearly broke our hearts to have to stand off and watch her burn to death." The newspaper also reported that a preliminary inquiry was being started by the Hong Kong Marine Department as to how the fire broke out. However, it was the view of one senior marine officer that it would be very difficult to find out what the cause of the fire was.

The New York *Daily News* carried a picture of the blazing liner on its front page with the succinct caption: "Queen

Dead in Hong Kong." In the newspaper's centre pages were pictures of the *Queen Elizabeth* at New York during wartime, pictures of glamorous celebrities of stage and screen who had sailed on her and another picture of the ship burning. The caption was "Queen of Atlantic dies in exile".

Seawise University had been insured as a conversion for $5 million, with the coverage increasing to $8 million as the work neared completion. In the following months a marine court held several hearings in an attempt to ascertain the cause of the blaze. The general conclusions of the court were that there were at least three major sites of fire, all of them occurring within minutes of each other, and that there may have well been other independent sites as well. This, combined with size of the independent outbreaks and the speed with which each of the fires became uncontrollable, possibly enhanced by some highly inflammable reagent, and the fact that the outbreaks occurred at a time when virtually all of the workmen had withdrawn for lunch in either the Restaurant or ashore, led the Court to the same conclusion as that of Commodore Marr on first hearing about the fire – sabotage. The Court, however, stated this view in more circumspect tones: that while there was no direct and conclusive evidence on the matter, the Court was satisfied that by far the most likely cause of these fires was a series of deliberate acts by 'a person or persons unknown'.

From a reborn beauty to a charred hulk, the wreck of the *Seawise* now sat in Hong Kong harbour as both an eyesore and a hazard, lying as she did in one of the world's busiest harbours.

One year later, on the anniversary of the fire, one of the *Queen Elizabeth*'s former Masters, Sir Ivan Thompson, along with a small group of men, held a memorial service at the end of New York's Pier 90. The Grand Old Lady was never going to arrive there in glory after all.

As had been the case in her later years, there still remained those who hoped to squeeze a bit more money out of the old ship. So even as a wreck she was seen as having some potential and as such served as a backdrop to some scenes for the James Bond film 'The Man with the Golden Gun'. It could hardly be reckoned as a moment of fame as few of the film's fans could have been expected either to know about the *Queen Elizabeth* or to appreciate her significance.

Such was the intensity of the fires that parts of the superstructure collapsed completely.

A striking aerial view of the fire-ravaged hulk.

In August 1973 C. Y. Tung was given an order by the Hong Kong authorities to clear the wreck from the harbour as soon as possible, warning him that further delay would not be tolerated. To have 1,031 feet of rusting steel, the world's largest wreck, in the very centre of one of the world's greatest harbours was very obviously an enormous embarrassment. Any hopes that the wreck could be refloated had been dashed by marine engineers having finally concluded that resurrection of the devastated liner was impossible and that she would therefore have to be cut up and her remains hauled away to the scrap yards. Oil had gradually begun to seep from the ruptured fuel tanks and an inflatable boom was floated around the rusting hulk to try and contain it. Engineers from Hong Kong's Marine Department pumped 3,000 tons of oil from the wreck. This, they believed, saved the island's beaches.

It was estimated that it would cost up to £50 million to remove the wreck and despite the warnings to C. Y. Tung, the Marine Department were unwilling to begin such a massive task, even though the law gave them the right to clear wrecks and recover the cost from the owner.

As the smoke clears, the pathetic remains of the once-proud liner are revealed.

Meanwhile, as the insurance talks continued in London, the scarred and twisted wreck encouraged fish, and Chinese fishing from sampans – and the tourists. Even as a wreck, the tourists still gazed upon her in awe.

A further year would pass before work began on removing what remained of the former *Queen Elizabeth*. She was cut or blown into sections of up to 250 tons with 45,000 tons of metal being lifted from the wreck. A great deal of it was used in the construction of the new buildings that were being created in Hong Kong. In January 1975 a memorial to the *Queen Elizabeth* was unveiled in New York by Mayor Lindsay outside the Orient Overseas Line's offices. Made of granite, the memorial contained the letters Q and E, salvaged from her bows, along with carved copies of letters from the Queen Mother and from the Secretary General of the United Nations.

Not all of the wreck was easily salvageable, so some of it remained there on the harbour bottom. It was ultimately covered, lost forever, with the creation of Hong Kong's vast new airport. In the end the airliner triumphed over Cunard's mightiest liner.

THE MERCHANT SHIPPING ORDINANCE
(Chapter 281 of the Laws of Hong Kong)

REPORT OF THE MARINE COURT

S.S. *SEAWISE UNIVERSITY*

In the matter of a Formal Investigation made by a Marine Court held at the Legislative Council Chamber on the 8th, 10th–28th (inclusive) (Mondays to Fridays only) of February, 1972, and in Room 150 on the 29th February to 30th March, 1972 (inclusive) (Mondays to Fridays only) and also on 4th April, 1972 in the Colony of Hong Kong before Mr. Justice A. M. McMullin assisted by Mr. John Robson, M.B.E., B.Sc., F.R.I.N.A., C.Eng., and Captain John d'Oyly Green, RNR (Retired) to enquire into the casualty of the S.S. *Seawise University* which occurred on the 9th January, 1972.

The Court, having carefully enquired into the circumstances of the said casualty, finds that said *Seawise University* became a constructive total loss as a result of several fires which broke out on board in the forenoon of that day. The Court regrets that it is unable to assign a certain cause for any of these fires but considers for the reasons given in the Annex, that the most probable cause in each case was the act or acts of a person or persons unknown.

Dated this 29th day of June, 1972.

ART MICHAEL McMULLIN,
Puisne Judge.

We concur in the above report.

JOHN ROBSON,
Assessor.

JOHN D'OYLY GREEN,
Assessor.

NOTE: To reduce printing costs the Appendices to this report have been omitted.

1

R.M.S. QUEEN ELIZABETH

RECORD OF VOYAGES

HMT Queen Elizabeth's troopship voyages

Note: Convoy numbers do not necessarily indicate that the
Queen Elizabeth was sailing with other vessels – she may have
been sailing on her own.

1940
Clyde dep. 2 March
New York arr. 7 March
New York dep.12 November
Singapore arr. 26 November
1941
Singapore dep. 11 February
Sydney dep.11 April – Convoy US10
Fremantle, Trincomalee
Suez dep. 8 May – Convoy US10A
Singapore dep. 3 June
Fremantle
Sydney dep. 29 June
Fremantle dep. 9 July – Convoy US11A
Suez dep. 2 August
Fremantle dep. 18 August
Sydney dep.2 September – Convoy US12A
Trincomalee
Suez dep. 25 September
Trincomalee
Fremantle
Sydney dep. 23 October
Hobart dep. 31 October
Sydney dep. 3 November – Convoy US13
Fremantle, Trincomalee, Colombo
Suez dep. 24 November
Trincomalee, Fremantle, Sydney
1942
Sydney dep. 6 February
Auckland
Esquimalt dep. 10 March
San Francisco dep. 19 March
Sydney dep. 19 April
Fremantle, Cape Town, Rio de Janeiro
New York dep.4 June – Convoy AT15Z
Clyde arr. 9 June – dep. 17 June Convoy WS19Y
Suez dep. 19 July
Cape Town, Rio de Janeiro
New York dep. 30 August – Convoy AT21
Clyde dep. 8 September – Convoy TA21
New York dep.5 October – Convoy AT25

Clyde dep. 17 October – Convoy TA25
Halifax dep.30 October
Clyde dep.8 November – Convoy TA26
New York dep. 24 November – Convoy AT 29
Clyde dep.4 December – Convoy TA29
Halifax dep. 13 December – Convoy AT31
Clyde dep.21 December – Convoy TA31
1943
New York dep.6 January – Convoy AT 34
Clyde dep. 19 January – Convoy TA 34
New York dep. 10 March – Convoy AT38
Clyde dep.20 March – Convoy TA38
Halifax dep. 29 March – Convoy AT40
Clyde dep.7 April – Convoy TA40
New York dep. 5 May – Convoy AT42
Clyde dep. 16 May – Convoy TA46
New York dep. 27 May – Convoy AT46
Clyde dep. 7 June – Convoy TA46
New York dep. 1 July – Convoy AT54
Clyde dep. 10 July – Convoy TA54
Halifax dep. 23 July – Convoy AT56
Clyde dep. 30 July – Convoy TA56
New York dep. 20 August – Convoy AT62
Clyde dep. 31 August – Convoy TA62
Halifax dep.14 September – Convoy AT64
Clyde dep. 23 September – Convoy TA64
New York dep. 13 October – Convoy AT69
Clyde dep.23 October – Convoy TA69
New York dep. 3 November – Convoy AT71
Clyde dep.13 November – Convoy TA71
New York dep. 23 November – Convoy AT 75
Clyde dep. 2 December – Convoy TA75
New York dep. 14 December – Convoy AT80
Clyde dep. 22 December – Convoy TA80
1944
New York dep. 2 January – Convoy AT84
Clyde dep. 13 January – Convoy TA84
New York dep. 2 February – Convoy AT91
Clyde dep. 12 February – Convoy TA91
New York dep. 31 March – Convoy AT104
Clyde dep.10 April – Convoy TA104
New York dep. 20 April – Convoy AT108
Clyde dep. 30 April – Convoy TA108
New York dep. 30 May – Convoy AT120
Clyde dep. 9 June – Convoy TA 120
New York dep. 22 June – Convoy AT125
Clyde dep. 1 July – TA125

New York dep. 15 July – Convoy AT132
Clyde dep. 25 July – Convoy TA132
New York dep. 6 August – Convoy AT140
Clyde dep. 14 August – Convoy TA140
New York dep. 28 August – Convoy AT146
Clyde dep. 11 September – Convoy TA146
New York dep. 24 September – Convoy AT152
Clyde dep. 5 October – Convoy TA152
New York dep. 17 October – Convoy AT159
Clyde dep. 28 October – Convoy TA159
Boston dep. 13 November
New York dep.21 November – Convoy AT169
Clyde dep. 2 December – Convoy TA169
New York dep. 16 December – Convoy AT174
Clyde dep. 28 December – Convoy TA174
1945
New York dep. 8 January – Convoy AT180
Clyde dep. 20 January – Convoy TA180
New York dep. 31 January - Convoy AT187
Clyde dep. 13 February – Convoy TA187
New York dep. 28 February – Convoy AT193
Clyde dep. 13 March – Convoy TA193
New York dep. 25 March – Convoy AT200
Clyde dep. 7 April – Convoy TA200
New York dep. 14 June
Clyde dep. 24 June
New York dep. 5 July
Clyde dep. 15 July
New York dep.26 July
Clyde dep. 6 August
New York dep. 15 August
Southampton dep. 26 August
New York dep. 5 September
Southampton dep. 14 September
New York dep. 24 September
Southampton dep.4 October
New York dep.13 October
Southampton dep. 22 October
Halifax dep.31 October
Southampton dep.15 November
Halifax dep. 23 November
Southampton dep. 2 December
New York dep. 11 December
Southampton dep.22 December
New York dep. 31 December
1946
Southampton dep. 9 January
New York dep. 18 January
Southampton dep. 28 January
New York dep.6 February
Southampton dep. 15 February
New York dep. 28 February
Southampton arr. 6 March

Note: On voyage AT174, New York to Clyde 13,057 troops
were carried.
On voyage AT180 New York to Clyde 12,664 troops were
carried.
On voyage AT187 New York to Clyde 12,295 troops were
carried.
On voyage AT193 New York to Clyde 12,285 troops were
carried.

Voyages during re-fitting of *RMS Queen Elizabeth*
30 March Southampton
31 March Gourock
16 June - 6 October Southampton
7 October Firth of Clyde Trials
9 October dep Firth of Clyde
10 October Southampton

The commercial voyages of the *RMS Queen Elizabeth*
1946
Southampton 16 October
New York 21-25 October
Southampton 31 October – 6 November
New York 11-14 November
Southampton 19-22 November
New York 27-29 November
Southampton 4-7 December
New York 12-14 December
Southampton 19-27 December
1947
New York 1-4 January
Southampton 9-11 January
New York 17-18 January
Southampton 23-29 January
New York 3-5 February
Southampton 10-13 February
New York 18 - 20 February
Southampton 25- 28 February
New York 5-7 March
Southampton 13-15 March
New York 21-22 March
Southampton 28 March-2 April
New York 7-9 April
Southampton 16-19 April
New York 25-26 April
Southampton 1-4 May
New York 9-10 May
Southampton 15-18 May
New York 23-24 May
Southampton 29 May - 4 June
New York 9-11 June
Southampton 16-25 June
New York 30 June – 2 July
Southampton 7-10 July
New York 15-17 July

Southampton 22-25 July
New York 30 July – 1 August
Southampton 6-9 August
New York 14-16 August
Southampton 21-27 August
New York 1-3 September
Southampton 8-11 September
New York 16-18 September
Southampton 23-26 September
New York 1-3 October
Southampton 8-11 October
New York 16-18 October
Southampton 23-26 October
New York 31October – 1 November
Southampton 7 November

1948
Southampton 3 January
New York 8-9 January
Southampton 15-17 January
New York 23-25 January
Southampton 30 January -4 February
New York 9-11 February
Southampton 16-19 February
New York 24-26 February
Southampton 2-5 March
New York 10-12 March
Southampton 17-20 March
New York 25-27 March
Southampton 1-7 April
(calls at Cherbourg reinstated from this voyage)
New York 12-14 April
Southampton 19-22 April
New York 27-29 April
Southampton 4-7 May
New York 12-14 May
Southampton 19-22 May
New York 27-29 May
Southampton 3-9 June
New York 14-17 June
Southampton 22-24 June
New York 29 June – 1 July
Southampton 6-9 July
New York 14-16 July
Southampton 21-30 July
New York 4-6 August
Southampton 11-14 August
New York 19-21 August
Southampton 26 August – 2 September
New York 7-8 September
Southampton 13-16 September
New York 21-23 September
Southampton 28 September – 1 October
New York 6-8 October
Southampton 13-16 October

New York 21-23 October
Southampton 28-31 October
New York 6-7 November
Southampton 12 November – 1 December
New York 6-8 December
Southampton 13-16 December
New York 21-23 December
Southampton 29 December
1949
Southampton 11 February
New York 16-18 February
Southampton 24 February - 2 March
New York 7-10 March
Southampton 15-18 March
New York 23-26 March
Southampton 31 March – 6 April
New York 11-13 April
Southampton 18-21 April
New York 26-28 April
Southampton 3-6 May
New York 11-13 May
Southampton 18-21 May
New York 26-28 May
Southampton 2-8 June
New York 13-15 June
Southampton 20-23 June
New York 28-30 June
Southampton 5-8 July
New York 13-15 July
Southampton 20-29 July
New York 3-5 August
Southampton 10-13 August
New York 18-20 August
Southampton 25-27 August
New York 1-4 September
Southampton 9-14 September
New York 19-21 September
Southampton 26-29 September
New York 4-7 October
Southampton 12-14 October
New York 20-21 October
Southampton 27-29 October
New York 3-5 November
Southampton 10-16 November
New York 21-23 November
Southampton 28 November – 2 December
New York 7-10 December
Southampton 15-21 December
New York 26-29 December
1950
Southampton 3 January – 15 February
New York 20-23 February
Southampton 28 February – 3 March
New York 8-11 March

Southampton 18-22 March
New York 28-30 March
Southampton 4-6 April
New York 11-14 April
Southampton 19-21 April
New York 26-29 April
Southampton 4-10 May
New York 15-17 May
Southampton 22-25 May
New York 30 May – 1 June
Southampton 6-9 June
New York 14-16 June
Southampton 21-24 June
New York 29 June – 1 July
Southampton 6-15 July
New York 20-22 July
Southampton 27 July – 1 August
New York 6-8 August
Southampton 13-16 August
New York 21-23 August
Southampton 28-31 August
New York 5-7 September
Southampton 12-14 September
New York 19-21 September
Southampton 26-29 September
New York 4-7 October
Southampton 12-17 October
New York 22-25 October
Southampton 30 October – 1 November
New York 6-9 November
Southampton 14-16 November
New York 21-23 November
Southampton 28-30 November
New York 6-8 December
Southampton 13-16 December
New York 21-24 December
Southampton 29 December

1951
Southampton 8 February
New York 13-16 February
Southampton 21-23 February
New York 28 February – 3 March
Southampton 8-13 March
New York 19-21 March
Southampton 26 March – 14 April
New York 19-21 April
Southampton 26 April – 2 May
New York 7-8 May
Southampton 13 – 17 May
New York 22-24 May
Southampton 29 May – 1 June
New York 6-7 June
Southampton 13-15 June
New York 20-22 June

Southampton 27-30 June
New York 5-7 July
Southampton 12-21 July
New York 26-28 July
Southampton 2-7 August
New York 12-14 August
Southampton 20-22 August
New York 27-29 August
Southampton 4-6 September
New York 11-14 September
Southampton 19-21 September
New York 26-28 September
Southampton 3-6 October
New York 11-13 October
Southampton 18-23 October
New York 28-31 October
Southampton 5-7 November
New York 12-14 November
Southampton 19-21 November
New York 26-28 November
Southampton 3-5 December
New York 10-14 December
Southampton 19-22 December
New York 27-29 December

1952
Southampton 4 January – 12 February
New York 17-20 February
Southampton 25-28 February
New York 4-7 March
Southampton 12-15 March
New York 20-22 March
Southampton 27 March – 1 April
New York 6-9 April
Southampton 14-16 April
New York 21-23 April
Southampton 29-30 April
New York 5-7 May
Southampton 12-14 May
New York 19-21 May
Southampton 27-28 May
New York 2-4 June
Southampton 10-11 June
New York 16-18 June
Southampton 24-25 June
New York 30 June – 1 July
Southampton 6-8 July
New York 13-16 July
Southampton 21-30 July
New York 4-6 August
Southampton 11-13 August
New York 18-20 August
Southampton 25-28 August
New York 2-3 September
Southampton 8-10 September

New York 15-17 September
Southampton 23-24 September
New York 29-30 September
Southampton 6-8 October
New York 13-15 October
Southampton 21-22 October
New York 27-29 October
Southampton 3-6 November
New York 11-13 November
Southampton 18-21 November
New York 26-28 November
Southampton 4-8 December
New York 13-17 December
Southampton 22 December

1953
Southampton 11 February
New York 17-19 February
Southampton 24-27 February
New York 4-6 March
Southampton 11-14 March
New York 19-21 March
Southampton 26 March – 1 April
New York 6-8 April
Southampton 13-16 April
New York 21-22 April
Southampton 27-30 April
New York 5-6 May
Southampton 11-14 May
New York 19-21 May
Southampton 25-28 May
New York 2-3 June
Southampton 8-11 June
New York 16-17 June
Southampton 22-25 June
New York 30 June – 1 July
Southampton 6-29 July
New York 3-5 August
Southampton 10-13 August
New York 18-19 August
Southampton 24-27 August
New York 1-2 September
Southampton 7-10 September
New York 15-16 September
Southampton 22-24 September
New York 29-30 September
Southampton 5-October
New York 13-14 October
Southampton 19-22 October
New York 27-28 October
Southampton 3-5 November
New York 10-12 November
Southampton 17 November – 10 December
New York 15-16 December
Southampton 21 December

1954
Southampton 10 February
New York 15-17 February
Southampton 21-25 February
New York 2-5 March
Southampton 11-13 March
New York 18-20 March
Southampton 25-31 March
New York 5-7 April
Southampton 12-15 April
New York 20-21 April
Southampton 26-29 April
New York 4-5 May
Southampton 10-13 May
New York 18-19 May
Southampton 24-27 May
New York 1-2 June
Southampton 7-10 June
New York 15-16 June
Southampton 21-24 June
New York 29 June – 1 July
Southampton 6-8 July
New York 13-14 July
Southampton 20-28 July
New York 2-4 August
Southampton 9-12 August
New York 17-18 August
Southampton 23-26 August
New York 31 August – 1 September
Southampton 6-9 September
New York 14-15 September
Southampton 20-23 September
New York 28-29 September
Southampton 4-7 October
New York 12-13 October
Southampton 18-21 October
New York 26-27 October
Southampton 1-3 November
New York 8-10 November
Southampton 16-19 November
New York 24-27 November
Southampton 2-9 December
New York 14-15 December
Southampton 20-24 December
New York 29-30 December

1955
Southampton 4-7 January
New York 12-15 January
Southampton 20 January – 27 March
(Trials after installation of stabilisers)
Southampton 30 March
New York 4-6 April
Southampton 12-14 April
New York 19-20 April

Southampton 26-28 April
New York 3-4 May
Southampton 10-12 May
New York 17-18 May
Southampton 24-26 May
New York 31 May – 1 June
Southampton 7-9 June
New York 14-15 June
Southampton 21-23 June
New York 28-29 June
Southampton 4-7 July
New York 12-13 July
Southampton 18 – 28 July
New York 2-3 August
Southampton 8-11 August
New York 16-17 August
Southampton 23-25 August
New York 30-31 August
Southampton 6-8 September
New York 13-14 September
Southampton 20-22 September
New York 27-28 September
Southampton 3-7 October
New York 12-13 October
Southampton 19-20 October
New York 25-26 October
Southampton 31 October – 3 November
New York 8-10 November
Southampton 15-18 November
New York 23-25 November
Southampton 30 November – 3 December
New York 8-9 December
Southampton 14December

1956

Southampton 25 January
New York 30 January – 1 February
Southampton 6-9 February
New York 14-17 February
Southampton 22-25 February
New York 1-3 March
Southampton 8-14 March
New York 20-21 March
Southampton 26-29 March
New York 3-5 April
Southampton 10-12 April
New York 17-18 April
Southampton 23-26 April
New York 1-2 May
Southampton 7-10 May
New York 15-16 May
Southampton 21-24 May
New York 29-30 May
Southampton 4-7 June
New York 12-13 June

Southampton 18-21 June
New York 26-27 June
Southampton 2-5 July
New York 10-12 July
Southampton 17-26 July
New York 31 July – 1 August
Southampton 6-9 August
New York 14-15 August
Southampton 20-23 August
New York 28-29 August
Southampton 3-6 September
New York 11-12 September
Southampton 17-20 September
New York 25-26 September
Southampton 2-4 October
New York 9-10 October
Southampton 15-18 October
New York 23-24 October
Southampton 29 October – 2 November
New York 7-8 November
Southampton 14-16 November
New York 21-23 November
Southampton 28 November – 1 December
New York 6-8 December
Southampton 13 December

1957

Southampton 23 January
New York 29-31 January
Southampton 5-8 February
Halifax 14-17 February
Southampton 21 February
Halifax 27 February – 3 March
Southampton 8-13 March
New York 18-20 March
Southampton 25-28 March
New York 2-3 April
Southampton 8-11 April
New York 16-17 April
Southampton 22-25 April
New York 30 April – 1 May
Southampton 6-9 May
New York 14-15 May
Southampton 20-23 May
New York 28-29 May
Southampton 4-6 June
New York 11-12 June
Southampton 18-20 June
New York 25-27 June
Southampton 2-4 July
New York 9-11 July
Southampton 16-25 July
New York 30-31 July
Southampton 5-8 August
New York 13-14 August

Southampton 19-22 August
New York 27-28 August
Southampton 2-5 September
New York 10-11 September
Southampton 16-19 September
New York 24-25 September
Southampton 30 September – 3 October
New York 8-9 October
Southampton 14-17 October
New York 22-23 October
Southampton 29-31 October
New York 5-6 November
Southampton 12-14 November
New York19-20 November
Southampton 26-28 November
New York 3-6 December
Southampton 12 December
1958
Southampton 22 January
New York 27-29 January
Southampton 3-6 February
New York 11-14 February
Southampton 19-22 February
New York 27 February – 1 March
Southampton 6-12 March
New York 17-19 March
Southampton 25-27 March
New York 1-2 April
Southampton 8-10 April
New York 15-16 April
Southampton 22-24 April
New York 29-30 April
Southampton 6-8 May
New York 13-14 May
Southampton 20-22 May
New York 27-28 May
Southampton 2-5 June
New York 10-11 June
Southampton 16-19 June
New York 24-25 June
Southampton 30 June – 3 July
New York 8-10 July
Southampton 15-24 July
New York 29-30 July
Southampton 4-7 August
New York 12-13 August
Southampton 19-22 August
New York 26-27 August
Southampton 2-4 September
New York 9-10 September
Southampton 16-18 September
New York 23-24 September
Southampton 30 September – 30 October
New York 7-8 October

Southampton 13-16 October
New York 21-22 October
Southampton 27-30 October
New York 4-6 November
Southampton 11-14 November
New York 19-21 November
Southampton 26-29 November
New York 4-6 December
Southampton 11 December
1959
Southampton 21 January
New York 26-27 January
Southampton 1-4 February
New York 9-11 February
Cherbourg 16 February
(struck a submerged object)
Southampton 20 February – 11 March
New York 16-18 March
Southampton 23-26 March
New York 31 March – 3 April
Southampton 8-9 April
New York 14-15 April
Southampton 20-23 April
New York 28-29 April
Southampton 4-7 May
New York 12-13 May
Southampton 18-21 May
New York 26-27 May
Southampton 1-4 June
New York 9-10 June
Southampton 15-18 June
New York 23-24 June
Southampton 29 June – 2 July
New York 7-9 July
Southampton 14-23 July
New York 28-29 July
(in collision put back)
New York 30 July
Southampton 4-6 August
New York 11-12 August
Southampton 17-20 August
New York 25-26 August
Southampton 31 August – 3 September
New York 8-9 September
Southampton 14-17 September
New York 22-23 September
Southampton 28 September – 1 October
New York 6-7 October
Southampton 12-15 October
New York 20-21 October
Southampton 26-29 October
New York 3-4 November
Southampton 9-12 November
New York 17-18 November

Southampton 24-26 November
New York 1-2 December
Southampton 9-10 December
New York 15-17 December
Southampton 22-30 December

1960
New York 4-6 January
Southampton 11-14 January
New York 21-22 January
Southampton 27 January – 9 March
New York14-16 March
Southampton 21-24 March
New York 29-30 March
Southampton 4-7 April
New York 12-13 April
Southampton 19-21 April
New York 26-27 April
Southampton 2-5 May
New York 10-11 May
Southampton 17-19 May
New York 24-25 May
Southampton 31 May – 2 June
New York 7-8 June
Southampton 14-16 June
New York 21-22 June
Southampton 28-30 June
New York 5-7 July
Southampton 13-21 July
New York 26-27 July
Southampton 1-4 August
New York 9-10 August
Southampton 15-18 August
New York 23-24 August
Southampton 29 August – 1 September
New York 6-7 September
Southampton 12-15 September
New York 20-21 September
Southampton 26-29 September
New York 4-5 October
Southampton 10-13 October
New York 18-19 October
Southampton 25-27 October
New York 1-2 November
Southampton 8-10 November
New York 16-17 November
Southampton 22-25 November
New York 30 November – 1 December
Southampton 7-9 December
New York 14-16 December
Southampton 22-29 December

1961
New York 3-4 January
Southampton 9-13 January
New York 18-20 January

Southampton 25 January – 8 March
New York 13-15 March
Southampton 21-23 March
New York 28-29 March
Southampton 4-6 April
New York 11-12 April
Southampton 18-20 April
New York 25-26 April
Southampton 2-4 May
New York 9-10 May
Southampton 16-18 May
New York 23-24 May
Southampton 29 May – 1 June
New York 6-7 June
Southampton 12-15 June
New York 20-21 June
Southampton 26-30 June
New York 5-6 July
Southampton11-20 July
New York 25-26 July
Southampton 1-3 August
New York 8-9 August
Southampton 15-17 August
New York 22-23 August
Southampton 29-31 August
New York 5-6 September
Southampton 12-14 September
New York 19-21 September
Southampton 26-28 September
New York 3-4 October
Southampton 9-12 October
New York 17-18 October
Southampton 23-26 October
New York 31 October – 1 November
Southampton 6-9 November
New York 14-16 November
Southampton 21-24 November
New York 29 November – 1 December
Southampton 6-9 December
New York 14-16 December
Southampton 21-28 December

1962
New York 2-4 January
Southampton 10-12 January
New York 17-19 January
Southampton 25 January – 7 March
New York 12-14 March
Southampton 19-22 March
New York 27-28 March
Southampton 2-5 April
New York 10-11 April
Southampton 16-19 April

.... continued after fold-out plan.

New York 5-6 May
Southampton 11-14 May
New York 19-20 May
Southampton 25-28 May
New York 2-3 June
Southampton 8-11 June
New York 16-17 June
Southampton 22-25 June
New York 30 June – 1 July
Southampton 6-9 July
New York 14-15 July
Southampton 20-23 July
New York 28-29 July
Southampton 3-6 August
New York 11-12 August
Southampton 17-20 August
New York 25-26 August
Southampton 31 August – 3 September
New York 8-9 September
Southampton 14-17 September
New York 22-23 September
Southampton 28 September – 1 October
New York 6-7 October
Southampton 12-15 October
New York 20-21 October
Southampton 26 October – 16 December
New York 21-23 December
Nassau 25 December
New York 28-29 December
Nassau 31 December

1965
Nassau 1 January
New York 3-5 January
Southampton 10-13 January
New York 19-20 January
Southampton 25-28 January
New York 2-4 February
Southampton 9-12 February
New York 17-18 February
Nassau 20-21 February
New York 23-26 February
Las Palmas 3-4 March
Tangier 5 March
Cannes 7-8 March
Naples 9-11 March
Piraeus 12-14 March
Gibraltar 16 March
Lisbon 17-18 March
Madeira 19 March
New York 23-24 March
Southampton 29 March – 1 April
New York 6-7 April
Southampton 12-15 April
New York 20-21 April

Southampton 26-29 April
New York 4-5 May
Southampton 10-13 May
New York 18-19 May
Southampton 24-27 May
New York 1-2 June
Southampton 7-11 June
New York 16-17 June
Southampton 22-24 June
New York 29-30 June
Southampton 5-8 July
New York 13-14 July
Southampton 19-22 July
New York 27-28 July
Southampton 3-5 August
New York 10-11 August
Southampton 17-19 August
New York 24-25 August
Southampton 31 August – 2 September
New York 7-8 September
Southampton 14-16 September
New York 22-23 September
Southampton 28 September – 1 October
New York 6-7 October
Southampton 13-15 October
New York 20-21 October
Southampton 26-29 October
New York 3-6 November
Bermuda 8 November
Nassau 10-11 November
New York 12-13 November
Southampton 18 November – 4 December
Greenock 5 December

1966
Greenock 9 March
Tail of Bank 12 March
Southampton 13 March
Southampton 29 March
New York 4-7 April
Bermuda 9 April
New York 12-13 April
Southampton 18-21 April
New York 26-27 April
Southampton 2-5 May
New York 10-11 May
Southampton 16 May – 2 July
New York 7-9 July
Southampton 14-16 July
New York 21-22 July
Southampton 27-29 July
New York 3-4 August
Southampton 9-11 August
New York 16-17 August
Southampton 22-25 August

New York 30-31 August
Southampton 6-9 September
New York 14-15 September
Southampton 21 September – 8 October
New York 13-14 October
Cherbourg 19-21 October
New York 26-28 October
Bermuda 30-31 October
St Michael's 3 November
Lisbon 5-6 November
Gibraltar 7-8 November
Madeira 9 November
Las Palmas 10 November
Dakar 12 November
Barbados 16-17 November
Caracas 18 November
St Thomas 20 November
New York 22-23 November
Southampton 28 November – 16 December
New York 21-22 December
Nassau 24-25 December
New York 27-28 December
Nassau 30-31 December

1967
New York 2-4 January
St Thomas 7-8 January
Caracas 9 January
La Guaira 10 January
Trinidad 11 January
New York 15-17 January
Southampton 22-27 January
New York 1-3 February
Cristobal 7-8 February
La Guaira 9-10 February
Caracas 10-11 February
Barbados 12-13 February
St Thomas 14 February
Nassau 16 February
New York 18-21 February
Las Palmas 26-27 February
Gibraltar 28 February
Palma 1 March
Alexandria 4 March
Piraeus 5-8 March
Alexandria 8-11 March
Beirut 12-13 March
Haifa 14 March
Messina 16 March
Naples 17-18 March
Cannes 19-20 March
Barcelona 21 March
Lisbon 23-25 March
Madeira 26 March
New York 31 March – 1 April

Southampton 6-19 April
New York 25-26 April
Southampton 1-3 May
Cobh 5 May
New York 9-10 May
Southampton 16-18 May
New York 23-24 May
Southampton 29-31 May
Cobh 1 June
New York 6-7 June
Cobh 12 June
Southampton 13- 15 June
New York 20-21 June
Southampton 26-29 June
Cobh 30 June
New York 5-6 July
Southampton 11-13 July
New York 18-19 July
Southampton 25-27 July
New York 1-2 August
Cobh 7 August
Southampton 8-10 August
New York 15-16 August
Southampton 22-24 August
New York 29-30 August
Cobh 4 September
Southampton 5-8 September
New York 13-15 September
Southampton 20-22 September
New York 27 September – 5 October
Southampton 10-12 October
Cobh 13 October
New York 17-19 October
St Thomas 21 October
Nassau 22-23 October
New York 25-26 October
Southampton 31 October – 2 November
New York 7-8 November
Southampton 13 November – 14 December
New York 19-21 December
Nassau 23-24 December
New York 26-27 December
St Thomas 30 December

1968
Nassau 1 January
New York 3-5 January
Nassau 7-8 January
New York 10-11 January
Southampton 16-19 January
New York 24-26 January
Cristobal 29-30 January
Caracas 31 January - 1 February
Barbados 2-3 February
Fort de France 3 February

St Thomas 4 February
New York 7-8 February
Southampton 13-15 February
New York 20-21 February
Nassau 23-24 February
New York 26-27 February
Southampton 3-7 March
New York 12-14 March
Southampton 19-22 March
New York 27-28 March
Southampton 2-5 April
New York 10-12 April
Nassau 13-14 April
New York 16-17 April
Southampton 22-24 April
New York 30 April – 1 May
Cobh 6 May
Southampton 7-8 May
New York 14-15 May
Southampton 20-21 May
Cobh 23 May
New York 27-28 May
Cobh 2 June
Southampton 3-6 June
New York 11-12 June
Southampton 17-19 June
Cobh 20 June
New York 25-26 June
Southampton 2-3 July
New York 8-9 July
Cobh 14 July
Southampton 15-17 July
New York 22-23 July
Southampton 29-30 July
Cobh 31 July

New York 5-6 August
Cobh 11 August
Southampton 12-14 August
New York 19-20 August
Southampton 26-27 August
Cobh 29 August
New York 3-4 September
Cobh 9 September
Southampton 10-11 September
New York 16-17 September
Southampton 23-24 September
Cobh 25 September
New York 30 September – 1 October
Southampton 7-9 October
New York 11-15 October
Southampton 20-23 October
New York 28-30 October
Southampton 5-8 November
Las Palmas 11-12 November
Gibraltar 13 November
Southampton 15 November
Non-commercial voyage –
Southampton 29 November
Port Everglades 8 December

Seawise University Voyage
1971
Pt. Everglades dep. 10 February 1971
At anchor off Aruba 24 February
Departed 8 May
Rio de Janeiro 30 May
Cape Town 14 June – approx
Singapore 7 July
Hong Kong 14 July

BIBLIOGRAPHY

The North Atlantic Run (John Maxtone-Graham, Cassell, 1972)
Record Breakers of the North Atlantic (Arnold Kludas, Chatham Publishing, 2000)
Atlantic Liners of the Cunard Line (Neil McCart, Patrick Stephens Ltd., 1990)
The Queens of the North Atlantic (Robert Lacey, Sigwick & Jackson, 1973)
Damned by Destiny (David L. Williams & Richard P. De Kerbrech, Teredo Books Ltd., 1982)
The Liner – Retrospective & Renaissance (Philip Dawson, Conway Maritime Press, 2005)
British Superliners of the Sixties (Philip Dawson, Conway Maritime Press, 1990)
RMS Queen Elizabeth – from Victory to Valhalla (David Hutchings, Kingfisher Publications 1990)
Memory of a Queen, RMS Queen Elizabeth, Colin Walker (Oxford Publishing Co. 1972)
The Queen Elizabeth, P.R. Bird & Raymond Birt (Winchester Publishing Ltd. 1947)
The Big Ship – the Story of the SS United States (Frank O. Braynard, The Mariners Museum, Newport News 1981)
Warrior Queens: the Queen Mary & Queen Elizabeth in World War II (Daniel Allen Butler, Stackpole Books 2002)
Elizabeth, The Queen Mother (Hugo Vickers, Arrow Books, 2006)
The Journal of Commerce
Lloyd's List
The Syren & Shipping Illustrated
The Shipping World

PHOTO & ILLUSTRATION CREDITS

Australian War Memorial Museum collection: 40; 41.
Author's collection: 16 (three images); 17; 19; 22; 24; 26; 31; 35; 39; 45; 46; 50; 52; 55; 63 (lower); 68 (upper and lower); 69; 70 (upper and lower); 72 (upper and lower); 75; 76; 83; 87; 90; 92; 95; 97 (upper); 100; 101; 105; 106; 108; 110; 112; 113; 114; 115; 117 (six images); 119 (upper and lower); 120; 121; 122; 123; 124 (upper and lower); 125; 126 (upper); 127; 128; 130; 132; 137; 139; 140; 143; 148; 149; 158; 159; 169; 185.
Stephen Berry: rear endpaper; 168; 170; 172; 173; 175; 178-9; 180; 181; 182; 183; 184; 186; 187; 189.
Arthur W. Crook: 171; 174; 188.
Charles Dragonette collection: 12; 13; 15; 44; 58 (upper); 67 (lower); 78; 80; 81; 88; 91; 94; 131; 141; 150; 164;167.
Maurizio Eliseo collection: 11; 16 (ship profile); 25; 27; 36; 53; 93; 97 (lower); 98; 99; 103; 109; 138; 163; 190; 199.
David F. Hutchings collection: 152; 153.
Ian Johnston collection: front endpaper; 1; 30; 33.
Richard Maxwell collection/Charles Dragonette: 144; 145; 156; 160; 162.
Steven Moore: 146 (four images); rear cover.
Todd Neitring collection: 38.
Newall - Dunn collection: frontispiece; 8; 28; 30; 33; 43; 47; 48; 51; 56; 58 (lower); 59; 60; 61; 62; 63 (upper); 64; 65; 66; 67 (upper); 73; 86; 126 (lower); 129.
Don Stoltenberg: front cover.
Ringo Varisco: fold-out plan.

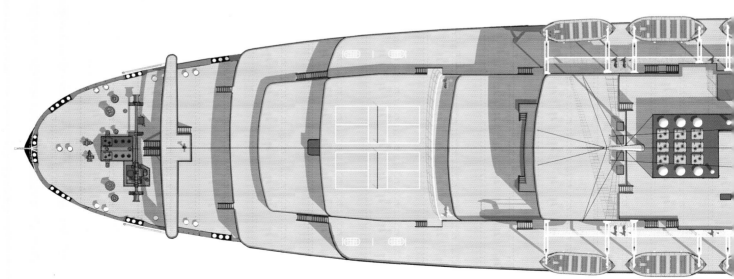

0   10   25   50m

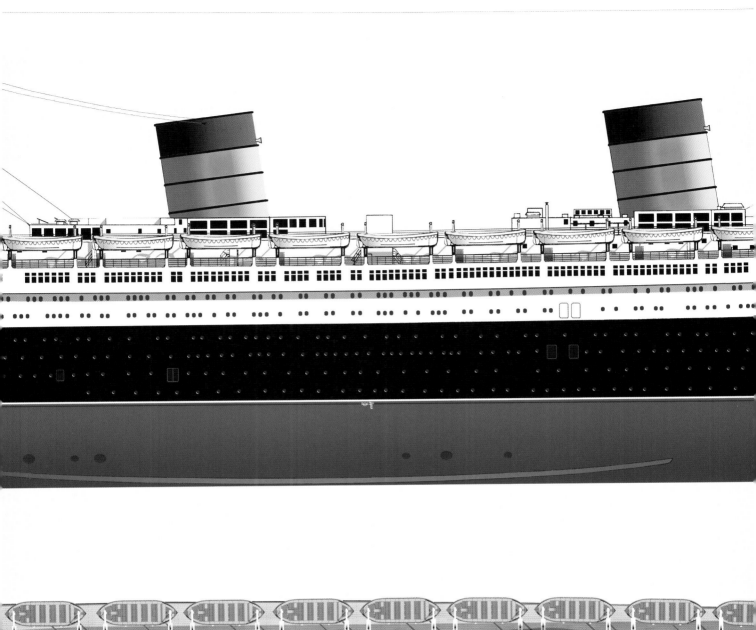
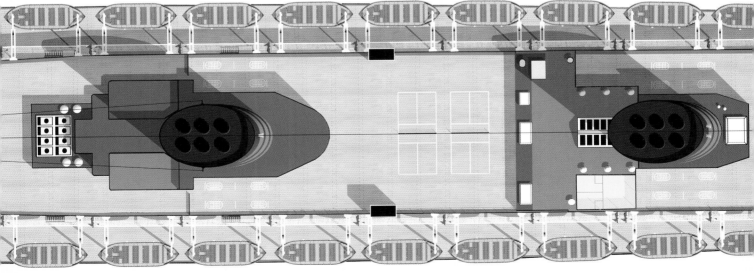

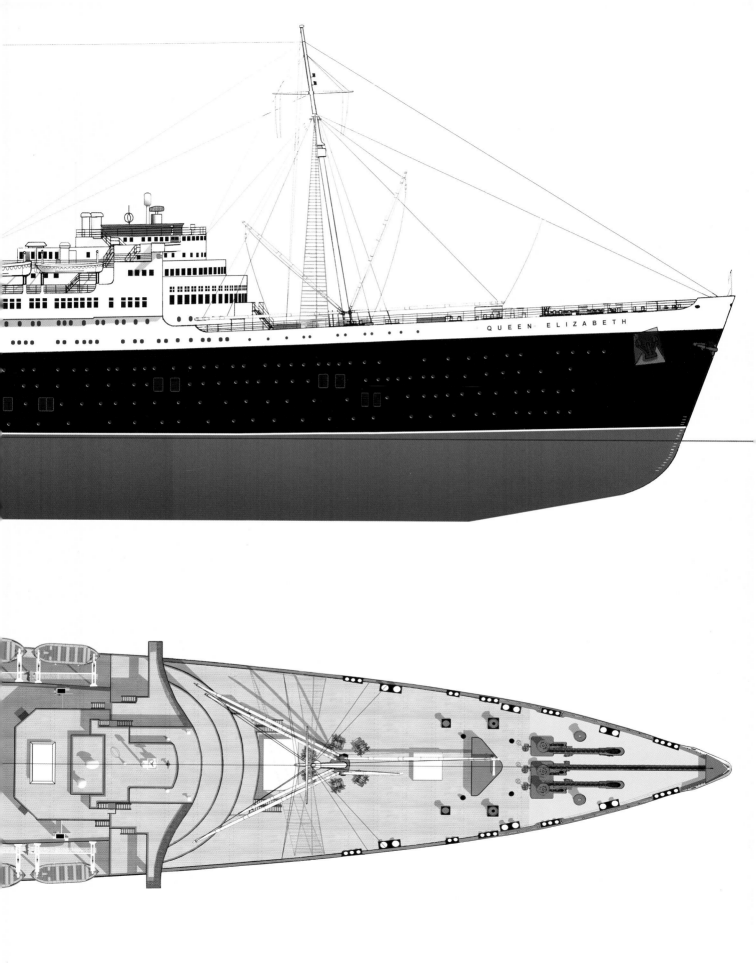

R.M.S. QUEEN ELIZABETH (1946) - © 2008 drawing by Maurizio Eliseo